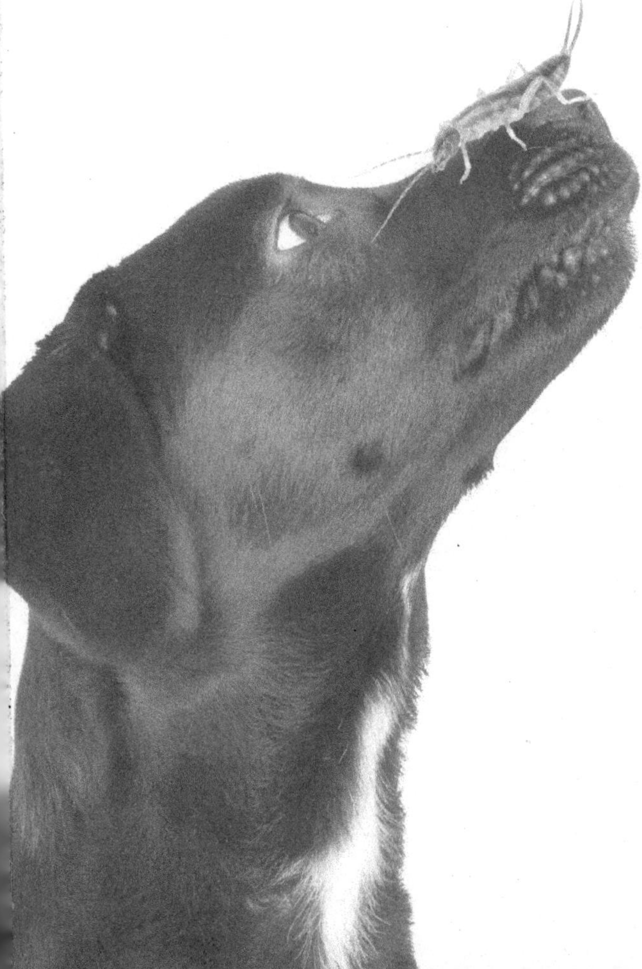

THERE'S AN EARWIG IN MY FISH TANK

HELEN COLLINS

THE STRIFE
AND CRIMES OF
AMOEBA MONTGOMERY
TWO-BY-FOUR
THE FIRST AND
HIS PALS

Copyright © 2017 Helen Collins

The moral right of the author has been asserted.

Apart from any fair dealing for the purposes of research or private study, or criticism or review, as permitted under the Copyright, Designs and Patents Act 1988, this publication may only be reproduced, stored or transmitted, in any form or by any means, with the prior permission in writing of the publishers, or in the case of reprographic reproduction in accordance with the terms of licences issued by the Copyright Licensing Agency. Enquiries concerning reproduction outside those terms should be sent to the publishers.

Matador
9 Priory Business Park,
Wistow Road, Kibworth Beauchamp,
Leicestershire. LE8 0RX
Tel: 0116 279 2299
Email: books@troubador.co.uk
Web: www.troubador.co.uk/matador
Twitter: @matadorbooks

ISBN 978 1785899 867

British Library Cataloguing in Publication Data.
A catalogue record for this book is available from the British Library.

Printed and bound by CPI Group (UK) Ltd, Croydon, CR0 4YY
Typeset in 11pt Adobe Garamond Pro by Troubador Publishing Ltd, Leicester, UK

Matador is an imprint of Troubador Publishing Ltd

ACKNOWLEDGEMENTS

There are many people who became part of the creation of this book and who offered continued support and encouragement as it unfolded. A heartfelt thank you is expressed to the following:

To Sarah Brown and her family, for giving us the chance to love Monty.

To Julie Grady Thomas for her editorial knowledge, constructive advice, help and for getting me past my writer's block with her wise words.

To my family for their love and belief in me.

To Anna Jones who inspired me to start this project and made me believe I could do it.

To everyone who followed Monty's story and pushed me to turn it into a book, especially Carolyn, Denise, Kerry and Mila.

To Daniel Rhodes for editing the final draft with dedication, humour and endless patience.

And to John, who remains my soul mate, my rock and my everything.

TABLE OF CONTENTS

Foreword	ix
Introducing	xiii
Be careful what you wish for	1
First Night Chaos	6
How Muttley became Monty	10
My First Walk with Monty	14
Operation Turd and Wazz	19
Dirty Protests and an Obsession with Cat Pee	25
These Nuts are Toast	38
Bad News for Megan	44
Culinary Capers	50
Puppy Playtime	55
Christmas is Coming	65
Discovering his Woof	70
Doctor Monty	75
Puppy turns to the Dark Side	82
Tasty Morsels and Bits of Sheep	87
Roll Over and Give us a Kiss	93
Havoc from Dawn to Dusk	99
Scaredy-Pooch	108
Megan's Story	111
Megan meets the Locals	117
Fish Tank Maintenance, Monty style	122

The Saga of the Tropical Fish	126
Tropical Fish begin to take over the House	131
Déjà vu on the Fish Front!	135
Fish Funerals: to Flush or not to Flush?	139
All about Goebbles	143
The Amazing Rat Killing Cat settles in	149
And not forgetting Micky	155
Micky's Story	158
There is only one 'F' in Tufty	165
Alpha Female in Control	173
Tripe, Training and Facials	178
Monty has a Smashing Time	183
Goebbles comes for a Walk	189
Lost in Translation	195
Still Lost in Translation	199
There's an Earwig in my Fish Tank	203
Little Birds	207
Goebbles reclaims her House	217
Ball Training (Indoor Rounders)	221
Me Master, You Dog	225
The Battle Plans of General Cow	230
The Stream eats my Wellies	238
Cold Storms and Hot Rocks	245
Summer Walk	252
Revenge of the Sheep	260
Guns and Crowses (and a Wood Pigeon)	266
Winter Walk – The Song of the Gate	273
Tribute to a Dying Ewe	278
Monty is a Legend after all	284

FOREWORD

I have always had a passion for animals. My dad came home with a couple of gerbils for my brother and me when we were about four and seven respectively. To my knowledge they were our first true pets if you discount goldfish that you could win at the fair in those days. We never became bored and carried out our pet-keeping duties diligently, which is probably why I was then given a budgie for my twelfth birthday. This ignited my lifelong burning love for birds.

In fact, before long my mum, dad, brother and I ended up with a budgie each, all living in large indoor aviaries in harmonious chirpiness; mine was Perry (I was learning French, budgie in French is *Perruche*), my mum's was Banana (it was yellow), my dad's was Grey Thing (work it out) and my brother's was Joey.

Having a pet taught me responsibility, duty, sharing and an early understanding of the laws of circumstantial evidence when Perry was blamed for the untimely demise of Joey. The fact that Banana and GT were immaculate while Joey reposed in bits on the floor of the aviary he shared with Perry, and Perry looked like she had been showered with the contents of an abattoir, seemed a bit like jumping to conclusions to my thirteen year old self and remains a sibling argument to this day.

We progressed to guinea pigs, more budgies and holiday-sat various specimens from school including gerbils, stick insects and silkworms. The last of which pre-dated my horror of caterpillars and introduced an early understanding of the laws of trespass when the science teacher in charge of pets failed to inform the school secretary, who owned a mulberry tree, that two oiks would be prowling round her garden in search of mulberry leaves instead of him. Disaster was averted by our polite demeanour and the fact that we only had armfuls of foliage and woeful tales of peckish grubs instead of the family silver.

I cared for injured birds that fell from their hangar nests at my dad's work, feeling a sense of achievement and privilege when I was able to return them back into the wild, healed and fully fledged. The early summer of 1986 was memorable for the dawn to dusk rearing of two baby starlings, one of which had a broken leg that my dad and I set with a matchstick and surgical tape. The vet who checked it over praised us for the quality of our efforts and the leg healed perfectly.

When our starlings fledged the one with the broken leg returned each dawn to tap on my bedroom window. Knowing it would not open it then flew to my brother's window next door and waited for me to come and let it in. It would then go back to sleep on the top of my doll's house until the chill of early morning had worn off, when it would fly down to my pillow and prod me with its beak until I let it out again. My doll's house has not been played with for many years but, sentimentally, I have still never felt able to clean the last vestiges of starling poo from its roof.

For my eighteenth birthday I received Olly, an umbrella cockatoo and then, eight months later I went to university in Aberystwyth where I rediscovered the beautiful Welsh countryside I had enjoyed on holidays as a child. I made an amazing set of friends who gave me hamsters on my birthdays and, as with so many students at Aber, I later found the person I wanted to spend the rest of my life with and we settled in the hills. John had a rescued cat when we met, the rest is history.

This book is written as a tribute to rescue animals and pets everywhere.

To earn the trust of a previously abused or abandoned animal is a blessing.

To be accepted unconditionally by an animal is a privilege.

To be welcomed home, no matter what mood you are in, as a friend, playmate, provider and member of the pack by a creature that before knew only fear is a joy.

To accept that life into your home, with all the associated mishaps, responsibilities and pitfalls, and know that your commitment is total and lifelong is a lesson.

To care for an animal in health and in illness, providing proper treatment and if necessary, at the end, ensuring the ultimate gift of a pain free passing is a duty.

To experience all these together and to love a pet, rescue or otherwise, is an honour.

INTRODUCING

Megan: A Border Collie sheepdog, who turned up one summer, starving and injured, and took over our lives.

Micky: A bald, middle-aged Blue-Fronted Amazon parrot, who barks like a dog and looks like an oven ready *poussin*.

Bobby: A Ring Neck Parakeet on a mission to wind up all things canine.

The Budgies: Originally, a potential breeding pair, Perry and Huckleberry. But, two boys, so slight technical hitch in the breeding programme.

The Tropical Fish: Of various sizes and completely unrestrained reproductive ability.

Goebbles: Elderly cat with attitude and an aversion to wearing a large, black dog.

And Monty...

BE CAREFUL WHAT YOU WISH FOR

Megan had been with us for two years. She had flourished from the starving scrap that appeared outside the front door scavenging potato peelings from the bins, all bleeding pads, ribs and bruises. She still had the issues with sudden noise that had probably caused her to be beaten as a sheepdog and then abandoned, but she had settled into a happy existence with us, the parrots, fish and the cat.

From being someone who had run the full gamut of pets since childhood, from hamsters to stick insects and even a stint arriving home from school to announce cheerfully to my unprepared mother that we were holiday-sitting the psychotic school gerbils, I had never wanted a dog. But now I was hooked on all things canine. Friends visited with their dogs and Megan behaved impeccably. She was a bit clingy and hated to be left if we needed to pop out so, one day in early September 2012, watching her surveying the yard and digging holes I had a light bulb moment. What about getting her a friend?

Once John's eyebrows had returned to their normal position I put forward all the possible benefits of a second dog, carefully gleaned and edited from the Internet. It was just as cheap to feed two dogs (dog food website). Meg would stop missing us if we went out and would spend the time chilling with her new companion. Having a second dog also means happier, healthier pooches all round (dog insurance website). One dog brought so much fun, enjoyment and enrichment to our lives; it would be absolute nirvana with two dogs.

John presented alternative views. I called this being a spanner in my works. Feeding two dogs would actually cost twice as much. Meg occasionally displayed her annoyance at being left while we went shopping by chewing furniture and shoes; it was perfectly possible that chilling with her new companion would involve teaching it to wreck the house. However happy and healthy our new little pack would undoubtedly be, they *would* occasionally be ill and having a second dog would mean double insurance, double jabs, double boosters and double vet bills.

We already had a medium sized dog bouncing round our little home, unless the proposed second dog was going to be a chihuahua, how exactly were we going to accommodate another one? Another dog in our lives would not measure up to any concept of nirvana that John had ever understood.

Sensing a little resistance I left the idea for a while, but then took to casually dropping into conversations more second dog benefits. If Megan barked outside I suggested that she wouldn't do so if she had a little friend to play with; I mentioned how much nicer it would be of an evening if we each had a snoozing dog at our feet; I accidentally kept leaving the computer logged onto dog rescue websites and extolled the virtues of giving a rescue dog a loving home. I painted an idyllic picture of walks being so much easier if you could lean on the various farm gates with a benevolent smile as a well-trained Meg gambolled around with her equally well-behaved new mate.

John agreed with me on all my points but insisted on pointing out the practicalities. We had a little house and little money. However friendly Megan had been with the dogs she had met so far, our choice of new doggy pal might not be to her liking and then where would we be? Taking on a second dog would involve much planning and soul searching and if I could possibly stop banging on about it through every single television programme he wanted to watch, he would be very grateful. Very occasionally, John did make reference to the possibility himself and I would then dive back into selling the second dog idea with all the enthusiasm of a salesman on commission.

One Saturday morning before work I happened to mention in passing our ongoing second dog discussions to Denise, my assistant manager. Being a dog owner herself, we spent an agreeable twenty minutes chatting about our dogs and the benefits they bring us. I said that the idea of a friend for Megan was being bounced around at home as the merest, vaguest hint of something we were pondering as a remote, but unlikely, scenario.

A few days later, while working at the bottom end of the shop I noticed Denise in earnest conversation with Sarah, who had worked for us previously. Denise eventually sent her in my direction, they were both smiling.

Sarah advanced, beaming at me, "Denise says you are looking for another dog!"

Casting an exasperated look back towards the till area, to find Denise scooting rapidly out of my sight, I mentioned that John and I had discussed the idea.

"Good," said Sarah. "Because we have got an abandoned one year old collie at home, no one in the village knows where it has come from, there is no microchip or collar, it is skin and bone, starving and terrified but the vet can't see anything majorly wrong with it. We have to keep it for ten days while we check with the police, vets and dog wardens, but then we need to find it a home as our dogs don't like it very much. Oh, and if we can't find it a good home it might have to be put to sleep as all the animal charities are inundated with strays. So?"

All this was delivered with a suitably sorrowful tone and all in one breath. "What sex is it?" I wanted to know.

Cue another cascade of information from Sarah. I found out that he was a boy, looked like he was neutered, very friendly but absolutely emaciated. He had been lying in long grass at the side of a road in pouring down rain and was totally soaked through when found. At first it was thought that he had been hit by a car as he would not walk, but it turned out that he was just too terrified to move. By now wondering if Sarah ever needed to draw breath, I promised to talk to John about the abandoned dog that night.

Still beaming, Sarah left, but not before Denise popped up from her tidying to give her the thumbs up.

In the car on the way home from work, I casually enquired of John, "When do you think Megan would like to meet her potential new poochy friend?"

A sideways glance in my direction, "What new poochy friend would that be, darling?"

This prompted an enthusiastic and unstoppable torrent of information from me, along with numerous references to fate and coincidence that finally ceased about four hours later. We went to bed that night with an agreement that the abandoned dog could meet Megan on her own territory. Then, *if* initial introductions proved favourable, we might, possibly, nothing decided yet or set in stone, consider whether to take in the abandoned dog.

A few days later a car pulled up in our yard. Sarah and her father, Barry, hopped out and a scrawny dog was duly offloaded from the back. He was quite clearly very, very thin, with long gangly legs and a large head topped by cute fold over ears. Mainly black with a white blaze on his chest and neck, his collie pedigree was decidedly open to debate and he also possessed the most enormous set of paws I had ever seen on a collie.

As he scrabbled across the yard in our direction I called, "I think he has a bit of growing to do yet."

"Vet thinks there is a bit of lab in him," Sarah's dad responded cheerfully.

Megan eyed the newcomer. Suspect collie came through the door and made an immediate dive for her food bowl which earned him a snarly lunge to teach him some ground rules.

Once in the lounge he did his best to jump up on the settee and was promptly hauled back by Sarah. There was some grumpy growling from Megan when he walked over her rather than round her and then stood on her tail but she generally showed signs of tolerating this intruder. I positioned myself next to the birdcage as Micky started to yell and squawk, working on the principle that exposing a starved dog to a parrot with the outward appearance of an oven ready chicken was probably inadvisable. The dog came and sat in front of me and looked up with hypnotic pale-ringed eyes.

"We have been calling him Muttley. He is really friendly," said Barry, as Muttley drooled hungrily at Micky.

With the introductions going well, we promised to discuss and give a final answer as soon as possible. The deadline for needing to keep him in case his former owners claimed him was a couple of days away. Watching as he was being loaded back into the car I almost threw caution to the winds and wondered whether he could move in immediately but sense prevailed and off he went.

"Isn't he gorgeous? Megan loved him," I enthused to John the second that the car disappeared out of sight.

"That is going to be a BIG dog," came back the reply.

I immediately countered, "No, no, no, he is tiny. He is so thin."

John raised his glance heavenward, "What reality are you living in, didn't you see his paws? He is bigger than Megan."

"His paws only look big because the rest of him is so scrawny. He would love it with us."

"Big paws mean BIG DOG."

Discussions continued for the rest of the weekend. I saw a tiny, helpless scrap in need of some tender care who was meant to be ours, John saw a rangy mutt of questionable heritage who would turn into a massive mutt of questionable heritage, but eventually we reached a consensus.

We had analysed the situation carefully in a logical, well thought out rational way until we adopted the most sensible and responsible option in the circumstances. Notwithstanding the potential final dimensions of Muttley, the existing dimensions of our little house, our precarious finances and the fact that he appeared to have a few obedience issues, Muttley was to come and join our happy throng.

And that is when our ordered existence went totally and completely pear shaped.

FIRST NIGHT CHAOS

The due day soon came when Muttley was officially abandoned and homeless. We set off to pick him up and he came home with us. We took him out with Megan for an orienteering session and he bounced, snuffled and rolled around the fields on a training lead in ecstatic joy. Back at home, in the warm, it took all of about thirty seconds before we planned bath time. He stank! To high heaven! Sensing the shower being turned on Meg disappeared, solidarity with her new friend instantly forgotten.

We picked up Muttley, popped him under the spray and got to work with the suds. Once he was wet, we realised just how skinny he was; basically legs, a ribcage and a head, with a tail firmly clamped between his legs and two huge, amber-ringed eyes looking up at us. John gently washed his head and then I lathered up the other end. It was then that I discovered that, although not very well endowed, he most definitely had not been neutered.

Clean and dried off, although not entirely pleased with this bathing lark, he drooled hopefully while we assembled two teatime bowls. Megan nibbled delicately at her bowl of kibble. Muttley stuffed his whole face into his, scattering kibble everywhere and gobbled and slurped without chewing. Hiccoughing wildly, he then drained an entire bowl of water before trawling the floor with his tongue, mopping up loose kibble and spilt water. He then sat back on his haunches, threw the whole lot back up onto the floor, gobbled it all up again and then looked hopefully up at us as though to say, *'Well, that was all right for starters, what's next?'*

Megan eyed him with what passed as a fairly impressive expression of doggy disgust. She then eyed us with an even more pained look of amazement that we had brought this total slob into her nice, ordered life.

Preparations for bedtime involved taking dogs out for evening constitutionals, covering parrots and turning off the fish tank lights and then moving to the bedroom to watch television and relax. Megan would settle on her bed, Goebbles would appear for a cuddle and all would be calm and mellow. That was BM (Before Muttley). At about ten thirty we were rather worriedly pondering the fact that Megan had gone to bed an hour before, Goebbles was happily tucked up in her nest, while the fish, Micky, Bobby and the budgies were all fast asleep. Muttley was still destroying the house.

Eager to share our new addition, I had previously posted Muttley's arrival on my social networking page. In response to queries I had proudly introduced him as Megan's new friend, a lab cross collie, although, based on his antics so far, I preferred tornado cross dustbin cross drooly cross mutt. Proudly, I announced that we loved him to bits already but I also added that we were shattered. After the latest crash from the other end of the house I logged back in to read the most spectacularly, unintentionally insightful comment one of my friends could ever have posted at that moment in time.

"Wow Helen…Lab x Collie…two of the most hyperactive breeds!! Are you a glutton for punishment or what?! xx"

Showing Muttley his lovely, cosy bed once more and deciding that all he needed now was some peace and quiet and pitch darkness to settle down, all lights were firmly switched off. We listened as he stayed in bed for all of thirty seconds before disappearing back into the hall. There was a tell-tale tick, tick, tick of claws on tiles, a long pause, then the tick, tick ticks came nearer, sensation of the dog getting back into bed and a slurping, chewing investigation of whatever he had brought back with him.

We realised that he had found Megan's toy pile, which was wedged between the floor steamer and the wall at the very far end of the hall. Aha, the poor little pooch just wanted a comforter for his first night in this strange new house. However, the comforter quite obviously did not pass comforting muster a minute later when Muttley bounced up again and tick ticked off once more. Another pause, more tick ticking back to bed, more slurpy chewing, and another toy bit the dust in the dog-settling stakes.

At the time there were about twenty toys in the pile, Muttley set about systematically relocating them, one by one, to our bedroom floor, with a relentless determination that lasted most of the night. Each return involved making the effort to get back into bed, followed by a lengthy examination of his prize. This dog did not sleep.

"At least when the steamer appears, he has brought all the toys down," I whispered to John, somewhere around three in the morning.

After a particularly prolonged absence around three thirty, I decided to see what was up. I turned the hall lights on to find he had peed up against the bookcase and was squatting on the rug, finishing up the business of depositing a rather large turd. Also, bored with shifting toys he had obviously decided that the current configuration of house and ornaments was not to his taste and needed urgent rearrangement. Adopting my most sympathetic 'I know it is all new, but you will settle in and if you would please go to sleep now' look I escorted him back to his bed, where he fell asleep instantly. John snored quietly, breathing with uniform deep exhalations.

Wondering what part of cleaning up dog poo and rescuing pee soaked books at the crack of dawn was part of the second dog benefits I had so vigorously extolled, I eventually stumbled through a minefield of scattered toys and fell onto the duvet. John continued pretending to be asleep as Muttley, refreshed and alert after his ten minute nap, leapt into action and began exploring the bedroom.

We both gave up trying to sleep around six, when a malodorous whiff permeated the air, the hall décor was now enhanced by another turd the size of the Bismarck and enough pee to sink it. Ecstatic at the thought of an eight hour shift after no sleep, my mood was enhanced no end by a series of chirpy texts from Sarah enquiring after our new arrival's first night.

HOW MUTTLEY BECAME MONTY

About a week after Muttley arrived I injured my foot at work and after a morning at casualty and being sent home to rest up, was confined to a hobbling existence around the house. This meant me directing household operations from the settee or bed and feebly wheedling for cups of tea or glasses of wine, depending on the time of day. It also meant that I was taking approximately zero physical participation with regards to Muttley's day to day routine. Despite his weak appearance and scrawny size, he was actually surprisingly strong for a dog so thin, a fact that was pointed out emphatically and regularly by John as he reappeared from being hauled round the fields to find me lying in injured repose.

"My foot hurts," I'd whimper.

"My bloody back hurts," John would retort. "Not to mention my shoulders, and he has nearly broken my wrist!"

This dog did not do 'heel', or 'come here', or 'stay'. Becoming used to his field surroundings now he allegedly had one top gear speed and he used all four large, splayed, scrabbling paws to achieve it as fast as possible. He was also, apparently, deaf. As the fields were wet and muddy after a summer of relentless rain, the ground underfoot was soft and slippery and treacherous. Numerous near misses as Muttley changed tack suddenly and caught John off balance, nearly landing him in the mire, were grumpily reported. Secretly pooh-poohing John's obviously crap dog-walking skills I counted down the days to when I could walk Muttley myself.

One night John had disappeared with Megan for her final dog

training class. This had involved six weeks of trying to introduce her to structured training. While she was well-behaved around livestock owing to her sheepdog heritage and would respond to whistled commands in the fields, she was not very good on the lead. She was also definitely a country dog rather than an urban dog and going into town in the car stressed her out. Dog training in an environment where there was a car park, a strange building and people she did not know would do her good.

Except that she hated it. From day one she and a muscled female staffy with a studded collar and a kerchief took an instant dislike to one another and eyeballed each other across the room. She completely failed to see any point at all in walking round a room full of dogs while on a lead. It became patently obvious, by her fixed collie stare at the other trainees, that what she really wanted was either to round up this bunch of growling rabble, or go home. She would vent her nervous energy with a series of gaseous emissions that would dissolve a nuclear reactor, leading to John and me standing in a noxious cloud, reassuring ourselves that this was really a productive way to spend our evening.

At least Megan stopped short of expressing her delight at the training in a more tangible fashion, as did an excitable and bouncy cockapoo one session. This dog decided walking to heel was boring, stopped dead and squatted in the middle of the training area and then produced an impressive pile of dog shit entirely disproportionate to its size.

As more and more logs added to the pile, its owner's eyes saucered in embarrassment, while the trainer in charge observed, "No problem, but we do normally see that more in *puppy* training class."

The hapless owner's night went from bad to worse as, after much frantic rooting through pockets, she turned to her neighbour and squeaked, "Excuse me, but could I possibly borrow a poo bag?"

Training suspended for the purpose of cleaning up I had whispered to John, "Borrow a poo bag? Borrow?!"

The graduation class for Megan coincided with Muttley's arrival week and my bad foot. Off John went to earn her rosette and I settled down for an evening with limited mobility and a pup clearly intent on taking advantage. Muttley charged around, bouncing on and off furniture and walls, before collapsing for a quick snooze. In typical puppy fashion, he was up and about completely refreshed after about twenty minutes, ready for more mayhem. Taking the opportunity during one nap, I hobbled to the kitchen and defrosted some dinner. Limping back through to the lounge I switched on the television and started on my tea.

Muttley's sleeping nose twitched and he sprang instantly awake. Leaping vertically and sideways in one movement onto the settee next to me he sniffed hopefully as I used an elbow to lever him back onto the floor. Not put off in the slightest he immediately stood on his back legs and firmly extended one paw over the edge of my plate. Bad dog! At that moment my phone beeped, it was Sarah wanting an update on Muttley's progress. Glaring at Muttley, who was now busy licking my dinner off his foot with a self-satisfied look, I enlightened her that I was learning Italian. A puzzled query pinged my way. '*Chilli con Carne*' I informed her, now translated as 'Sodding Great Paw on edge of Dinner Plate'.

John arrived home with Megan. She had completed basic training and was the only one to do so, seeing as no one else had turned up to the final session. Nevertheless, she sat proudly in the lounge as John placed her graduation rosette on the coffee table for due admiration. Straightaway Muttley sidled up with a view to eating it so John whipped it back out of the way.

A bottle of wine was cracked open to toast our clever Meg and we looked at our little pack. Muttley sat next to Megan, still gangly, not as confident, with his head cocked. He sat tall and, in profile, he actually looked quite handsome. We looked ahead to when he was the proper size and weight; Muttley might suit him now but it wouldn't when he had filled out. We pondered, it wasn't fair to change his name again as he had already had too much disruption in his short life but Muttley would not do justice to the dog he was going to become.

A long discussion on the variety of suitable dog names followed, it had to be similar to Muttley but proud and distinguished, something our scrawny mutt could grow into. He looked unusual so we did not want a name that you heard all the time but we also aimed for something that was a sensible name for a dog that was living in a farming community. If we had to call both dogs at the same time, their names had to flow together to avoid a delay in any command. Finally it clicked, after many tryouts and rejections, by the end of the evening Muttley had a new title.

"Megan and Monty," I tested. "Monty and Megan."

"They even work shortened," said John. "Meg and Mont."

And then, by one of those strange coincidences that seem to affirm decisions sometimes John scrolled through the channel guide on the television, ready to set a recording for the next day. As he found the timings he was looking for we both noticed a programme title on a World War Two history channel, 'Monty – Legend in the Desert'. It was meant to be. Whether our scrawny dog would turn out to be a legend was moot but the name stuck. Muttley belonged to his old life, Monty represented all he could and would be from now on.

MY FIRST WALK
WITH MONTY

My foot took a while to heal and even when back at work a week later I could only wear ballerina pumps that left the top of my foot open to the air. Although I could limp about I could not stand any pressure on it. Ballerina pumps were completely unsuitable for taking the dogs into the fields which meant that I was excused walking duties until such time as I could actually tolerate socks and wellies. Eventually though, the time came when it was my turn to head for the hills with what I had been assured was a totally undisciplined mutt, with no sense of recall and a penchant for changing direction without warning.

Looking at our scrawny little dog sat wagging his tail and looking innocently up at me, I mentally put Monty's alleged bad behaviour down to John's obvious deficiency in dog-walking skills. Togging myself up in coat and scarf, ready to brave the elements, I squeezed my feet into my welly boots, attached Monty's lead, gathered up Megan and breezed a cheery 'goodbye' to John, who immediately wound me up with a smirk and an equally cheery 'good luck'.

Shutting the door I turned in the direction of the gate. My arm was instantly pulled rigid with a sharp jerk as Monty showed that he was evidently not going to put up with any dawdling by hurtling to the end of the lead. John had moved halfway down the house to the hall window and was now smugly observing as I reeled in Monty with as much aplomb as I could muster. The gate was the entrance to the lane that ran past the end of our house, about fifty metres down the lane was one of the gates to our main walking field. It had been a very wet summer and the ground in the lane was a muddy quagmire of slimy, sticky mud, liberally churned with sheep droppings.

It made for an environment that you needed to tread with care, slowly and steadily, to avoid slipping over. It was not the environment in which to discover that your footwear had all the grip characteristics of bald tyres on ice and that you were being hauled along by a skinny mutt powered by about eighty horsepower.

As Megan headed through the gate and waited for me to close it, Monty heard Goebbles behind the house, meowing to be let in the bedroom window. He shot off again at speed to investigate. I had not yet shut the gate and found myself clinging to it for dear life while locking every finger muscle I had around the handle of the lead, the ratchet within it making an ominous grinding noise as Monty bounced around on the other end. Goebbles did not help matters by deciding that she was quite safe on the other side of the fence, she took up a lurking position on the garden bench to wash her face and watch me slither past, making frantic lunges at the fence to try to stop my momentum.

Using an elbow to anchor myself to a fencepost I dragged Monty back to my side. Plodding with baby steps and the lead as short as I could make it, I let go of the now leaning fencepost and made a lunge for the next one. In this way I slowly made it to the field gate.

Catching my breath, with Megan huffing impatiently, I looked across the field. No sheep in the near vicinity so we all headed through the gate, with me mightily relieved that the worst was over. Unfortunately, in the neighbouring field about half a mile away, there were a few sheep that merited immediate investigation. Squeaking every training club command I knew to try to get Monty's attention I realised with a rising sense of discomfort that he had me running. Trying to brace my feet enough to bring myself to a halt and regain control was not happening. He was off like a rocket, clawing through the grass, with me scuttling along behind him with ever longer strides. The only thing that stopped me falling and then being surfed face first through the molehills and sheep poo was Megan. She heard a car heading up the adjacent road and started barking, Monty came to a halt momentarily, which gave me a nanosecond to regain my balance and haul him back.

This was not on. My second dog benefits had never included this.

A walk lasted an hour, we had been out for five minutes and Monty had tried to kill me and turn me into an Olympic sprinter at the same time. Proceeding with more caution I headed down into a dip in the field that hid the sheep from view. Megan decided it was high time for playing and chased Monty in circles. She maintained a rough sense of clockwise direction, Monty did no such thing. He changed tack frequently in an attempt to cut Megan off, which meant he wound the lead round my ankles and then hurtled off, hobbling me and threatening to upend me into the sludge.

Bellowing at Monty to slow down I decided it would be safer to hold my arm above my head, all this did was to cause me to take on the attributes of a fifties western cowboy as my arm swivelled manically with Monty's revolutions and I came to the realisation that the whipping lead was coming perilously close to decapitating me.

In the interests of self-preservation I made the most of the next pause in frantic chasing to summon the dogs into some sort of order. With my sternest expression I informed them that we were going on a fence inspection and I would be very grateful if they would kindly behave for two seconds. Megan ambled off to roll in a pile of sheep poo while Monty planted two filthy paws halfway up my chest and lunged at my face for a lick.

The hedgerow was a goldmine of rabbit holes, fox runs, old bird nests and various deposits of scat, ripe for examination. Megan had an ongoing inclination to roll in sheep droppings but would merely sniff and scent her way along the hedge, happy to explore. It was at this point that I found out that Monty was also intrigued by the new experience of the fence and all its offerings, but he saw the whole length of the hedge as a running buffet of unmentionables, to be scoffed down at rapid speed. Seeing him chow down on the latest juicy fox turd while developing sudden, acute deafness I hauled him away from the fence, crouched down to his level and instigated a little motivational chat. Obviously having the time of his life, Monty happily panted a miasma of fox crap into my face until Megan, hearing another car head up the road, charged off and he promptly lost interest in me and followed suit, pulling me prone onto the grass.

Just when I thought I would lose my grip on the lead, he veered suddenly into the hedge, jamming his head through the fence, and started drooling at a startled blackbird perched in the depths. Calling Meg back, I freed Monty's ears, reeled the training lead in to a length of about three feet and headed for home.

Reaching the stream Megan took a break for a refreshing slurp while Monty, obviously deciding that this walking business was hot work, picked the muddiest section of slime for a cooling lie down. As I watched him turn from black and white to a rather disturbing brown and green I contemplated the fact that I could feel every muscle in my body tensing in protest at the onslaught of the previous hour. Begrudgingly accepting that John's tales of woe on his return from his walks with Monty may possibly have had a ring of truth to them, I set off for the last lap home.

Back through the gate, Goebbels was still hovering. Megan suddenly realised that she had not had her afternoon constitutional and squatted by the fence. Monty hurtled past her to aim one last lunge at the cat, catching me in the complacency of practically being home, and nearly depositing me up close and personal with Megan's pile of logs.

John was in the kitchen making dinner when I finally opened the front door a few minutes later and fell into the hall.

"How was your walk? I've already poured you a glass of wine, thought you might need it." He smiled and extended a brimming glass. Resisting the temptation to throw the glass at him and grab the bottle, I smiled back.

"Our walk was absolutely peachy, thank you. I don't know what you were making such a fuss about."

"Good, good, glad you enjoyed it, you go and sit down and relax, dinner won't be long. Oh, by the way, why has Monty turned green?"

OPERATION TURD AND WAZZ

Of all the teething troubles we encountered as Monty began to settle in three issues demanded our immediate attention. Firstly, he seemed to have a terror of all things textile. Secondly, he crapped everywhere. Thirdly, he peed everywhere. It became a mission to resolve these problems as a matter of urgency, the first to ensure Monty's psychological welfare, the second and third to ensure ours.

We had found out very quickly that we could not even pick up a tea towel to dry dishes, unload the washing machine, shake out any bedding without Monty flattening his ears, crouching down, and scuttling off with worried whimpers and the whites of his eyes showing.

We could only presume that he had been punished for his misdemeanours by having fabric flicked at him. As he seemed to have a complete lack of training in anything at all, his perceived misdemeanours must have been many and his punishments frequent which had developed his shaking fear of material being handled in any shape or form.

We could cope with his general lack of training and looked forward to helping him develop into a well-behaved and obedient dog. What we hated and what upset us greatly was seeing him shoot off in panic when I inadvertently shook a cushion to plump it up, or John emptied his shirts out of the ironing basket. Consulting the training manuals, we knew that it would reinforce his fear if we made a fuss, so in the early days we concentrated on minimising the handling of fabrics whenever Monty was in the near vicinity.

If something spooked him because we had absentmindedly forgotten, we made no issue but praised him with treats and fuss when he reappeared. Gradually, we would show him what we were doing and would hold out the duvet cover, tea towel, or ironing and let him approach and sniff. More treats would follow if he stayed put and did not run away. It took time and patience, and more than one occasion where Monty would turn tail and scarper.

One such morning, emerging from the shower on the first day of a week off, I flung the curtain back with an exuberant swish, not realising that Monty had let himself into the bathroom and was sat on the bathmat looking for me. He promptly squeaked a whimper and legged it straight into the wall, rebounding into a quivering heap on the floor while I stood over him, dripping, apologetic and freezing, too scared to grab a towel in case he decided to try to stick his head through the wallpaper again.

A frequent invader of the bathroom up until that point, the shower curtain incident meant that his visits were restricted for quite a while to a nose slowly nudging the door open and a wary peek inside before he hastily withdrew on seeing the curtain hanging from the rail. Slowly however, he came to realise that we were not going to hurt him and we could actually do the drying up or change the bedding without him having a nervous meltdown, but his fear was ingrained and it was an ongoing learning curve for all of us.

His other initial problem was a complete and total lack of housetraining. Megan had soiled on her first night with us, but that was the only time she ever toileted indoors. Cutting Monty the same slack on his first night, we empathised with him over this strange new environment that must be causing a nervous loosening of the bodily functions.

What we were not expecting was a dog that had reached his age without any concept of housetraining at all. He freely used all parts of our little house as a bespoke toilet. He had no favoured space; he did not try to hide his activities. If he needed to go, there was no clue, no looking at the door with his legs crossed, nothing. The canine grey cells had obviously assessed the whole house as a potential dumping zone for his comfort and convenience. *'Need a crap in the lounge? No problem, squat on the carpet. Hang on, I am on the settee, hey ho, this cushion will do nicely. In the hallway? Let's add to the décor with a nice mound of stinky logs and, while I am at it, I think I will offload about a pint of pee onto this bookcase.'*

As Monty was also very underweight we were doing our best to build him up with three meals a day. In the early days this copious amount of food showed no signs of sticking to his ribs and every sign of shooting straight through his digestive system and sticking itself to our carpets.

Monty would also drain water bowls in one go, which led to a consultation with the vet. No, he did not have a kidney problem. What he was doing was applying the same reasoning to water as he did to his food. Being starved, he did not know when he would be fed again, hence his frantic gobbling of every meal. If his previous owners had been lax with feeding him, they had probably not been too fussy with ensuring an adequate water supply either, so Monty slurped up water at every opportunity in case no more was forthcoming.

This behaviour would ease with time and a regular and consistent availability of food and water, as Monty learned to trust that another mealtime would follow. This, however, did not help us now. Gallons of water going in one end had to come out of the other in equal quantity and Monty adopted the same free abandon with cocking his leg as he did with squatting for a dump.

John regularly picked me up from work with the car full of the latest odour-removing cleaning fluids and we both became experts on the efficacy, or lack of, of the anionic surfactants and bacteria digesting enzymes in posh pet shop sprays, designed to remove the smell of dog pee from our carpets. Our house, despite our best efforts, began to assume the unappealing atmosphere of an unemptied festival portaloo in high summer.

We cleaned the mats and had a stack of poo bags strategically sited around the house. Then we cut the more soiled chunks out of the hall runner and threw them away. Finally, the rest of the hall runner went for a burton and was relegated to the skip, by now more bacteria digesting enzyme than carpet. Books were removed to higher shelves and I tried to ignore the fetching yellow tint my white wood bookcases were sporting anywhere up to a height of about two feet.

I dug out the training books and hopped on the web for advice. Much of the training was directed at puppies, little fluffy scraps that you could forgive for their tiny offerings, as they looked at you helplessly with outsize innocent eyes. While Monty was still, technically, in puppyhood, it was not practical to pick up this pup and move him to a training mat when he was in the process of crapping something the size of a bag of sugar, and eyeing you with a self-satisfied gleam that told you, *'Aaaah, better out than in, eh?'*

Finally, we found some advice on housetraining adult and rescue dogs. Although out of order that Monty had been allowed to get to his size without learning to control himself, nevertheless we had to work with what we had. Surveying our dripping wine rack one evening and wiping off a soggy bottle of Merlot, I would have liked to have had a friendly little chat with Monty's previous owners, but instead, we threw ourselves into 'Operation Turd and Wazz'.

We gave Monty every opportunity to toilet outside. One of us would take him out regularly after meals and about half an hour after we had seen him drinking. If he did anything outside, regardless of the time during the day or night we would leap about as though we had had won the Premium Bonds jackpot. If an accident occurred indoors I would get on the case with cleaning up, but we would not admonish Monty, we just ignored the transgression.

At night, we decided to take a risk and closed the bedroom

door. Whereas before, the door had remained open in case either dog needed a drink, now we made sure neither dog was thirsty before settling down time, then that was it on the water front until morning. This also meant that Monty did not have free access to the hall as a toilet and, if he was going to soil, he would have to do it in his sleeping area, which, all the training guides assured us, he would not want to do.

Fervently praying that the authors knew what they were talking about on the grounds that sleepily squelching barefoot through one of Monty's deposits on the way to the loo in the middle of the night would really test our love for the Mont, we put our trust in the manuals and in Monty.

Finally, we both attuned ourselves to the slightest behaviour that would indicate Monty was planning to offload – sniffing the side of the armchair – looking round at his back end – passing explosive wind – circling, and always had his lead ready in the speed of light, just in time to take him into the yard. Turds were left in the turding area and we took him to the same patch of grass to pee, working on the principle that the scent would tell him what to do. For weeks John and I breathed, slept and lived Monty's copious excretions.

We had good days and bad ones; one morning I had praised Monty to the heavens for not having an accident indoors for two whole days, treats and cuddles were unlimited. Monty repaid my new found faith in him by emptying his bladder over Megan's food bowl and crapping in front of my little fish tank.

Gradually, all our efforts seemed to be paying off. We realised we were getting somewhere when Monty would occasionally issue a little whine and look uncomfortable. To start with though he left it until he was absolutely bursting to go to let us know and you would head towards the door with him leaving a trail of little bullets or a wavy line of pee along the tiles. Taking him outside in these circumstances was mainly academic but we heaped on the praise when he squeezed the last drop over the grass, or dropped the last five grams in the turding area.

The advice I had downloaded indicated that, although harder than training a puppy, owing to ingrained behaviours and routines, housetraining an adult dog was not impossible if you persisted. It gave a timescale of about three months for your recalcitrant pooch to get the idea on a permanent basis, as long as the training had been consistent and your trainee had a reasonable level of intelligence. Two weeks before this deadline was due to be up we realised that Monty was regularly giving a little whimper when he needed to go out, furthermore, he was able to hold on if you needed to put on shoes or a coat.

It did mean that sometimes the whimper came in the very early morning for his first constitutional of the day, but more scrutiny of the guidebooks and an adjustment of the timing of his last meal of the day soon sorted this out. Tea had been given at around six in the evening for both dogs, in line with Megan's usual routine. With Monty's digestion still being in juvenile mode, he had been processing this by about four in the morning, which meant he then needed to go out. Moving teatime to eight and then gradually bringing it back to an earlier time as he grew older solved this and saved sanity for all. Monty was, at last, a fine upstanding housetrained member of the canine community.

DIRTY PROTESTS AND AN OBSESSION WITH CAT PEE

Whilst we were over the moon that housetraining Monty meant our house was no longer used as a toilet, there had been a time, only a couple of months before Monty arrived in our lives that we had been doing everything we could to persuade our cat to oblige us by peeing indoors.

Goebbles came and went as she wished. Although we had no cat flap she would meow outside a window or door when she wanted to come in from her explorations of the barns and fields. Likewise, if she wanted to go out, she would park herself by the front door and wait until one of us opened it for her. This way we could keep an eye on whether she turned up with a rodent in her mouth, which minimised the chances of her letting it loose inside until she felt the urge to hunt it down.

In the brief but very fine period of weather at the end of summer 2012 the door was left open to keep the house cool and let some air circulate, on these occasions we sometimes realised, usually at some ridiculous time of night, that Goebbles had managed to sneak in one of her unfortunate furry friends. She would then spring into action at hearing scratchy scuffling and proceed to rampage around the house in pursuit. Dawn would reveal the mauled corpse displayed for our appreciation and Goebbles, exhausted by her nocturnal activities, would settle down to clean mouse intestines off her paws and enjoy a morning's snoozing.

After the initial settling in period we had also been able to dispense with a litter tray. The cat preferred to find private spots in the garden to toilet in peace, which was absolutely fine by us. The litter tray was relegated to the shed. Although an elderly cat, Goebbles prowled her territory with sprightly determination and enjoyed reasonable good health for a cat of her age.

There were odd visits to the vet for routine check-ups and one time when she had to make several trips to be treated for pain while urinating. This did not go down at all well with Goebbles and she decided to show her disgust at the situation with a dirty protest. Yowling in indignation at being put into her cat carrier she had glared balefully out at us as we loaded her into the car. On the first trip we made it halfway down the lane before the car filled with an eye watering stench and the cat carrier shifted and wobbled on the back seat as Goebbles flung herself around the interior.

Arriving at the surgery to find it packed we sat and tried to look nonchalant as the waiting room filled with the overwhelming odour of cat poo.

"Grotty animal!" commented our vet, as he examined the liberally coated cat and brushed turdy lumps off her fur onto the examination table. "She has a temperature, she's got cystitis."

Apologising profusely for her unsavoury condition we headed home with antibiotics and an instruction to return in a few days.

"She has never done that before," I said, with my head stuck out of the car window.

"Mmm," John mumbled through tightly clenched lips, grimly trying to drive the nine mile journey holding onto the one fresh breath he had taken before getting into the car. "Exime uhat ioin itha oot."

I pulled my head back inside. "Next time the cat is most certainly not going in the boot! It is probably just a one off because she isn't feeling herself."

Goebbles, however, had other ideas. For the next visit we had taken precautions by giving her less to eat the night before and no food before we set out but John had barely pulled out of our yard before she conducted a repeat performance. This time though there was an ominous squirting noise and we realised with horror that Goebbles had upped the ante with a hefty dose of nervous diarrhoea. The basket shook and bounced round the back of the car as she engaged energetically in 'Dirty Protest: The Sequel'. By the time we parked up in town John and I were light headed with trying to hold our respective breaths.

"There is no way we can go and wait with her smelling like this," I said. "I'll go and check her in and then wave for you to bring her when we are called."

John was not very enthusiastic about my plan. "Oh thanks! I'll just wait here with the shitty cat then, shall I?"

I sought help from the receptionist who looked absolutely ecstatic to have me back in the waiting room. "We're here with Goebbles."

"That stinky cat?"

"Um yes, but she is a bit more stinky than last time so John is staying outside with her. I don't suppose you do cat laundering?"

The receptionist raised her eyebrows. "You can book her in for a hygiene appointment now and she can see the vet at the end of surgery."

"Great," I was relieved. "And how much would …?"

"Fifteen pounds."

"No problem."

"Plus VAT."

"That's fine. Although I do feel a bit sorry for whoever is going to clean her, she really is humming."

"And that would be me!"

"Right, oh dear, well, I'll just go and fetch her then." I retreated with a distinct feeling that a pair of eyes were boring into my back.

Duly cleaned off, Goebbles saw the vet in a decidedly more acceptable condition and was given the all clear from her cystitis. Her urine had shown signs of struvites so a new magnesium light diet was recommended and we headed home. This was the last time we needed to seek the vet's advice about the cat until the summer before Monty's arrival.

I had seen Goebbles skulking in the bathroom and went to investigate. She was perched on the edge of the sink lapping drips from around the plughole.

"What are you up to cat?" I wanted to know.

Seeing me she hopped down, gave her damp paws a quick lick and sauntered off. Glancing round I couldn't see anything untoward so made to follow her out. It was then that I noticed my shoes, neatly side by side where I had left them on arriving home from work the previous evening. One was now full of a dark red fluid, as though a glass of blackcurrant juice had been poured into it. Crouching down, I dipped a finger into the liquid and sniffed, there was the unmistakeable scent of urine.

"John," I called down the hall. "The cat has wazzed in my shoe, we need to ring the vet."

"Why? What have you done to her?" John appeared in the bathroom door way.

"I haven't done anything to her, but look at this." I proffered my shoe, red liquid slopping into the toe and back to the heel.

John took one look and agreed with me. On the phone to the veterinary surgery a few minutes later I asked the receptionist for a home visit.

"There are only a few available and there is a charge, can't you bring your cat in to see us?"

"The cat is Goebbles."

"Oh, that cat! Well of course we can sort out something for you. We can't give an exact time but is early afternoon all right?"

"That is fine, we are in all day."

At lunchtime, I went in search of Goebbles, who was sunning herself under the lounge window and was most unhappy at being brought inside. She proceeded to stalk around the house in search of an open window to escape through, meowing and complaining bitterly. Eventually she huffed off in a sulk to sleep on the settee.

When the vet arrived it was entirely in keeping with living in a friendly local farming community, a sharp knock followed by announcing who you are as you came through the door. We were expecting this and had been keeping a constant eye on the yard but, in the end, were neither observant nor quick enough.

As soon as we heard the rap John shouted, "Don't open the…"

"Vet here," called the vet, stepping into the hall.

"…door," finished John as a hairy tabby missile shot through the vet's legs, hurtled across the yard and disappeared into the barn.

Our vet looked down and then around, "I take it that was my patient?"

"It was."

A quick check of the barn revealed absolutely no sign of Goebbles. With the subject of the visit AWOL we were at a slight diagnostic disadvantage but the vet gave it his best shot. I showed the sample of liquid I had salvaged from my shoe.

"Looks full of blood to me," came back the gloomy response. "How old is this cat now?"

"About fifteen and a half," I replied.

"Is she eating okay?"

"She eats like a horse."

"Has she been losing weight at all?"

"You have got to be joking, she looks like a barrel."

"Is she showing pain when peeing?"

"She always goes outside so we don't know. If she hadn't done this in my shoe we would have had no idea anything is wrong," I waved the sample.

"She certainly didn't look very ill," commented the vet, glancing across the yard towards the barns. "Right, she could have cystitis again, there could be struvites in her urine again or," he paused, "There is a possibility, and this is quite common in elderly female cats, that she has a tumour in her bladder. I need an uncontaminated urine sample and I could do with seeing her at the surgery. We will analyse her pee first, get some idea of what's happening and then we can look at giving her an x-ray."

With one last look across the yard in case Goebbles suddenly felt the urge to reappear and submit to an examination the vet took his leave. We were left with some special cat litter, designed not to absorb urine and an instruction to bring Goebbles's sample in as soon as possible. As soon as the car disappeared up the lane we heard annoyed meowing from the barn, the cat homed into view and stalked across to the house.

"Great timing cat," I said, picking her up to give her a stroke. "Now you decide to show yourself. Twenty-five quid for the vet to see your furry backside disappearing into the distance and you still have to go to the surgery." Goebbles purred and rubbed her face into my neck as I carried her inside.

John rooted the litter tray out of the shed, gave it a wipe over, and poured the special sachet of litter into the bottom. It amounted to no more than a handful of little white balls.

"I bet she will be well impressed with those," he commented, rolling them around.

I decided to give Goebbles a pep talk. "Right puss, it is a lovely sunny day. If you want to be back outside get on the case with giving us a sample. No pee, no sunbathing. Got it?"

I moved the litter tray into the bathroom. Goebbles wandered off to the lounge and settled down to sleep. Maintaining litter watch was boring so I headed off to clean the bedroom. Stripping the bed and flinging the bed linen in the laundry basket, I changed sheets and vacuumed, then collected polish and duster. Opening a window to shake the duster off periodically I moved around the room. About halfway through my dusting the phone rang, it was work with a payroll query that took a while to go through in detail, so I moved to the office to sit down. Finishing up the call I attempted to go back to my cleaning, just as John appeared in the doorway.

"Where's the cat?" he asked.

I shot back into the bedroom to see Goebbles's tail disappearing out of the window that I had forgotten to close when the phone rang.

"Bloody cat has legged it," I reported.

"She hasn't gone very far," John replied, looking out of the kitchen window. "She seems to be providing her sample all over Pest."

He was right. Goebbles was busy digging a hole in front of Pest's gravestone. Squatting, she peed, circled and sniffed and then moved a few inches to dig again. Using the earth from her new excavation to cover the old one she then took a dump on her predecessor.

I flung open the kitchen window to protest. "Oi cat! Do you mind? Knock it off with the lack of respect, if you need a pee, get in here and have a pee." Goebbles looked up with a total lack of inclination to comply and carried on crapping. She then studiously buried the mound and slunk off.

"At least the bulbs I planted around Pestie should be well fertilised," John mused, watching the proceedings at my side.

Clearly deciding to spend an afternoon enjoying the sunshine we did not see the cat again until early evening, when she reappeared for dinner. Sat at my feet yowling in disgust at my slow preparation she stalked round my feet, rubbing her head on my ankles as I cleaned bowls and mixed food. Then I poured fresh water, trickling it noisily into the bowl from a height.

"Now doesn't all this tinkling water make you want to go for a nice pee Goebbles?" I smiled down at her.

With dinner gobbled up, my plan seemed to have worked. Goebbles checked for any open windows but, finding none, she prowled down the hallway. I had left the bathroom door open with the litter box in the position it had always been in when the cat first came to stay. The only thing that was different was the medical litter itself. Goebbles went into the bathroom. I sneaked up to peek round the door as she pushed the swing door to the covering lid and stepped inside.

"John, Goebbs is in the litter box," I hissed, in a stage whisper, in the general direction of the lounge.

"Jolly good," the reply came back.

I could now hear scuffling and knew that she was circling and digging in preparation, hopefully, for giving us our awaited sample.

"John, Goebbles is scuffling round in the litter box," I stage whispered again.

"Jolly good."

There was a pause in the digging noises and I listened with bated breath, hoping she was getting down to business.

"John, it has gone quiet in the litter box, I think we may have peeing in progress," I only felt it fair to keep John informed with the latest update.

"Jolly good."

And then the scuffling started again, briefly, followed by another pause, then the cat climbed out of the box, cast a disdainful look over her shoulder, squatted and relieved herself on the floor in front of the box. Her sample tracked along the grouting of about four floor tiles and a little pink pool spread slowly across the floor. To add insult to injury, Goebbles was still crouched as it spread around her feet so she left a trail of wazzy paw prints as she exited the bathroom.

"JOHN! Goebbles has just pissed all over the bathroom floor!" I dispensed with the stage whisper and yelled down the hall.

"Jolly good."

I stomped into the lounge. "It would appear, John, that I do not have your complete attention in this matter. We still do not have a sample and now I've got to mop the floor. And don't even think about saying 'jolly good' or you're toast."

"Perhaps she just needs more of that litter stuff. Chuck another bag in and see if that makes a difference." John attempted to be helpful.

With the floor cleaned and disinfected I took his advice and added another miniscule sachet of granules to the base of the tray.

Replacing the lid, I put the litter box back in its usual place and we went back to waiting. Next morning I happened to see Goebbles heading for the bathroom again, I resumed my waiting position by the door and watched. Goebbles once more pushed the door open and climbed in, once more there was scuffling and pausing followed by more scuffling. Once more the cat climbed back out, but this time she did not squat and pee on the floor. Had we been lucky at last?

I approached the litter box in high anticipation. Lifting the top off I discovered that the cat had indeed come to terms with the idea of this strange rationed litter and had made the most of the facilities. In the centre of the tray sat a large pile of cat crap, studded with just about every single granule of the litter. This pile was sitting proud in the middle of a little puddle of pink urine.

"Well?" John came through the door. "Have we got a ... what is that bloody awful smell?"

I looked up. "She has crapped in my sample."

"Back to square one is it?" John commented, peering at Goebbles's latest offering. "I don't think we can pass that off as uncontaminated."

"We need a plan B. I have already put all the granules in," I pondered.

This litter box idea was not going to get us a sample easily or quickly and from the state of the urine I had seen, whatever was wrong with the cat was not getting any better. Then I saw Goebbles sniffing the shoe she had initially peed in. I had rinsed it out and put it outside to be thrown into the rubbish. Could we con the cat into giving us what we needed? Fetching an old metal tray I sterilised it and put it on the bathroom floor. I then moulded cling film to my shoe and put it on the tray. For the rest of the day the cat was allowed to come and go as usual, we did not try to keep her in at all.

Somewhere in the early afternoon I saw Goebbles coming out of the bathroom. Hardly daring to hope I went to see if anything had happened. On the tray were a few pink drops, in my shoe with its cling film liner was a pool of red urine, completely isolated from its surroundings and uncontaminated. Using a disposable pipette we used to measure fish tank treatments I sucked up a decent amount and transferred it to a glass vial, again from our fish tank equipment supply. Within a few minutes our hard won sample was *en route* to the veterinary surgery for testing.

The test results showed, unsurprisingly, a high level of blood but no signs of bacterial infection. Worryingly, there were markers present that the vet would expect to see if the problem was caused by a tumour. Goebbles was promptly booked in for an x-ray. If anything suspect showed up the vet would conduct a biopsy via the urethra under the same anaesthetic, thus saving the cat, us and his long suffering receptionist the stress of a return visit. As sedation would be required it meant that she was not to have any food for several hours before the appointment. We had no problem with this as we worked on a less in, less out theory of digestive processing.

"She must be getting used to these trips now, I reckon we can make it to the end of the lane before she craps," I said hopefully.

John did not look convinced, so I tried offering helpful non-driver driving tips instead. "Why don't you just drive faster? Put your foot down a bit? If we have the windows down, more air will blow the smell away and we'll also get there more quickly?"

"Oh, I see. So the fact that I already do these jaunts at the safest legal speed possible has escaped you, has it? What do I now say to the copper sat with his speed gun then? 'Sorry Officer, was I really doing eighty? Is it a thirty zone? Well I never! No, no, I'm not related to Lewis Hamilton. It's like this Officer, our cat has dropped her load on the back seat and I am trying to drive nine miles without passing out. No, why don't you come and sit in my car instead and you'll see what I mean?'"

In the end I picked up a tip from the forensic dramas we liked watching on television. Before we set out I advanced on John with a tub of menthol ointment from our medicine cabinet. "Put some of this under your nose."

Suitably prepared, we loaded up our complaining moggy and set off. My estimate of the end of the lane was wildly optimistic and Goebbles chose to perform the second John started the engine. Despite there being a lack of food in her system, what she had retained, she had matured and fermented to pungent perfection.

Before I lost mobile signal I quickly rang the vet, "Hello, this is Helen here. Yes I'm fine thank you, how are you? Great stuff. Um, we are bringing Goebbles in for her x-ray, is it possible to book one of those hygiene appointment thingies?"

Once John had parked up in town I hopped out of the car. "Righto, see you back at the car in a wee while then."

"Hang on just one second," John said. "Where do you think you are going?"

"She honks, it's embarrassing, your turn to charm reception. I will go and buy the papers and the lottery while you hand her over."

I returned about ten minutes later to find John standing by the car and all the windows down. "Is she charmed?" I queried.

"Oh, she's chuffed to little mint balls. Nothing like having a cat covered in poo dumped on you to really make your day. We should be able to pick Goebbles up at lunchtime."

Back at the veterinary surgery later we consulted with our vet and found out the results of the x-ray. A shadow had shown up in Goebbles's bladder wall. The vet had attempted to perform a biopsy but, unfortunately, our cat had a very narrow urethra and it proved too difficult to access the area. It was probable that she did have a tumour and that it was bleeding, causing the red urine.

We now had several options to consider. A biopsy could be obtained surgically but then the vet could also try to remove the mass at the same time, the problems he outlined with this approach would be that it was an invasive and very serious procedure for any animal. For such an old cat the risks were much higher. She would have to recuperate slowly from major surgery and there was the possibility that he may not be able to remove the entire tumour. Disturbing it, if it was relatively stable, may cause it to spread and conversely there was the chance that, even if he could cut all of it out, major trauma could result to the structure of the bladder wall depending on how much it had been infiltrated.

Our other option was to leave the tumour *in situ* and treat it with steroids. This would act as a sort of feline chemotherapy and keep the tumour at bay. It would not be a cure and at some point the treatment might stop working but it was something to consider as an alternative to an operation.

The vet laid all the facts, possible complications, outcomes and options out for us in a compassionate matter of fact way. He did not rush us but really, there was no debate. I knew John was thinking along the same lines as me as we contemplated our still slightly groggy cat. We were not going to put her through a major operation that might not solve the problem and could well finish her off. At fifteen and a half she had earned a peaceful retirement.

"If we go down the steroid route, what does it entail?" John asked.

"A short intensive course of tablets and then a maintenance dose daily."

"How are the tablets given?" I wanted to know.

The vet smiled, "You can hide them in her food, they are not very big."

This was a relief. Goebbles did not do tablets. Administering medication normally involved John holding the cat while I poked the tablet into the business end. I would then stroke her throat while we both tried to ignore her attempting to excavate arteries in our arms with her claws. Once we were absolutely, one hundred percent sure that the tablet had been swallowed, we would let her go, at which point she would spit it onto the floor with a smug *'puhh'* and disappear.

Round two would involve John telling me that I had done the whole thing wrong and he should have done it himself in the first place. I would tell John that he was entirely welcome to the end with all the teeth and to feel free to educate me and, by the way, if he had bothered to hold the cat more securely then I would have been able to complete the job properly.

John would huff off to retrieve the tablet and I would huff off to collect the cat. The whole procedure would then be repeated with a slightly soggy tablet which was now losing its anti-foul-tasting-coating. I would then adopt a smug manner as I picked the mushy remains off the floor while John glared at the cat. Depending on how many tablets we actually had at our disposal we would then commence with a new one or smudge the mush into peanut butter and smear it down Goebbles's leg for her to lick off. Tablets that went straight into food were a bonus.

"Do you think the tumour is causing any pain?" asked John.

The vet was honest. "Animals can be very good at hiding pain but she isn't giving any outward signs. She is not losing weight, she's active, she is grooming herself regularly and is eating and drinking normally. If any of these change, it may be an indication that she is uncomfortable but we can cross that bridge if we come to it."

John and I looked at each other, we both knew what direction to take. "Let's go with the steroids," I said.

The vet sorted out a prescription. "You should start to see more normal urine but I will need samples to check. Do you need more of our litter?"

"No, we are okay, we have a way of collecting pee."

My shoe was needed for another couple of months. Goebbles obliged by providing regular samples. Checks at the vet showed a gradual reduction in the markers for the tumour and visually, we could see ourselves that the vivid red colour was diminishing. The tablet regime became second nature and my shoe was finally relegated to the bin when a week's samples had been crystal clear and blood free. We knew that, at some point, the tablets would cease to do their job but as Goebbles pottered into her nineteenth and then her twentieth year with no further signs of ill health we felt that we had definitely made the right decision for her.

THESE NUTS ARE TOAST

Sunday mornings tended to follow a relaxed and established routine. Not generally being a working day for me I would try to sneak a lie in. What usually happened was that John would get up to make me a cup of tea, there would then be a gentle thump on the duvet as Megan hopped up, she would give one gentle lick on my ear and I would roll over to give her a cuddle. This particular Sunday started no differently. It was cold and wet outside so I welcomed the chance to stay snuggled up. John headed off to make me my tea, there was the usual soft thump on the duvet, a quick lick on my ear and I rolled over to find myself eye level with three inches of doggy dong.

At that moment, John appeared in the bedroom doorway, tea in hand to find me speedily propelling myself backwards into the still sleeping cat, spluttering my disapproval at Monty, while Monty stayed where he was, his dog-hood still in all its proud glory.

"Well, that's not something you see every day," he said. "Why is there a dog sat on my pillow with its knob hanging out?"

My lie in that morning came to an abrupt end. Very shortly afterwards, discussions commenced on when to do the deed and to have Monty snipped.

A couple of days later I was sitting on the floor cushions cleaning books after the latest drenching from Monty's bladder, when two paws appeared over my shoulders and a tongue lazily licked my ear. As I was also sat fairly near to the television with a dog programme showing, I thought Monty simply wanted a better view so did not immediately throw him off. That was until I sensed the paws tighten over my shoulders and a rather rhythmic motion began emanating from behind me. Monty was busily humping me. Springing up, I stomped down the hall to find John. These nuts were going to be toast.

Checking back with the vet, we found Monty was nowhere near the weight he should be yet, but at least he was heavy enough to undergo an anaesthetic safely. The appointment was made for a couple of weeks' time.

Within this time his exuberant libido managed to upset relations with Megan, who very nearly attempted to do the vet's forthcoming job for him. Wanting a cuddle at around five one morning, Monty decided to ignore the usual protocol of a light tap with a paw and a nose nudge. Launching himself onto the bed in a flying leap from around ten feet away, he stood on me, clubbed John round the head with a foot, farted and was then most put out not to receive a favourable reception.

Undeterred, he bounced off the bed, obviously labouring under the impression that giving a sleeping Megan a full genital examination was a better idea. It wasn't. Most unimpressed at having a cold, wet nose rammed up her fundamentals at the crack of dawn, without so much as a by your leave, Meg exploded awake in a snarly, growling, black and white ball of indignation.

Eyeing Monty later and with Megan maintaining an affronted distance from him, we pondered his uncertain genetic heritage.

"You, mate, are not a collie lab cross," I said, ruffling his ears. "You are quite clearly a doughnut crossed with a plank."

Monty was completely unperturbed by this dismissive analysis of his genes and reared up to park two huge paws on my chest, his tail waving frantically.

"Get down, naughty dog." I pushed him back to the ground. "You should have a more impressive name. You could be the sire of a unique breed."

I watched him wiggle a paw at me, his tail sweeping the tiles then, as soon as my back was turned, he planted his feet on the draining board and started slurping the washing up water.

"Monty, no! Off, now."

The perfect name popped into my mind and I passed it by John for approval. "What do you think of 'Amoeba Montgomery Two-by-Four the First' as his breeding title?"

John nodded as he emptied the dish bowl while Monty burped suds back on all fours. We felt it represented his key attributes. It reflected his tendency to utilise all of one brain cell in everything he undertook, it accommodated a posh version of Monty in an attempt to bestow a vestige of pedigree, it allowed for recognition of the fact that no matter how rebuffed, snarled at or told off he was, he blundered happily through his daily existence with all the common sense of a lump of timber and it also declared to the world that he was unique.

Following the trend to merge names when two distinct breeds coupled, rather than admit that an unexpected shafting by a wayward, randy hound resulted in random mutts, his puppies would create a new pedigree. Aware that his breeding potential was due imminently to be curtailed, I advertised his services on my networking site, 'Available at stud for approximately one week, Amoeba Montgomery Two-by-Four the First. Roll up, roll up if you want your own little Doplanks'.

Unfortunately, our pedigree sire's reputation was becoming well known in cyber world by this time and there was a singular lack of enthusiasm for populating the county with mini Montys. Although I felt everyone should have a hairy tornado with no body clock and the social etiquette of a hippo in their lives, the opportunity was missed and the chance of seeing a Doplank parading the ring as Best in Show at dog shows of the future was lost forever.

The due day of Monty's snip soon arrived. Instructions from the vet were not to let him have any breakfast and to present him at the surgery for nine. In the interests of keeping the peace, we decided that Megan would have her breakfast once Monty had gone. This course of action was most unpopular, both dogs sat in their normal feeding places looking disgruntled and hungry. They were then duly loaded into the car; Monty breakfastless and bemused, Megan breakfastless and cross, we arrived at the vets and Monty was handed over into the care of the nurses.

We could ring at two in the afternoon to check that all had gone well with the anaesthetic and the operation. By twenty past nine I was on tenterhooks, by lunchtime I was pacing the floor, by five to two I had the phone in my hand, counting down the seconds. We had read up on canine castration, the plus points would hopefully be a calmer dog; he should be less prone to scenting all over the place, more inclined to pay attention to command. Without all that testosterone coursing through his system he should also pack it up with humping anything that moved and his tendency to drag the cushions behind the settee for the purpose of conducting illicit liaisons should cease.

The down side could be that he would be a little depressed and sore and would have to wear a cone to stop him worrying the wound site. He would have to be walked gently for a few days and rough and tumbling would be out while he recovered but, as he would probably be feeling bruised and uncomfortable, he would most likely not feel like much vigorous activity anyway.

From our point of view, a couple of days of gentle pottering instead of Monty dragging you around the fields were an added plus. Once the vet had given the all clear to pick him up, John set off to reclaim our wounded warrior. They arrived home and Monty hurtled through the door. As per the care sheet, we offered a meal but were prepared for him not to be very interested. Monty pounced on the food, scoffed the lot in record time and then upended the bowl in case he had missed a scrap hiding underneath. He then set about charging round the house to check everything was as he had last seen it.

"We are supposed to ensure a calm environment for his recovery," I said, waving the care sheet as John tried to catch Monty to put the cone on him.

I grabbed the treat box and rattled it and Monty skidded to a halt wagging his tail. Duly fitted with a cone we then realised that it essentially provided him with the equivalent of a bucket on the front of a digger. Totally unconcerned, he used this new tool to blunder round the hallway, scooping toys and shoving his water bowl along the tiles.

"He doesn't appear to be very depressed and sore, does he?" John observed, as Monty careered through the lounge door to pounce on Megan.

Eventually, the rigours of the day caught up with him and we were able to settle Monty down quite easily. Reading the care sheet in more detail once Monty was asleep we noticed that the vet doing the operation had assessed him as only being eight months old. We had had him for about a month, which meant that he had only been a seven month old pup when he came to live with us. A puppy with the energy of a nuclear power plant and no training!

Next morning, Monty's excitement levels were off the scale, he bounced out of bed and swiped Megan round the chops with his cone while trying his usual trick of attempting to chew her face off. Setting off down the corridor we heard a crash as he scooped the brush attachment of the vacuum in passing and knocked it over. Arriving in the kitchen for breakfast, he planted the cone over his bowl and chomped away as though we hadn't fed him for a week, an echoing slurping issuing through the plastic.

There was absolutely zero indication that he was remotely bothered that some rather important additions to his person had been removed. We watched our little house being slowly reduced to rubble as Monty refused to be slowed down or distracted from his usual rambunctious activities by the addition of his odd headgear. We then watched him instigate a new game with Megan. Pouncing in front of her with his bottom in the air, he waited until she grabbed the edge of the cone with her teeth. He then proceeded to bounce backwards, dragging her with him as she chewed a fetching frill of mangled plastic all around the edge. As the structural integrity of the cone was slowly reduced to a scattering of little plastic bits all along the hallway, we made the decision to chance taking it off.

We watched Monty carefully over the next few hours, waiting for him to lick the bruising or worry the wound site. None of the dire complications that came with the care instructions came to fruition.

John was amazed, "Numbnuts has become nonuts and he hasn't even noticed!"

BAD NEWS FOR MEGAN

Our pets bring us untold entertainment, unconditional love and we would never be without them. Sometimes, however, things go wrong. Monty may have been completely unconcerned by his surgical experience, but it had not been such an easy ride with Megan early in 2012, about seven months before Monty's arrival. She had been snoozing on the chair next to John and, as usual, he had reached over and given her a gentle stroke on the head, she responded by wriggling round and upending, exposing her under side. Lazily ruffling the fur on her belly he suddenly stopped, then concentrated on one spot.

"I think Meg might have picked up some bites from being in the long grass," he said.

I hopped off the settee and came to add my own inspection. Meg thought this was great, two people stroking her was an unexpected bonus and she obligingly stretched her front legs out, giving an unobstructed view of her tummy.

"I don't think they are bites," I said, parting Meg's fur and examining the area where there were a few raised bumps. "They feel like little lumps."

Next morning saw us at Megan's favourite place in the entire world – our local veterinary surgery. While her first few trips to see the vet had been uneventful, a later one had involved him lifting her tail, without so much as a by your leave, to take her temperature and empty her anal glands. This effrontery caused Meg to whip round in indignant rage and snap an impressive set of gleaming teeth in the general direction of the vet's hand. From then on Megan was muzzled for surgery visits and she developed an abiding dislike of our entirely likeable vet. Checking her in with the receptionist we took our place in what was a crowded waiting room. The usual arrays of worried looking owners, holding cat baskets or rabbit carriers, were sat among people with well-behaved dogs waiting their turn.

Megan glared round suspiciously then disappeared behind John's legs to peer out at her fellow patients and growl whenever the vet appeared from the treatment room. Finally it was our turn.

"Megan please," called the vet.

Megan poked her head out from under John's knee and started with the growling again.

The vet looked over at us and raised his eyebrows. "The feeling's mutual dog, come on."

After a good look at the offending lumps it was time for a plan of action.

"They are mammary tumours," he said. "We need to have her in and whip them off. I can send off for a biopsy and that will give us an idea of whether they are sinister or not."

This was worrying news to hear but Meg was a young, strong dog and there was always a chance that they would prove to be benign. She had, by now, had two clear seasons so we also arranged to have her spayed during the same operation. It was something we had been planning anyway but now it was medically recommended to maximise the chances of the tumours not recurring at a later date.

A couple of days later a grumpy and starved Meg was delivered to the surgery for her operations. I was due to be at work all day so I had arranged with John that I would get a taxi home and he would pick Megan up when she was released by the vet. However, if there were any problems whatsoever with either Megan's operations or her subsequent recovery I would be rung at work immediately. A quick courtesy call to let me know that she was safely back at home would keep my worry levels in check until I could get home and see her for myself.

Reaching home that evening, I dumped my bag and keys in the hall and raced into the lounge. Megan was groggy but awake. She had been injected with painkillers and a long lasting antibiotic but was quite obviously a little uncomfortable, shifting awkwardly as she tried to change position to greet me.

"If she shows any signs of licking or worrying the wounds, we have to put a cone on her." John waved a hand towards an as yet unused cone.

We decided that the best thing to do was to coax her down to the bedroom, where she could stretch out in comfort on her bed and we could watch television without having to disturb her again. A bowl of water was placed nearby, Megan clambered gingerly onto her duvet and settled down, seemingly only too happy to be in her own bed with us by her side. She fell asleep straightaway, exhausted by the trauma of her day.

I awoke in the early hours. Soft licking sounds were coming from Meg's bed. As I hopped out of bed to investigate John whispered in the darkness, "She started licking a few minutes ago, I have got my hand between her tongue and the wound sites so she is licking me at the moment."

Crouching down by her bed I said to John, "I'll stay with her for a bit, you go back to sleep." John withdrew his hand and sighed, which led me to think that he had been stopping Megan licking for a lot longer than the few minutes he had told me about.

"Right Meg," I soothed. "What's going on?"

I cradled her head and she seemed to go back to sleep. I stayed with her until she appeared to be breathing deeply and then crept back under the duvet. Instantly the licking started again.

"Don't worry, I'll take the next shift," came a voice from the darkness.

Just as dawn was breaking I headed for the bathroom. Coming back to bed I noticed that Meg was awake. John's arm, at an angle that was bound to give him severe grief when he woke up, was still hanging out of bed cuddling her side. Gently lifting his arm back into bed, I snuggled down next to Megan and scooped her to me. Pulling my dressing gown close I settled down and curled up next to her. She did not seem in too much discomfort but would instantly head for the wound sites the second she was not being watched.

This led to a council of war over breakfast. We were both exhausted and it had only been the first night of Megan's recovery. The care sheet issued dire warnings about infection and wound damage resulting from licking and pulling at the stitches. We decided to put the cone on her. When Monty had been fitted with his he became a little more clumsy but was completely unperturbed by its presence, Megan, by contrast went completely mad.

She careered off in a panic, pawing at her head and whimpering. A trail of damp paw prints on the kitchen tiles indicated her stress levels and she blundered into walls and doors in her efforts to escape.

"She should hopefully get used to it if we don't make a fuss," John said.

As we went about our business, studiously not making any sort of issue about the cone, we waited for Megan to settle down. She didn't. Still crying and shaking her head she looked up at us with the whites of her eyes showing before colliding with the kitchen cupboards. We gave it an hour but Megan still showed no signs of tolerating the cone and was becoming more distressed by the minute.

"She is going to hurt herself if she doesn't calm down," John observed. "We will just have to go back to keeping an eye on her."

So the cone was removed, to Meg's immense relief. But watching her twenty-four hours a day was not going to be a feasible option for either of us. We had a consultation with the vet. It would be completely possible, he informed us, for Megan to reopen the wounds by licking them. If she pulled at the stitches she could cause nasty infections in a major surgery site. If we were not going to subject her to the cone then we would absolutely have to make sure that she did not have access to the area. To emphasise the point he mentioned a recent emergency he had been called to where a local dog had succeeded in licking open a wound site and creating a large enough hole for its innards to escape through.

Chastened by this alarming prospect, we resolved to try the cone again. As soon as John picked it up, Meg flattened her ears, whimpered and shot off to hide.

"This isn't going to work, is it," he muttered despairingly.

"Hang on a minute, I have just thought of something." I headed off down to the bedroom and reappeared a few seconds later.

"That's your favourite swimming costume," John looked surprised.

"It is, but it is worn out. I just didn't want to throw it out. With a bit of modifying it might just be the next best thing in doggy couture." I fetched the scissors and cut a tail-sized hole in the seat, then called Meg. Wary, but relieved that I did not have the dreaded cone in my hand, Megan sidled up.

Between us we manoeuvred her back legs through the existing leg holes and her tail through the new one I had created. Pulling the body of the costume up her torso, her operation sites disappeared under a layer of protective fabric, and I then tied the halter straps to her collar.

"Won't she be too hot?" John asked.

"No, the material is breathable, she will be fine."

I sat back to admire my handiwork. Megan was a dog with medium length fur. The end result was a fluffy head and neck sticking out of one end with a fluffy waving tail and haunches at the other. Four legs with feathering at each corner while in the middle, my black swimming costume snugly encasing the rest of her body.

"She looks like a collie with a poodle cut," John smiled.

Meg sniffed over her new outfit, she then attempted a cursory examination of her operation sites but soon gave up. Evidently deciding that a little sartorial indignity was infinitely preferable to the cone she sauntered off for a nap.

With the recovery process protected from unwanted ministrations, the scars healed well. It wasn't long before we were back at the vet for the stitches to be removed and a check-up. The news was good on the healing, no infection and nice neat scarring. It was not so encouraging on the lumps that had been removed. We knew that with mammary tumours in bitches roughly fifty percent prove to be benign with the other fifty percent being cancerous. Of the half that is malignant, half of those are fast developing and dangerous, the other half is slow growing.

The vet got straight to the point. "Megan's tumours were malignant," he said, consulting the results on his computer screen.

John and I exchanged worried looks.

"But," continued the vet. "They were very slow growing ones. I have taken out a lot of surrounding tissue as well as all the tumours, it looks hopeful that they were localised and there has been no spreading. Megan should make a full recovery."

Bitter sweet news to hear but if Meg had to have cancerous growths then she had the best kind to have. We were instructed to complete regular checks of her tummy area as a precaution but the operation had been a success.

"Come on then, daft dog," John said, ruffling a muzzled head. "Let's all go home."

As we both conveyed our thanks to the vet for his help, Meg added her own comment, diving for the door and growling all the way.

CULINARY CAPERS

Being semi-vegetarians, there does not tend to be a lot of meat in our house, but, living with a couple of alpha predators, I opted to spend a productive afternoon one day making a meaty casserole for the dogs.

Money being tight, I found some reduced pre-packaged cuts in the local supermarket and set about preparations. Congratulating myself on just how cheaply I was able to obtain prime protein I cut the wrapping and dumped the pigs' kidneys on the chopping board. One promptly slid off the board and into the washing up bowl. I grabbed the other to stop it following suit, only to find that it had all the culinary characteristics of a bar of wet soap as it shot out of my hand onto the floor and skidded under the kitchen table, hotly pursued by one of the alpha predators.

Retrieving the kidneys, I rinsed soapsuds off one, fluff and dog hair off the other, with a mental note that I would have to start taking more care of the housekeeping standards of the kitchen floor. Then I commenced chopping them up ready for quick frying to seal in the flavours, in what was to be the ultimate in bespoke dog dinners. I was, however, totally unprepared for the smell that arises when you chop up kidneys and the fact that my one large piece of culinary soap became lots of little soaplets, all intent on slithering everywhere.

Eventually I managed to turn them into the pan for sautéing, where they all immediately stuck fast to the bottom and I realised that hot kidneys smelled even more repulsive than cold ones. With the flavours now permanently sealed to the base of my best frying pan, I added vegetables and a stock and left the foetid stew simmering on the hob. John emerged from the office, sniffing the air and muttering darkly.

"What the hell is that stink? Don't say the drains are blocked again."

He lifted the lid on my concoction and prodded a greyish floating lump with a wooden spoon while the alpha predators positioned themselves in front of the cooker and drooled.

"It's kidney and swede casserole for the dogs," I explained, as another waft of fermenting septic tank drifted upwards.

John replaced the lid, wrinkled his nose and went back to his computer. "I hope you are going to get on the case with the washing up, your casserole smells like something has died in here."

The dogs disagreed with his assessment and hung around looking hopeful. Monty tried to save me the effort of cleaning at least part of the kitchen floor by energetically following the skid marks left by the erstwhile escaping kidney with his tongue. While watching him drool what looked like a giant slug trail across the tiles, I absentmindedly brushed my fringe back and then made a disturbing discovery. Not only did the scent of fried and boiled kidney permeate every nook and cranny of the vicinity, but also the raw ingredient also firmly impregnated the skin on my fingers. I washed my hands again. I used hygiene spray. I used scented bath oil. But, I could not get the smell of pigs' kidneys off my skin.

Sitting in the lounge later that evening I morosely sniffed the end of my fingers after raiding my bedside cabinet for the strongest scented hand cream I could find.

John saw an unmissable opportunity to take the mickey. "What's up? Do your pinkies still smell offal?"

I glared across at him, "It's horrible, and the smell just won't come out."

Notwithstanding the unexpected odours of my first attempt at gourmet dog food, the speed with which both bowls were emptied and then licked clean of every last remaining scrap proclaimed my cooking a success. I decided that a casserole would be on the menu every week or so as a special treat.

A couple of months later I was happily pottering around the kitchen, chopping and blending. My latest offering was bubbling on the stove and I was doing my best to stack all the remaining washing up in the sink. As I perched the last spoon on the teetering pile I heard sighing behind me.

"What's been going off in here?" queried John, glancing around.

Admitting that the level of disarray exceeded even my usual ability to wreak havoc while cooking, I cast a guilty look over my shoulder, just as my washing up stack collapsed sideways onto the draining board, evicting the pots I had washed onto the floor.

"The BBC could pass this off as a war zone. Do you have to use every single utensil going? And, just a tip, but I tend actually to start some washing up when I can still see the taps."

I glared up from where I was scooping the escaped pots from the floor.

"You could help. I'm trying to beat the thirty second rule."

"The what rule?"

"The thirty second rule. If it lands on the floor in a dog household, there's no contamination if you can get it back off the floor in under thirty seconds."

John raised his eyebrows, "Great, everything is so much better with mud and hair on it. I have a feeling you have wildly overestimated your timing, it's actually a three second rule." He gestured at my armful of crockery, "Which means that lot needs washing again."

As he turned to go, he cast an appreciative glance at the hob and sniffed, "Mind you, that cooking smells yum, what is it?"

"That is a stew of ox hearts and chicken with peas for the pooches."

"Lovely. And what are we going to be having?"

"Oh, I'll rustle up some crap from the freezer in a minute."

With a look and a set of newly raised eyebrows, John left the kitchen. I put the ox heart stew to cool and ferreted about in the freezer. I had decided to run our stocks down so that I could plan a defrosting and clean so I was using up trays of cling-filmed portions from earlier meals. Peering at my freezer burned selection dredged from the depths I was happy with sausage casserole, mashed potatoes and some sort of green veg and put the trays in the oven to heat through.

An hour later and I was ready to dish up. Megan and Monty bounced around my feet as I filled their bowls, while Goebbles huffed and yowled her annoyance at being third. Then I retrieved our tea from the oven to find that a year lurking at the bottom of the freezer had given my casserole, spuds and veg an oddly exotic aroma. Plating up revealed a slight menu change which was going to take some explaining.

I decided to wing it. Taking cutlery through to the lounge along with a saucer for Micky I announced that dinner was ready.

"*Hello mate, I'm a good bird,*" warbled Micky the second he spotted the saucer. We had long ago realised that if we were eating in the lounge, Micky expected to join in. Not including him would result in a cacophony of squawks that lasted through dinner. His Micky plate consisted of a tiny bit of whatever we were eating that was safe and suitable for a parrot and would ensure that we had peace and quiet.

"Smells nice, what are we having then?" John asked as I delivered his plate.

"This is a medley of international fusion cuisine for your delectation," I replied, putting Micky's saucer sample of our dinner in the bottom of his cage and settling down to eat my own.

John poked around his plate and seemed to be examining things perched on the end of his fork.

Megan and Monty had finished their tea and were now sat either side of me looking hopeful. "Yum," I declared, tucking in. "Mmm, mmm, mmm."

John appeared to be having difficulty in getting to grips with his dinner and now seemed to be conducting a forensic dissection of his greens.

"Um darling, about your medley…"

"... of international fusion cuisine, yes John?"

"Well, much as I admire the chef's bold use of colour and adventurous technique."

"Thank you. Are you delectating?"

"I wouldn't exactly call it that. Correct me if I'm wrong but we appear to be having cod gratin, prawn tomato satay and hot guacamole for dinner?"

"Yes John. International and Fusion."

"Hot guacamole?"

"All the best chefs push the boundaries of flavour and texture. Megan! Stop drooling on my foot."

Micky had now cleared his saucer and had climbed back up onto his perch to wipe his beak. Seeing that we still had food on offer he started squawking *'Hello Mickys'* at us.

"See, Micky loves my fusion idea. And the dogs are positively salivating."

"Glad to see someone likes the idea of hot guacamole," John sniffed.

"Ah, well they've passed on the guacamole, it is avocado; it would poison them."

"I know the feeling."

A few minutes passed, then John piped up again.

"While I would agree that the boundaries of flavour and texture have certainly been pushed, I'm just wondering, is this international fusion idea going to be a regular thing?"

"No, but I must admit I am going to make more effort to label tubs in the freezer from now on."

John looked relieved, then commented once more as he grudgingly added a satay prawn to his gratin, "Interesting, we've got dishes from Europe, Asia and the Americas here, shame the Indian sub-continent is missing from your medley."

I looked down at my plate and then across the room. "You're quite right John, very remiss of me but I can resolve that right away. Would you like a poppadum to go with it?"

PUPPY PLAYTIME

When Megan turned up the vet assessed her as being about a year old. This meant she was still young enough to get up to mischief if left unsupervised for a moment. On one occasion, she munched the strap off a pair of shoes that had only been bought three days earlier that I'd left lying around. The floor standing bathroom cabinet was also subjected to a spot of illicit chewing. Coming back from shopping one day we found a pile of splintered wood and Megan giving us her best *'That will teach you for leaving me'* glare.

However, being partly trained as a sheepdog meant that Megan responded relatively quickly to boundaries being set. Catching her in the act of chewing something she shouldn't we issued a firm 'no' and the sternest looks we could muster; she soon cottoned on to the fact that toys were for playing with, furniture and footwear were most definitely not.

Monty's arrival soon enlightened us that an untrained pup with a Labrador persuasion was quite possibly the most destructive thing in the known universe. His life philosophy revolved around eating things, wrecking things or dragging things off to be eaten or wrecked out of sight of a telling off. Megan had amassed a huge pile of toys; mainly furry, stuffed animals that squeaked or honked when chewed. Whilst a couple of less robust specimens had been disembowelled and de-squeaked, generally Meg treated her toys well. The reason her toy pile was so extensive was because I could not resist adding to it every time I visited the pet shop. Megan played but did not destroy which meant that, by the time Monty came, an enormous mound of fluffies had taken over the hallway.

With eager relish Monty pounced on this new source of entertainment. Within a few weeks virtually every soft toy had been decapitated and de-stuffed. We became used to seeing our hallway covered in tufts of white foam or kapok and gathering up the sorry remnants of a cloth tail, leg or head. Visits to the pet shop for toys to replace the casualties now involved an assessment of their Monty-proof qualities. No longer would I spot a furry snake and think how Megan would enjoy dragging it around the yard before settling down to mumble it in the sunshine. Now, unless toys displayed the potential to survive the average nuclear strike they were replaced on the shelf immediately.

"What about this one?" I would ask, proffering a rugged looking specimen designed for the active puppy.

"Wouldn't last five minutes," John would respond.

"This then? It provides stimulation and hours of play for the inquisitive dog." Reading from the label I would hand another possible toy to John.

John would examine my new find. It would then invariably be handed back.

"It might stimulate Monty for about ten minutes, but then it would be in pieces and another ten quid would be down the drain."

We ended up with the 'extreme' ranges, the ones designed for the toughest of tough chewing. Labels on the toys we selected now displayed huge dogs with enormous teeth and promising descriptions like 'virtually indestructible'. The toy pile continued to take over a substantial corner of the hallway but now it consisted of solid rubber, robust antlers, unbreakable plastic and weighty rope. With the arrival of Monty, Megan's heap of feminine fluffiness metamorphosed into a mound of playthings with industrial lasting qualities.

Both dogs played tug together, or they would select the toy of the moment and retreat to a comfy spot to inspect and chew on their own. What we soon discovered, however, was that we had ended up with a minefield of objects designed to bruise and stub our unsuspecting toes as the dogs scattered them with free abandon along the corridor. Stepping on a furry sheep caused no problems, kicking an eight-inch antler was another matter entirely.

Having such an extensive supply of toys and being such a friendly dog meant Monty was only too happy to share with his human companions too. When I came home from work I laboured under the mistaken impression that I was entitled to sit down, kick off my shoes and relax with the papers while John rustled up dinner. What I was actually entitled to was Monty's undivided and exuberant attention and a session of rough and tumble play time.

"Clear off Monty, I'll play with you in a minute, just give me a second to unwind," I would sigh as my daily mantra.

Monty took me literally on these occasions and after allowing exactly one second of unwinding he would pounce on me. The daily paper did not usually stand a chance of survival and would be dispatched as a rival for my attention in a flurry of paws.

"Get off me, I hadn't read that."

Pushing him off and surveying the remains of the dailies I turned the television on to catch the early evening news. And then tried to catch up on what was happening in the world while trying to ignore the fact that the throw I was sitting on was slowly moving in a little series of shifting tugs. At the corner of the throw was Monty, fabric firmly clamped in his teeth as he jumped and flexed backwards in an increasingly successful attempt to relocate the throw, with me on it, to the lounge floor.

"Will you pack it in, you'll make holes."

Monty paused, but did not drop the corner. He knew, though, that he was on to a winner. By this point I would invariably be reinforcing my mean alpha female dominance by being unable to stop laughing. Another little bounce backwards, another inch or two of movement and that would be it. There was nothing for it, I could continue to try to fend off a dog intent on getting my undivided attention or I could indulge in a quick spot of 'wear the Mont out so I can chill' playing.

"Come on then, what shall we do?" I asked him.

Monty wagged his tail but didn't relinquish the throw. He wanted to wait until he was certain this was not just a ruse to get rid of him. John came into the lounge to sit down, Megan trotting behind him.

"Dinner will be about half an hour. What on earth has happened to the papers?" he said.

"Monty."

"I see, and what has happened to the settee?"

"Monty."

John assumed the position in his recliner while Megan, sheepdog duties over for another day, hopped up into the chair next to him and settled down.

"Any idea where the remote control has gone?" he asked.

"Monty."

"Or the stylus for my tablet?"

"Monty."

"Chatty this evening, aren't we? What is he now, the universal answer?"

"You know as well as I do, if in doubt blame the Mont." I replied. "Anyway, puppy wants to play."

John glanced away from the news, "Any chance you two can possibly refrain from destroying the house this time?"

"I am actually about to engage in a period of structured yet energetic interaction for the benefit of Monty's ongoing socialisation training and psychological welfare."

"That'll be a 'no' then, will it?"

Monty followed me into the hall. I stopped by the toy pile. "Which one Mont?" I gestured at the heap. Monty wagged his tail, waiting.

"What about the purple dumbbell?" I poked a rubbery tooth cleaning toy out of the basket. The tail wagged at the same speed as before.

"Okay, the knotty rope? The squeaky Wubba?" Monty ratcheted

up the pace of the wagging and sat to wave a paw at me.

"All right, it just has to be," I hovered my hand over the remaining toys. "The tuggy bone!" With a flourish I whipped a tough red bone, made from the same fabric car seat belts are constructed from, out of the pile and plonked it in front of Monty.

He instantly dropped his front paws to the ground and stuck his backside in the air, waving his tail so much now that his whole back end swayed from side to side. With a little bark he pounced on his end of the bone and began dragging it imperceptibly away from me. I backed off down the hall but Monty knew the game inside out. He stayed put, panting and wagging, until I turned and with exaggerated steps plodded towards him.

With each step I smiled at our routine, "I'm – coming – to – get – you Monteee!"

That was his cue. As soon as he heard his name he grabbed the bone, turned tail and hurtled into the lounge. Just inside the door, but out of my sight, he dropped the bone and stood over it, waiting. I sneaked silently to the doorway popped my head round so he could see me and then withdrew to stand back against the wall. Monty would take a step with his toy closer to the door. I crept forwards again and poked my face round the frame, this time Monty would track me out into the hall when I pulled back.

Tail waving like mad and his whole body quivering he waited for what came next. With a couple of hops I advanced on him.

"Oh Monteee! I'm coming to get youuu!"

Monty grabbed the toy and shot back into the lounge, with a leap he cleared the footstool and dived onto the settee where he positively radiated excitement. At this point he would leave the bone so I could grab it and retreat to the kitchen doorway. A thud would indicate he had jumped back to the floor so I wiggled the bone up and down the doorframe until he skidded into my sight. As soon as he sat I gave him back the bone and he would wait with it in his mouth, looking over his shoulder at me, eyes gleaming with the enjoyment of the game.

"Monteee! You're going to have to hiiide," I called, bouncing out of the kitchen, arms outstretched like a zombie. "Because I – am – coming – to – get – you!"

At this he headed at speed back into the lounge, bounded over the stool, and burrowed under the throw and cushions on the settee. As I zombied into the lounge, ignoring despairing looks from John, I asked, "Where aaare you?"

"What, the giant vibrating mound isn't a bit of a giveaway?" John said, with his arm over a sedate and snoozing Megan and trying to watch the television.

Lifting the edge of the throw I cooed "Hellooo Monteee!" which was Monty's cue to explode out from underneath it, fling himself onto his back and shimmy along the settee kicking the cushions and then the throw onto the floor. Panting with exertion and pleasure he lay with his paws in the air as I tickled his tummy and announced, "I've found you, shall we do it all again?"

After one particularly energetic session that left the lounge and hall looking like an earthquake disaster zone we decided that a new training regime was necessary. Monty needed to learn to play on his own occasionally. Whilst it was lovely, not to mention being a lot of fun, to interact with him, he had to learn that he could not have undivided attention on demand all the time. There would be times when he would have to occupy himself and playing nicely with his toys in a calm manner would be a good skill to take on board.

So, one Sunday seemed a promising day to start. The Grand Prix was on the television and I wanted to have a leisurely read of the papers while John watched it. Megan settled down behind his chair to chew an antler, gnawing away while holding it between her paws. Monty circled the toy pile. I left him to it and made myself comfortable on the settee.

A few seconds later came the unmistakeable sound from the kitchen of the lid being flipped upwards on the bin.

"John, Monty's in the bin again," I commented, engrossed in the enormous pile of bumf that comes with the Sunday paper.

"Well, go and sort him out then. The race is about to start."

There was a crunchy scuffling from the kitchen and then the sound of the lid flipping again. I was settled and comfy and reluctant to move.

"MONTY!" I yelled. "Get out of the bin. Now."

Monty showed his face in the lounge doorway, paper from the bottom of one of the bird's cages clamped in his jaws. As I pushed the supplements aside and stood up Monty disappeared with his prize, trailing debris back into the kitchen. He had long ago worked out that the bins offered a treasure trove of sniffable, edible contraband. It had taken him no time at all to learn that putting his foot on the pedal of our bin made the lid go up and he then had free access to the delights within.

So, when the bin needed replacing we opted for a pedal free version that you had to raise the lid up on by hand. My reasoning was, as we surveyed the various options in the hardware store, that even if he could work out the new bin Monty would not want the edge of a heavy plastic lid resting on his sensitive nose and our rubbish would be safe.

Once installed in our kitchen Monty looked it over, found that it did not have a foot pedal, and then set about solving his access problem with the enthusiasm and resolve of a professional safe cracker. It took him all of a day to learn how the lid flipped up and while I was correct in assuming that he would not want the nasty heavy lid resting on his delicate nose, the new bin was a couple of inches lower than the old one which meant that Monty was entirely unconcerned by it resting on the back of his thick skull while his sensitive nose rootled through the contents.

Now, as I heard the roar of engines signalling the start of the Grand Prix in the lounge, I grabbed the paper off Monty and stuffed it back in the bin. I then put the food recycling bin on top, the plastics and packaging bag in front and herded him out of the kitchen.

"These are your toys," I admonished, pointing back to the enormous pile at his disposal. "Leave the bin alone."

Leaving him to select something to play with, I went back to the lounge.

"I take it his new 'playing by himself' training session is not going so well," said John, beer in hand and engrossed in the race.

Settling back onto the settee, I picked up the papers again. "I've shut him out of the kitchen, he is now poking round the toy pile like a good dog."

Then there was a bang from the hall. "Sounds like your good dog doesn't like being shut out of the kitchen much."

Our house was a converted barn, the internal doors were rustic affairs that closed with a latch. A rather feeble and decidedly un-Monty-proof method of security if he was on the side where he could barge them open. Giving up on my reading I headed back into the hall to find the kitchen sporting a fetching council-landfill-site-look and Monty standing in the midst of a sea of recycling.

"Right. Out. Go find John." I ordered, pointing at the door.

Monty obligingly scarpered as I tidied up once more. Back in the lounge, he was standing on the armchair with his paws resting on the edge of John's chair, happily surveying his territory outside the picture window. This was a comfy armchair that my parents had been throwing out and which I had taken the opportunity to nab for our own house. My plan had been to install it next to John's recliner so that we could sit together and chat in cosy proximity. Its arrival had merited much interested sniffing and it was then instantly commandeered by both Megan and Monty as a premier snoozing spot. I was relegated back to the settee.

An even better view of whatever was happening outside could be achieved if Monty could get away with using John as a platform while he was reclining. As next door's cat homed into view and climbed onto our rockery he assumed the position, hind legs on the armchair, tail alert in pointer mode and two paws firmly planted in the middle of John's sternum.

Surprisingly benignly, considering the Formula One was in full swing, John patted the seat next to him. "Get down, next door's cat does not count as a toy."

Monty responded by edging his front paws a couple of inches further towards the window, eyeballing Kitty and drooling over John's sweatshirt. Trying to peer past him while not missing any of the action John patted the chair again.

"Lie down Monty."

Monty cocked his head, registering the instruction but keeping his gaze fixed on the cat.

"Will you get out of my face, dog? And lie down."

Finally the canine cogs whirred, ever willing to please Monty decided on compliance. Retracting his paws he instantly collapsed like a pole-axed bullock as John's head disappeared under a hairy torso and a muffled and fairly anguished squeak issued forth.

"Uumph. Not there."

Monty looked over at me with his best *'Is he going to make his mind up, or what?'* expression, at the same time wriggling to dislodge the annoying chin and nose bones from his ribs. Finding this new position offered the same viewing range, he turned his attention back to glaring at Kitty while I giggled on the settee.

Just as I was considering how the scene would look to forensics a flushed face reappeared and some less than polite gestures were issued as Monty was unceremoniously elbowed back to the floor. I decided to make it easier for the concept of playing alone to sink in and beckoned Monty to follow me.

"Here," I said. "This will do."

Pulling a toy from the pile I took it into the kitchen and spread peanut butter over it in patches. It was made of a tough fabric, designed for rough play and the picture of the obligatory dog on its packaging had shown what looked like a rottweiler on steroids, gnawing away with intent, with the toy maintaining its pristine appearance despite the onslaught of huge fangs.

Food always drew Monty's full attention and he trotted eagerly ahead of me back into the lounge. Handing the toy over I was pleased when he took a furtive look at Megan to check whether she had noticed what he had and then positioned himself out of her view and settled down to chew.

Half an hour later Monty had not budged from his spot, I had nearly finished the papers and the race was coming into its closing laps. John and I looked at each other and grinned, another milestone in training could be ticked off the list. I then smiled my appreciation at Monty but, in doing so, made eye contact and it all went awry. Leaping up, we could see why he had been so quiet; the toy had been denuded of its tough coating which lay scattered in shredded red scraps on the carpet and the pink stuffing was half in, half out of the sad remains of the shell.

Within a second he stuffed his head under the papers that were still spread on my knee and whipped it upwards, scattering them and upending my cup of tea down my top. He then cleared the side of the chair in one leap to land on John. While the commentator worked himself into a frenzy as two drivers took the result right to the wire on the last bend of the last lap of the Grand Prix, Monty parked his foot on the remote control and turned the television off.

We unticked the box and went back to training.

CHRISTMAS IS COMING

Our first prospective Christmas with Monty led to some lively discussions. We had always indulged in a few tasteful decorations and, for the past few years, having consigned our tatty moth-eaten artificial specimen to the skip, a real tree. The thought of introducing a tree when we now had a dog with only newly acquired housetraining skills and the tendency to see absolutely everything as a bespoke dog chew was daunting.

I started the debate early; to tree or not to tree? I happily pointed out the plus points of our tree; it would have beautiful lights and traditional charming tinsel. A warm Christmassy feeling would be created by its festive pine needle scent. Monty would easily pass the ultimate test that he was a fully integrated member of the household. John expounded upon a few incidentals being negative points of the said tree; the lights would end up wrapped round the dog and we would end up with a huge vet bill for munched tinsel. Both of us would end up having a nervous breakdown living with the festive scent of dog wazz on the tree and we would finally have proof positive that Monty was Tigger on acid.

We consulted friends and family. Some were decidedly emphatic, "In with the tree and out with the dog I say." Sarah, from the smug position of living twenty miles away adopted an encouraging approach. "Monty needs to get used to Christmas, I'm sure he will be just fine."

"Ok," I said. "Tell you what, he can come and settle into Christmas at yours and we'll have him next year. I take it this is a vote for a tree?"

"Dad says to decorate Monty instead, to save time and stress."

This was an interesting solution which left me pondering where to stick the plug for the lights? Needless to say, our first festive season with Monty ended up being an entirely tree-less affair.

The following year I instigated some tree training. In good time I decided to introduce some floor standing foliage in a carefully controlled environment to ensure Monty was completely comfortable with the idea. Firstly, I took him out for a pee. His bladder empty I carefully placed my prized and nurtured dragon tree on the floor and draped a bit of ribbon over it. Monty watched, his head cocked.

"Look Mont, this is a tree. Nice tree. Now get used to the nice tree and leave it alone, because its enormous big brother will be coming to stay soon."

A cursory sniff and a quick swig of the water out of the base container and Monty disappeared to find out what John was cooking in the kitchen. Thrilled that our well trained pooch had not made the link between what he did to trees outside and my inside tree I headed off to take over dinner preparations.

Returning to the lounge later, I found John engrossed in Bad Piggies and Angry Birds and came across a complete absence of dragon tree, also, a complete absence of Monty.

"Any idea where my tree is, oh love of my life?" I purred sweetly.

"It was there a minute ago," came back the unsatisfactorily unconcerned response as more piggies bit the dust.

I followed the trail of compost sprinklings, to find Monty proudly sitting in the hallway about to settle down to an impromptu spot of pruning, evidently pleased with this exciting, organic new toy. I palmed Monty off with a meaty twirler and relocated my slightly chewed pride and joy back to the safety of the windowsill.

"I suppose that is it in the tree stakes," said John later.

I was undeterred, "Not at all. We just need to plan the location and make sure that he can't get at any of the decorations. I will also probably have to desist from putting bleach, sugar and aspirin in the water I put in the trough this year."

"You put what in the water?" John stared at me in amazement. I sighed. Did men know nothing about Christmas tree care? "A teaspoon of bleach keeps the water fresh. Sugar feeds the tree so it stays lush and green and I think aspirin is supposed to help capillary action or something."

"What a load of old cobblers! In that case, why was our last tree dead and crispy within a week? Or was it possibly because it was drowning in the contents of our medicine cabinet and drinking sugary Domestos?"

"No," I countered. "Our last tree suffered from being crammed up against the radiator. It boiled. I did tell you that it would thrive better on the coffee table."

John put down his book. This conversation obviously merited full attention. "You put candle arrangements on coffee tables, darling. You might even stretch to putting ornamental Spode festive plates on coffee tables, with a few nibbles in them. You generally do not, however, put five-foot high spruce trees on coffee tables! And, if you are even going to contemplate this as an idea, do not buy a tree unseen, ready wrapped in that clingy mesh stuff."

Even I had to admit that this had not been the wisest way to buy our tree. It was the first time that I had insisted on taking the choosing and buying of the tree on myself and John had duly picked me up from town with my modestly sized offering ready wrapped for transit.

"I'm impressed," John remarked. "I was expecting to pick you up with something you could put up in Trafalgar Square. Is it a nice shape?"

"I have no idea, it was a couple of pounds cheaper to have one ready wrapped. The chap said it is easier to position in the base clamps if you bring it home like this. All the unwrapped ones looked really nicely proportioned though."

I got the look again. Later, in the lounge, I was smug when we found that it was indeed much easier to stand the tree in the base trough and adjust the holding bolts without having to grovel around under the branches. Once all was secure, I took a pair of scissors to the mesh and snipped, freeing the tree from its prison. Its branches instantly sprung outwards and showed the tree to be a healthy and bushy specimen. John watched on as the branches emerged and I carried on cutting away. At the base, the tree was about five feet wide, at the middle it was also about five feet wide. At the top, it did what any tree should and tapered elegantly; here it was about four feet wide.

"This is not a tree," John commented, trying to manoeuvre it against the radiator. "This would appear to be a hedge."

"Hang on, it can't go there. The heat will kill it."

"We are slightly limited though, on where we can put it, aren't we? On the grounds that you have bought a sodding forest and virtually every spare foot of available floor space is taken up with fish tanks."

"What about putting it on the coffee table?"

John looked incredulous. "On. The. Coffee. Table? Are you serious? We are going to be peering through the branches as it is, stick it on the coffee table and it is going to be like spending Christmas camping in a wood."

So, the tree stayed up against the radiator and within a week was dropping needles and looking parched. By twelfth night it was a giant twig and our vacuum cleaner was stuffed to the gunnels with pine needles. This year's tree was going to be a real one and it was most certainly not going near the radiator. John, however, would be back in charge of tree buying duties while I stuck to more suitable tasks like writing cards and buying presents and spending vast amounts of money we did not have. As it got nearer and nearer to Christmas Eve though, I started to notice that the necessary sense of urgency for installing a tree was decidedly lacking.

I opted for some subtle and gentle prodding, "It's the twenty-second, why haven't you bought a tree yet? Christmas will be over by the time you pull your finger out."

I came home from work that night to find our tree in the

lounge. Conceding to my demand that it be nowhere near the radiator, most of it was behind the settee. John had erred on the side of caution and left the lights off, stringing them over the pictures on the walls instead. The chocolate baubles were in a tin in the kitchen as he felt that this was a temptation too far on the Monty front and my lovely glass decorations were still in the Christmas box, replaced by shatterproof cheapo specimens from the local discount store. It was very pretty, festive and tasteful in a 'no great shakes if Monty wrecks it' kind of way. I loved it.

Monty completely ignored it for the entire Christmas period. Micky, on the other hand, for the first time in the seven years we had had him made a beeline for it every time I got him out, charging along the back of the settee and jumping onto a branch to bite chunks off and fling them on the floor. He would home in on the baubles, detach them and throw them, squawking *'I'm a good boy! I'm a good, good boy!'* as he did so. Our tree was safe from Monty, it was the parrot we had to worry about that year.

DISCOVERING HIS WOOF

For a long time after Monty arrived he hardly made a sound. Admittedly, he would whimper if he wanted something but generally he did not growl, he did not bark, he made no sound worth mentioning at all. We consulted Sarah, yes, he had barked very occasionally but not much and only usually one or two yips. Compared to Megan, who barked liberally at the Air Force overhead, anyone passing by the gate, us if her breakfast was late coming, we were not used to a quiet dog. It was uncanny, this was a virtually silent dog. He would fix you with his strange rimmed eyes but he would not bark.

We wondered if he had been punished by his former owners for barking and had decided it was safer to keep quiet. We just didn't know, but then, one fine, early winter day when both dogs were outside enjoying some rare sunshine it happened.

In the office checking emails a sudden, rumbling, abrupt noise stopped John and me in our tracks.

"What was that?" I commented, heading to the hall window to check on what was going on in the yard.

Monty and Megan were engaged in a spot of rough and tumble in the grass, with some energetic play fighting and fencing at each other going on. Taking it in turns to gain the upper hand, it looked pretty violent but the madly wagging tails and happy panting during breaks in play showed that there was no malice involved from either dog. I watched as Monty dropped to his front paws, his back end planted in the air, wagging frantically from his shoulders downwards, as he tried to get Megan to carry on with the game.

Megan half-heartedly chomped at his jaw but did not seem to

be showing the required levels of enthusiasm Monty expected. He backed off, pounced back in the paws down bottom up position and then barked. Or rather he emitted a noise that, on the Richter scale would register something between an earthquake and a meteor landing whilst wiping out known civilisation. Monty had discovered his woof.

John joined me at the window. Monty looked quizzically at us, cocking his head in surprise with a *'Did that noise just come from me?'* expression on his face. He then barked again, twice, before once more stopping in amazement, looking around for the source of this impressive new sound.

"I thought puppies were supposed to have sweet little puppy barks?" I said. "You know, to make you go 'aah' at your little pup and to look forward to lots of years of doggy companionship?"

John was eyeing Monty with his arms crossed. "It would help if the puppy in question was a little pup and not a bloody great dog. I think his bark is going to match his size."

Megan, who was used to being the centre of barking attention, was obviously unimpressed by this attempt to usurp her supremacy and decided to reassert her control of the situation. She wandered over to stand by Monty and give him a look.

"*Woof,*" she barked.

"*WOOF,*" Monty responded.

"*Woof, woof,*" Megan again.

"*WOOF, WOOF.*"

"*Woof, woof,*" Megan huffed, with a little growl for emphasis.

"*WOOF! WOOF! WOOF! WOOF! WOOF!*" Monty bounced around her in glee.

"Oh arse," said John.

Having belatedly discovered this new method of communication, Monty was justly proud of it and began to seek every opportunity to air it to a wider audience. He would wait until you picked up the phone and connected with the person on the other end, then he would begin with his own contribution to the conversation. It did not help one bit that this was a bark with the power to splinter concrete and bring the lampshades down.

This would invariably set Micky off, who would pitch in with his own terrier like bark. The usual result was for me to apologetically ring off with a promise to ring back when I had quelled the wolf and the parrot.

On another occasion a courier, trying to deliver a parcel, rang in despair when his Satnav had sent him up the side of the nearest mountain and he needed directions to find us. I had been snoozing with Monty on the settee and he voiced his disapproval at being disturbed the second I picked up the phone.

"You okay mate, I've got a package 'ere. Oi, what the chuff is *that?*"

"Hush Monty! Oh, hello, that's just our puppy."

"*GRRR ARF ARF GRRARF.*"

"Puppy? Wot of love? A chuffin' lion? I'll leave your parcel in the shed all right?"

Normal mail delivery time allowed more practice. Megan, never a fan of the postman, was happy to impart her ambivalent attitude to her new mate. On the arrival of the letters in the letterbox both dogs would now set up a cacophony of howling which set us looking to buy one of those post boxes you mount about fifty yards from your house. Unless we intercepted it first the post would be snatched out of the letterbox and given a damn good shredding while I peered fearfully through the glass for the quivering remnants of the postman.

"We need a baby gate," I announced one day.

"Is there something you need to be telling me, darling?" John queried.

"No, but the dogs are lurking in wait for the post, they might shred something important."

"We only ever get junk mail," John commented.

"I was thinking more of the postman's fingers," I clarified, picking bits of catalogue off the doormat.

Loading up the pooches for shopping meant heading into town with a fetching Boom Box effect rebounding around the interior of the car. Staying perfectly quiet in the countryside, Monty waited until the first sight of buildings and pedestrians before he started with the barking. Resisting the temptation to nod our heads and pretend we were listening to the latest heavy metal bass revival, we put up with the looks of smug owners, walking their beautifully behaved and utterly silent dogs, tutting at our total lack of dog discipline as we occasionally yelled, 'Monty, will you shut the **** up!'

The entire car park at the local supermarket glanced round with concerned looks when our car started shaking with the acoustics vibrating the metalwork. Being a university town, you could just see people speculating on possible dinosaur cloning as we sneaked in to the shop, *'GRAARF, AARF, GRARRF'* echoing behind us.

When we took Monty to our local pet store for one of his regular weigh-ins to check his progress he did not bark but planted two enormous puppy paws on the shoulders of the ever helpful sales girl.

As we logged his latest increase in weight, she rubbed his chest as he happily mined her ear with a huge tongue and commented, "Oh, he's got some growing to do yet."

We drove home to the usual din emanating from the back, until we exited town and headed back into the countryside. Monty promptly shut up but no one could see our now quiet well-behaved dog except the sheep and buzzards.

Glancing in the rear view mirror I expounded upon the development of the woof. "You know I came up with the doughnut and plank theory on Monty's genetic heritage?"

"Yes?"

"Well, I think I got it wrong, this dog is a great dane crossed with a T-Rex."

"I can live with D-Rex," John replied. "It wasn't right for him to be a silent dog."

Monty eventually became used to the novelty of barking. Both dogs indulged in a morning barking session as they woke up and chased each other round the house with tug toys and they always barked at the arrival of the postman, but generally Monty stayed quiet unless there was something to alert us to. It was reassuring, living in the middle of the countryside that we would receive a warning of visitors, because it meant that our little pack was looking out for one another.

Megan continued to be the noisy dog she had always been, thankfully, Monty joined in only at certain times. But, in the middle of the night, if something unusual broke the silence of the sleeping household; a late car on the lane, a strange scuffling outside of a visiting badger, someone lamping for rabbits in the fields we knew that Monty was alert to the risks and that both Meg and D-Rex had our backs.

DOCTOR MONTY

My first week off after the rigours of retail at Christmas was eagerly anticipated by me so I was totally unimpressed to come down with a cold on the first day. Snuffling valiantly, I threw gallons of vitamin C, zinc concoctions and cold remedies at it but it was determined to run its hacking, coughing, streaming course. Fresh air would do me good, I thought, heading out into the fields. Coming back into a warm house produced paroxysms of coughing and a need to harangue John about the unfairness of the cold versus holiday timing.

The weather was also threatening snow so one afternoon, feeling particularly weak and sorry for myself, I retired to bed. Laid low completely by the cold from hell I settled down in a sorrowful, spluttering heap. Luckily I had Doctor Monty on call. Not impressed with the fact that his patient had shut the bedroom door to keep him out, he conducted a short experiment on the structural integrity of its wooden construction versus the power of the modern dog claw. I gave up and let him in with strict instructions that, if he was going to join me then he was to lie down, stay still, not wreck anything and be a canine hot water bottle.

Monty sat by the door and listened intently. He then hopped up onto the bed and started snipping the sequins off the embroidered flowers on the eiderdown with his teeth. I dragged myself onto an elbow and glared at him. Yelling would start my cough off so I whispered my fiercest threats and prodded him with my foot. Monty made one last defiant chomp at a denuded flower and then started using his tongue to retrieve the sequins anteater fashion. He then ate them.

With the last of my energy I summoned John. "Your dog is eating my throw, tell him to pack it in or clear off."

By now Monty was curled up looking serene and innocent. I lay back on the pillows and shut my eyes. I snapped them open again a few seconds later when I heard an ominous ripping noise. Monty now had one of the small, decorative bed cushions braced in his paws. Taut between the cushion and his mouth was a length of ribbon which had, until that moment, formed an ornamental border. As I watched in fuming disbelief he gave a quick tug upwards and another couple of centimetres detached with a shredding of stitches.

I made a grab for the cushion but was not fast enough. Monty dived off the bed with his prize and made for the door, just as John reappeared with a hot toddy for me.

"Your rancid grotbag of a dog is now eating my cushion," I wheezed.

"Bit peckish are you Mont? Don't we feed you enough? Why don't you come with me and I'll find you something you are allowed to have?"

Monty trotted out of the bedroom and I heard the beginnings of negotiations to retrieve my mangled cushion. I lay down for the third time and tried to go to sleep. Just as I was beginning to drop off I heard the bedroom door bang open and a slinky black shape bounded in, Doctor Monty was back on a house call to check on me. His sense of medical urgency was enhanced by the fact that this latest visit involved arriving on the bed in a flying leap from about five feet away. He then pounced on my pile of tissues, giving those germs what for by head shaking them into a scattered mess of bits.

As I opened my streaming eyes he stood over me so that I had a view of his knob that only the vet should get and then he collapsed onto my chest for a cuddle. Concerned by my sudden apparent inability to breathe he then stuck his paw in my eye and swiped the empty packet of cold remedy, which he proceeded to shred all over the duvet. Working on the principle that if I could not see it then it wouldn't wind me up I pulled a pillow over my head and tried to ignore the tearing noises.

Monty decided that his patient should remain in view and began to dig me out. Adopting the same levels of emergency response as an avalanche rescue dog finding me under six feet of snow he set about unearthing me. Not really wanting to spend my afternoon retrieving clouds of duck down feathers, especially in my weakened state, I gave up and showed my face. I was flushed and wheezy. Monty paused and then set about concluding his rescue by resuscitating me, slurping at my feverish forehead and breathing a digested aroma of dog lunch onto my face, a pong that permeated even my blocked tubes.

John came in and watched the proceedings from the door. "Ah, he is such a caring dog really. I've just heard the weather forecast, they are predicting snow."

He gestured towards the glowering skies outside, heavy with menace in the early afternoon gloom. "It has turned really cold out there too. I will go into town and stock up."

As he spoke, the first big flakes began to drift down and the wind gusted the side of the house with a soft moan. We were not often affected by heavy snow, being relatively close to the sea, but the forecast was severe. On a couple of occasions in previous years our lane had become impassable with even the farmers struggling to access the steepest parts as they iced over. It made sense for us to have a few essential provisions in store; like wine, chocolate and whisky, to see us through the worst.

I however, was not going anywhere. I was ill and grumpy, but for the first time that day, with the duvet around me, and the heating on maximum, felt vaguely warm. I waved John off.

"See you soon, take Megan with you. Take a spade too. If you get stuck and you can't dig your way out you can at least cuddle Meg to keep warm. Oh, and if you find you are really stuck, you can eat Meg to survive, but don't eat her liver because it is too high in vitamin A and will poison you."

John moved his incredulous glance from the odd snowflake dropping past the window to me expounding survival techniques from my pit and sighed. "I am going into Aberystwyth for a couple of pints of milk and some bread. I can honestly say that eating Megan was not on my agenda for the day."

"Preparation is everything in a survival situation," I countered. "There is a pull out in this week's paper about having wellies in your car and checking your heating oil tank is full. It also says you should carry a spade and a blanket in the boot."

"And does it recommend chowing down on the family dog too? Must write to the editor. I will be a couple of hours, tops."

Monty was curled up next to me and Goebbles hopped up to snooze on my other side. This meant that I was now even cosier and their deep snoring had a soothingly soporific effect on me as I watched the snow falling gently. It looked like the ongoing turf war between dog and cat was temporarily suspended so John took Megan and made to leave.

"I wonder if Monty has ever seen snow before," I muttered. "I wonder what he will make of it."

"If you can hold off eating him while I am out surviving in the wilderness, we'll find out when I get back. See you later."

The snow fell lightly all afternoon but did not settle. It then fell heavily overnight and did. Morning revealed a beautiful winter landscape sculpted into drifts by the winds that had accompanied the blizzard. In places the fields were dusted by a mere sprinkling of snow with the sparse pasture poking grey green blades through an icy frosting. Against the fences and in the hollows of the hills deep drifts had built up in cushiony pristine swathes to a depth of several feet. In areas not swept by the wind the snow had fallen and settled in a three inch blanket of proper, fluffy, snowball snow and this included the part of our yard immediately outside our front door.

On opening the door for the first time that morning Monty had given the snow a frightened look and then backed away into the kitchen.

"Come on Monty, you need to have a pee." I gave the lead a little tug and scratched a trembling ear.

Presenting Monty with a completely different landscape was causing problems. While Megan dived across the yard, tracking paw prints through the virgin whiteness, for a steaming constitutional over by the barn, Monty had all four paws braced against the sill of the doorstep and was flatly refusing to cross the threshold.

"It is snow, it's fun, look." I stomped deep footprints and chucked a handful at Megan, who was now wriggling happily on her back, scuffling a deep impression and making dog angels.

Monty did not look convinced but tentatively extended one paw over the step and prodded warily. He then withdrew his foot as if scalded and looked in horror at the flakes now clinging to his pads. As they melted away and dripped onto the doormat Monty sniffed at his paw and then looked at me with a worried look. I gave the lead a little tweak once more as Megan gambolled around barking, poking her nose into the snow and tossing her head upwards, snapping at the scattered flakes.

Finally, the needs of Monty's bladder won out over his fear. He stepped over the sill, lifted each foot off the ground in turn in the manner of a dressage horse and skidded the ten feet over to the car, he then relieved himself at record speed and shot back into the house. As I closed the door, shutting out this strange new world, Monty visibly relaxed and charged into the lounge to pull the covers off the budgies. Opening the curtains allowed him to check on his territory at the back of the house. Standing with his paws on the windowsill he froze and then looked over his shoulder at us with a disgruntled expression. *'What's going on, this white stuff is out here as well?'*

A day in bed meant I was feeling a little better so we both decided to take the dogs out for the morning walk. An hour later we were all set to go, Monty was totally unimpressed to find the snow had not disappeared in the meantime and that more was now falling to boot. However, his choice was to come with us or be left behind so he adopted his bravest demeanour and sallied forth, mincing through the yard and shaking his head as fat flakes descended onto his nose. Once in the field, Megan set the pace with a joyous charge round the frozen expanses. She had always preferred cold weather and the snow provided her with a playground of rolling and diving opportunities as she squirmed on her back where the wind had scoured the grass and then plunged headlong into the drifts, sinking up to her neck and then digging her way out with nonstop happy barking.

Monty crept along by our side but we could see him taking sidelong looks at Meg as she obviously had the time of her life. I had brought my camera and it was when I was taking a shot of John standing thigh deep in one drift that he decided to see what all the fuss was about. Upending himself at my feet he rolled. When nothing disastrous happened to him he flipped over onto his tummy and nibbled at a frozen blade of grass.

Megan bounced up and tried to get him to play, chasing and tugging at a loop of lead, before once more ploughing through the nearest drift. Finally, Monty took the plunge himself and pounced into a snowy bank, his legs disappearing as he scrabbled sideways to free himself. Taking a cautious peek at the hole left behind he shook residual snow from his coat and then set about digging, scuffing a white shower past his back legs and over me.

We made our way to the top of the hill and paused to take in the view. The snow stretched to the far horizons and in all directions. The wind had dropped and the panorama was silent under its icy blanket, patch-worked by hedges and fences and broken only by black green woodlands, evergreen and frosted. Dotted about were wisps of smoke rising from the chimneys of local farms; distant muffled barking reached us from a sheepdog on a high field across the valley, its owner quad-biking across to a cluster of sheep to dispense feed, the bike bright red and the sheep dirty cream against the white.

The mountains stood stark against a granite coloured sky with clouds swollen with the threat of further snow building above them. In the opposite direction the sea was still, slate grey bordered with ivory for the whole sweep of the bay. The vista was serene and beautiful and we savoured this new outlook on our familiar surroundings, stamping to ward off the chill numbing our feet through thermal socks and wellies. Megan and Monty had pricked their ears at the distant barking but were happy to sit with us and regain their breath.

Our trip back to the house was punctuated with more mad excavations by the dogs as they dug through more drifts and snapped at flakes as they began to fall in heavy flurries. Monty realised that he could chomp frozen mouthfuls from the ground, shaking his head to scatter half melted snow and swallowing the rest. A frozen pile of fox scat unearthed from under a sheltered hedgerow provided a bespoke iced treat until we hauled both dogs away with disgusted admonishments. We returned home with Megan and Monty both panting and happy, puffing frozen clouds into the air. As John and I clapped and stamped life back into our chilled hands and feet and shed wellies on the doorstep Monty took one last chance to enjoy this new experience that had so scared him just an hour before.

Bounding over to the wall he took an interested sniff where the cat had recently relieved herself and then began energetically licking yellow snow. Pulling him firmly into the house and shutting out the cold we made coffee while both dogs settled down for a contented snooze. As Monty started snoring happily we realised what had provided the catalyst from fear to enjoyment. Yes, it was fun to bounce in drifts, it was also fun to roll on crispy grass and dig huge holes. But what was the most fun of all was that a walk in the snow provided Monty with a whole new world of something else he could eat.

PUPPY TURNS TO
THE DARK SIDE

As we concentrated on training Monty and teaching him to settle in, his amenable nature and general sociable demeanour stood out. For all the corrections he received he remained resolutely happy go lucky. Constantly aware that he was having to learn lessons that would normally have been taken on board much earlier in puppyhood we were, nevertheless, pleased with his abiding enthusiasm in the face of what must have felt to him like being at a rather intense school twenty-four hours a day.

We had had him for about five months. He had mastered housetraining and was filling out steadily. He had stopped guzzling every drop of water he could find and was coming to grips with basic commands. John and I were very pleased with how he was progressing. Having read in depth about rehabilitating a rescue dog we were expecting Monty, at some point, to test his new found security and push the boundaries but it was still a surprise when it happened.

One evening in February 2013 I was pottering around the kitchen making dinner.

"Hello Monty, what are you after?" I said, as a slinky black shape appeared in the doorway, sniffing hopefully.

Monty lay down on the tiles to watch proceedings as I stirred the contents of a saucepan and reached for the pepper grinder. "Sorry pooch, no casserole today, I'm doing veggie. You wouldn't like it."

Monty cocked his head and sidled a couple of feet closer clearly deciding that if food of any description was in the offing he most definitely would like it. I checked on the contents of the oven, turning away from the work surface for a second, and at that precise moment our sociable puppy turned to the dark side. Shutting the oven door I stood up and found Monty on his hind legs with his front paws on the draining board licking the washing up.

"Bad dog. Get down." I said sternly.

Monty dropped back to the floor but then braced himself square on to me and issued a rumbling growl. I faced him, shocked. "No," I said, putting the angriest look I could muster on my face.

Monty looked away from me and skulked over to the kitchen doorway where he sat watching me. Ignoring him, I collected up the food waste and peelings from my dinner preparations and opened the recycling bin. In an instant Monty was by my side trying to scavenge.

"No," I snapped. "You are really pushing your luck. Go away."

Monty did not go away. He backed up and growled again, then, in one quick movement, he made a snap at my hand. This was completely unacceptable behaviour and I was not going to stand for it.

"BAD DOG!" I said loudly, in a tone that gave absolutely no room for misinterpretation, at the same time tapping him sharply on the nose.

I faced him, mentally firing sparks from my eyes and with the meanest expression on my face. Monty growled once more, but more half-heartedly this time. I stomped a pace towards him, still scowling evilly. Monty assessed the situation and then, to my relief, wagged his tail, lay down on the floor in front of me and showed me his tummy.

"Good boy." I relaxed my body language and Monty returned to the light.

Later on, John and I discussed what had happened. Monty was now around a year old and he was progressing into adolescence. We knew little about his earliest life except that he had had no training and had been starved. He had learned a lot in the short time he had been with us but he still had a long way to go, it was not the most reassuring of positions to be in. Our scrawny pup was turning into a muscled dog, a large muscled dog with a correspondingly large set of teeth. It would appear that he was developing a case of adolescent angst and stroppiness that he felt was best resolved by whipping a gleaming set of canines perilously close to my soft little hand.

We went back to the training books. What I had experienced was not uncommon, ideally a dog should be trained in its place in the pack from its earliest age. Socialising a young puppy should be of maximum importance if it is going to grow into a well-adjusted dog. All too often this developmental milestone is overlooked and animal rescues are full of dogs who have never learned this and end up rejected when they try to work their boundaries out for themselves. If this involves chewing the family toddler it is never going to work out well.

Unfortunately, one of the busiest times for animal shelters is still late summer early autumn, when the fluffy little scrap that gambolled happily round the tree as a cute Christmas present is now an angry teenager with attitude and a chip on its furry shoulders.

What's worse is the dog who ends up being rejected, time and again, then begins a merry go round of being offloaded; from family, to friend, to mate down the pub, to rescue centre. Each disruption and abandonment just makes the poor dog even more confused and insecure when early training could have avoided the problem entirely.

Although Monty had been taught that his place right from the start was at the bottom of the pack with us, we had no idea what his previous socialisation had been. Rescue training advised that we may have a challenging time ahead. As he headed through his adolescence, up to a possible age of around two when he reached full maturity, Monty might decide on occasion to test his position in this new pack he had landed in. If and every time it happened the response had to be consistent, strict, humane and immediate.

It may not happen very often but as long as Monty was left in no doubt that a pack challenge was not going to be tolerated he would eventually happily accept the situation and the challenges would stop.

One evening about a month after the Great Kitchen Incident, Monty decided that it would be a good idea to disappear with John's pen. Settling down at the end of the hall to examine his latest contraband he was not impressed when John followed him to retrieve it.

"Drop it," John said.

Monty showed no signs of complying.

"Give it here, mutt."

Monty responded by growling.

John stood his ground and bristled with pack leader menace.

"DROP IT NOW."

As Monty started to look less certain of the success of this latest test John reiterated his command in his most severe tone. Monty relinquished the pen but as John bent to claim ownership Monty pounced. There was an angry shout of 'bad dog' from John and Monty immediately found himself outside the front door, in disgrace on the doorstep.

"Bloody dog nipped me," huffed John, nursing a bruised wrist as Monty peered through the glass.

He opened the door a minute later and brought Monty back in. Monty sat in the lounge with his ears flattened worriedly to his head until John called him over and the dog upended himself at his feet in complete submission.

There were a couple more small incidents over the following few months. At my parents' house just before Halloween I was pleased to see they were shutting out the cold night with a roaring fire in the lounge. It did make for a cosy atmosphere and I soon found myself taking off my jumper and relaxing in tee shirt and skirt.

"What on earth has happened to your arm?" queried my mother.

I had not mentioned Monty's latest challenge and she was looking at the ring of bruises circling my upper arm.

"Pup wasn't very happy about me stopping him eating the cat's food," I explained.

A few days before, Monty had got into the bedroom and was standing on the bed eyeing Goebbles's food bowl with intent. I had issued a forceful 'no' and moved to remove the temptation by pulling the curtain between Monty and the windowsill. Monty had snapped at me and closed his mouth briefly around my arm before realising the error of his ways.

"He bit you!" my mum was horrified.

I quickly reassured her. "If he really wanted to bite he could do a lot more damage, he hasn't broken the skin." I explained the behavioural process Monty had to learn and also that the challenges were diminishing.

By Christmas we had cracked it. There were no more growling sessions from Monty and he no longer tried to snap. He accepted his place a couple of months short of his being two years old, textbook rescue pup according to the guides.

TASTY MORSELS AND BITS OF SHEEP

"Well, it was a silly place to leave it, wasn't it?"

Whilst this might have been true, it was not the most helpful comment to make in the circumstances and it was winding me up.

"Are you cutting him off, or what?" I responded, as Monty shot between John and the settee and raced into the hall.

"Here Mont," called John. Monty bounced back into view, eyes gleaming.

"Okay, pincer movement. I'll herd, you corner and I'll grab," I outlined.

Opening my arms wide I advanced and coaxed Monty into the lounge. He took a flying leap onto the armchair and assessed our next move with his whole back end waving gleefully.

We were, by this point in our ownership of him, used to Monty charging round the house and purloining things he shouldn't. He would swipe slippers, socks or the recycling and we entered into negotiations to retrieve gloves, newspapers and the post that would put the United Nations in the shade, all with a treat in one hand and a benevolent smile on our faces.

But this time he had flashed past me in a blur of wagging tail and gleaming chompers, trailing drool over a twenty-pound note dangling from his mouth. I had put it on the dresser for a moment while I made a cup of tea and now Monty had it.

"This is not a game, dog," I said. "Hand it over mutt, or you're toast."

"Good job you are not a hostage negotiator," John commented, imperceptibly moving towards Monty, who was shifting his gaze excitedly between us.

"NOW." I plunged towards the armchair, arms akimbo, to retrieve my cash.

With lightning reflexes, Monty sprang from the chair onto the settee four feet away, cleared the back and dived straight into the hall again.

"You didn't corner!" I glared at John.

"Oh sorry. Was that herding? My mistake, but I didn't realise that flapping about like a rabid windmill was herding."

We began again but Monty had now sussed that his prize was forfeit. Retreating to the end of the hall he spat the now soaked note onto the floor and covered it with a large splayed paw. Keeping his attention firmly on us he bent his head without losing eye contact and delicately nibbled at Her Majesty's ear.

"Dangerous ground Monty, that is probably treason," I said. "How about a Kong instead?"

The nibbling paused for a second as Monty watched me edge his Kong from the toy pile. The dogs had one each and every evening after tea, I would put a smear of peanut butter inside and let them have it as a treat. Fetching the jar of spread and a knife I prepared it in front of him, he cocked his head but kept his foot on the note.

"Right, that's it. I'm going to give your Kong to the budgies," I told him.

Finally there was a temptation too far for Monty. Any opportunity to investigate the budgies and he was there. They were up on a shaded windowsill out of his reach but it was enough. He stood up and trotted into the lounge, peering up at the cage. I gave him his reward and John rescued my note, heading into the office to stick bits of the Queen back in place with sticky tape.

Later that day, with Monty still full of beans, I did some negotiating of my own. "I'll take the dogs out, you do dinner."

"Deal, what do you fancy?"

"I'm not fussed, anything will do."
"Curry all right with you then?"
"Oh, actually I'm not really in the mood for curry."
"Tuna steaks?"
"Ah, I've gone off tuna."
"I can rustle up a spicy chilli with rice?"
"Erm, well.."
"So, are you going to give me a clue what 'anything will do' means?" John sighed.
"How about prawn korma?" I suggested.
"Is that not a curry that you are not in the mood for?"
"Oh, but I thought you meant a tomatoey curry. I quite fancy a creamy curry, just not a tomatoey one."
"Of course you do. Sorry, my curry radar is not tuned in to my mind reading today."

With dinner arrangements sorted I left John in the kitchen and headed out into the fields. It was now early spring and lambing season was in full swing. The normally quiet countryside echoed to the calls of ewes and their offspring and on this lovely sunny afternoon groups of lambs gambolled and charged in play groups as their mothers grazed contentedly.

With the sudden influx of fragile new lives came the inevitable odd casualty and the kites and buzzards overhead were attentive to occasional buffet opportunities, stripping and carrying away carcasses in nature's efficient clean-up campaign.

Megan had gone to sit by the fence and survey the flocks as I ambled along with Monty through the sun dappled grass. All was going well until he spotted something that needed immediate investigation and which looked far more interesting than some boring paper money. With his prize firmly clamped in his jaws, I initiated my best training club commands.

"Leave."
"Drop it."
"DROP IT!"

"Monty! GIVE ME THAT BIT OF DEAD SHEEP NOW!"

With Monty dancing around me as though he'd won the lottery and with absolutely no intentions of letting go, I rang home for advice.

"No problem at all," John said. "All you have to do is to reel in the lead, grab the leg of lamb, fix the Mont with a steely glare and quickly tug it from his mouth."

"Really?" I said sceptically. "It's that easy?"

"You just have to show him who is in command," I was assured.

So I reeled in the lead, gave my best evil look and lunged for a rotting foot. Woohoo! Puppy playtime.

Monty was in heaven. My hand gripped woolly skin that slid over the decaying flesh underneath as he hopped about with his teeth energetically chewing the other end. An unseemly tug of war with the lamb's leg unfolded as I had visions of the next-door farmer coming over to investigate. *'Sheep? What sheep? No, no, it's the latest realistic training tug toy from the pet shop, honest.'*

I looked up across the field to see John standing by our lounge window laughing his head off. Miffed, I let go of the foot, wiped decomposing lamb slime off my hand onto the grass and hauled Monty over to the fence. Meowing announced the arrival of Goebbles so Monty dropped the leg in favour of a quick lunge in her direction.

By now John had joined me on the garden side of the fence. He whipped the leg out of sight, informed me that it was similar to the leg he'd had to post in a hedge in the next field the previous week and popped it in the tree out of canine reach but in view of the circling raptors.

"Great," I muttered. "So now our garden looks like a tyrannosaurus feeding station. There are dismembered sheep remains lurking in foliage all over the vicinity and, by my reckoning, we've the dubious anticipation of two legs still to discover."

"We'll just have to be a bit more observant," John said. "Keep an eye out, ward Monty away from things he shouldn't have. We are in charge, not him."

"I take it that is the 'we' that means me?" I said.

"Well you are a bit soft with him sometimes. That's twice today he has grabbed stuff on your watch. You just need to be a bit more dominant. Observe. Be in control."

"Is that so?" I bristled.

"Yes."

"Dominant and observant?"

"Yes."

"And then Monty won't nick stuff?"

"Exactly."

"Are you done?" I huffed.

"Don't take it personally," John said. "As pack leader I just have to make sure my little pack knows what's what."

Suitably enlightened I made my way back to the house. John carried on with dinner preparations as I settled down to read and Megan and Monty snoozed in the late afternoon sun coming through the window.

John came through from the kitchen. "Prep's done, I'll just catch a bit of the news and then dinner's a go," he said.

The dogs woke up and embarked on a spot of lazy play wrestling; all was well until I looked up and Monty was suddenly nowhere to be seen.

"I assume you shut the kitchen door?" I asked.

John gave me a horrified look and shot out of the armchair like a scalded cat. I followed him to the kitchen and looked past him to see Monty standing on his back legs with both front paws braced on the work surface. He was chomping away with relish on some key dinner ingredients that had been left uncovered and in reach.

"Bloody dog. Get off the bloody counter now, before I bloody STRING YOU UP," John shouted.

"Ooh, dominance in action," I commented.

Monty cast a glance over his shoulder, shifted his paws into a more secure position, licked his lips and side swiped the final prawn off the plate.

John turned a rather alarming shade of puce. "My last prawn has just disappeared down his sodding cakehole," he yelled in disbelief.

"Very observant, pack leader," I nodded sagely.

"What the hell am I going to make korma with now?" John grumped, with a cross stare at Monty and an incredulous glance at his decimated ingredients.

"It's such a shame we're veggie really," I mused. "Because there is half a sheep in the tree outside, we could have had lamb korma instead."

ROLL OVER AND GIVE US A KISS

I came off the phone one afternoon in a proactive mood. I had been chatting with my brother about the many accomplishments of his dog and had decided that it was high time Monty learned some tricks of his own. I would set about training him to do 'roll over'.

Megan was grumpy, her hip was sore again and she had ensconced herself on the armchair in the warm lounge for a bit of rest and recuperation. I made the most of the opportunity to head out for some quality one to one time with Monty. The weather was typical for early spring; when I had announced my training intentions the sun was shining brightly, by the time I left the house the sky had turned black and a hurricane was in force.

"Bit breezy out there," John commented helpfully, as green shoots detached themselves from budding trees and shot horizontally past the window. "Looks a bit like we're in for a shower too," he continued, glancing up at the biblically churning clouds threatening a deluge.

I was undeterred. "We'll be fine, I need some fresh air and Monty needs training. Labradors and collies are hardy outdoor breeds, he'll love it."

I found a slightly sheltered spot in the field and started with the basics.

"Come here." I yelled above the force ten gale.

Monty yanked away at the end of the training lead like a bulldog on steroids.

"Here boy." There was a brief pause in the tugging, Monty cocked one ear as though something fleeting had breached his auditory canal before he decided that he must have been mistaken and engaged in a further, sustained attempt to haul me off my feet.

"Get your scrawny butt over here now mutt, I'm freezing my tits off here," I bellowed, just as the wind died down completely for a minute, allowing my nippy state to be announced to the entire valley.

Monty homed in like a heat seeking missile and flattened me onto the grass while the farmer in his tractor sowing something in the field next door stopped to watch.

"Now that I have your attention," I said. "We'll begin shall we?"

"Sit," I said. Monty parked it.

"Paw." Monty offered his left foot.

"Other Paw." The right foot waved at me.

"Good boy." Praising my amazingly well trained dog for completing his commands with such aplomb, I carried on.

"Lie Down." No problem, he cocked his head and hit the grass.

Flushed with success I rubbed his tummy and commanded, "Roll Over."

Monty sprang up, pounced on a pile of sheep turds and started munching contentedly.

I reeled in the training lead and gave Monty a little pep talk. Having re-established behavioural boundaries we started again. Aware now of John observing proceedings from the lounge window, as well as the farmer watching I knelt down and repeated "Roll Over" with a helpful swirly hand movement to indicate exactly what I wanted. Monty eyed me and then flung himself on me upside down.

I had to admit that he was now rolled over but so was I, lying in a field full of sheep poo, in a howling gale, with an audience. Sighing, I mustered my rapidly shredding dignity, turfed Monty off and tried again, and again, and again. Finally, the canine grey matter fired a few neurons and it clicked. Monty upended to roll over, exposing his tummy for a tickle and lying happily with all four feet in the air. Exceedingly proud, I glanced around with a beaming smile at our onlookers, to find that the farmer had cleared off and John had gone back to his rugby.

Still buzzing, I decided to show John again once we reached home. In the confines of the lounge it was not so easy but Monty gave it a go and did me proud, wedging himself upside down between the coffee table and the settee and panting happily. Before settling down with a glass of restorative and congratulatory fruit punch I called the Mont over to me.

"You are such a clever pooch. Can I have a doggy kiss?"

Monty sat and waved a paw.

"No, that's 'paw', I want a doggy kiss."

Monty promptly lay down and rolled over again.

John started laughing. "I think you have a few translation issues," he said.

I persevered, sticking my tongue out and pointing at my nose. "Come on Monty, 'doggy kiss'."

Finally it sank in what I wanted. *'Ah, one of those my face in your face things'*. Backing up a pace he licked his lips and aimed a tongue at my nose, misjudged his distance and promptly head butted me in the mouth.

"Bonty, u've dust blit by'ip," I moaned.

Teaching the dogs to give a kiss was something that had arisen from a continued need to find something to do inside in bad weather. Quite often it was just not possible to put the dogs outside. Living in the hills near the coast, even in summer the gales and rain would drive periodically off the sea with a ferocity that could soak through the best of wet weather gear. Out on walks in these conditions meant even Megan and Monty would sometimes disappear under the nearest bushes and hunker down for shelter while you stood exposed to the elements. Constitutionals were a necessary evil and the wild weather did have an awesome beauty, but once back home the dogs had to be entertained indoors.

Notwithstanding their enormous pile of toys and the fact that they were happy to wrestle together in a growly, tuggy, slobbery tangle of paws and fur, sometimes it just had to be you that played with them. Tug toys and ball games aside, what really made both dogs' day was if you played on their level. I would start by kneeling, brandishing a toy and both dogs would home in for some sedate tugging.

In the interests of maintaining pack leadership I would endeavour to win all tug contests, grabbing the toy and throwing it over my shoulder. If it landed on the floor one of the dogs would retrieve and we would start again. However it could land on the settee and this would be the cue for Monty to spring up and turn both the throw and all the cushions onto the floor. Despite the fact that the toy would have been in plain sight he would pretend that it needed to be excavated from where it had sunk into the bowels of the upholstery.

The third option was that my random flinging would land the toy on John. Monty would see no difference between John and a settee and would then attempt the same excavations while I disappeared rapidly to make a cup of tea and find something important to do in the kitchen.

One such day had started with rain, continued with rain and finished with rain, turning the yard into a pond and the fields into a quagmire. Both dogs had given us a *'Are you serious?'* look at the prospect of a trek round the hills and I was now on a mission to keep them from getting cabin fever.

"Here Meg! Here Monty!" I called from the end of the hall.

No response. It was cold outside, the heating was on and both dogs were sat in the lounge by the radiator.

"Oi! You two, here now, I've got treeaats."

Both dogs turned up, collected treats and then disappeared back to the lounge again.

Coping with a bored dog meant thinking like a bored dog so I donned my best 'what would interest a dog stuck inside on a bloody awful day?' thinking cap.

Resuming my position I tried again, "Woof, woof, woof."

John, Megan and Monty appeared in the lounge door way and eyed me.

"Woof," I woofed.

"Is there something amiss with your arm darling?" enquired John.

"No John, it's my tail," I said, waving my arm behind me from my position kneeling by the bedroom door.

"I see. And is there any reason you are wiggling your backside in the air?"

"I'm wagging my tail."

"Of course."

Both dogs decided to investigate this new situation and a tidal wave of black and white fur bore down the hall. I was engulfed in paws and tongues and it was after this slobbery onslaught that I decided that we could refine this into another acquired skill. I would teach the dogs to give a kiss.

My plan was to get the dogs to sit nicely in front of me; I would then ask for a kiss, point to my chin and wait. The desired result of a quick lick before sitting again would elicit treats and my enthusiastic show of approval. It shouldn't be too difficult a task to master, both dogs were old hands at the 'sit' command and loved the chance to bond by licking.

I started with Megan. Originally trained as a sheepdog she was not generally fussed about learning tricks and had resolutely refused to 'give paw' despite numerous attempts to teach her over the years. However, this new session of training seemed to appeal and I soon had her sitting and watching my hand as I asked for a kiss, pointed the way and parked my face in front of her. With minimal coaxing and a couple of treats it wasn't long before Megan sat in front of me, waited for my request and then gave the merest flicker of a lick to my chin before backing up and sitting again.

John was impressed by Megan's ability to learn, less so with my sense of hygiene.

"You do realise where the dogs' tongues spend most of their time, don't you?" he observed, after Meg performed her new trick perfectly once more.

"I'm not asking for a Frenchie, it's just a tiny touch to the chin. You hardly even feel it."

"Come on then, let's see Monty do it too."

"Ah, well I am still refining the finer points of Monty's understanding of the request."

"He can't do it!" John patted Meg. "You're a clever girl though, aren't you?"

I bristled, "He can do it, he is just as clever as Megan."

"Let's see it then."

Monty had relished the chance to please and learn something new but as usual had added his own enthusiastic interpretation and style. With his reputation at stake I called him over.

"Monty. Sit." I said, kneeling by him. He sat.

"Good start," John observed.

I flipped him the bird and turned my attention back to the task in hand. Taking a deep breath I brushed my chin with my hand and hoped for the best.

"Doggy kiss?" I asked.

In an instant the whole of Monty appeared in my face as he happily attempted to suck out my eyeball before turning his attention to mining a nostril. Bracing his paws on my shoulders to better complete the command he then slapped me enthusiastically round the face with about four inches of wet tongue until I fended him off and sat gasping on the carpet.

John giggled as he addressed Monty, "A teensy bit forward in your approach there Mont." Then he looked to me, "I know it was only a tiny touch to the chin that you hardly even felt, but you appear to be a bit soggy, would you like a tissue?"

HAVOC FROM DAWN TO DUSK

Just occasionally there occurred a time when all the pets woke up wreaking havoc and kept it up until they crashed out at the end of the day.

One morning the dawn chorus woke Monty up and he decided everyone else should be awake to appreciate it too. After arriving on the bed like a crash landing jumbo jet, he discovered the occupants were not arranged to his satisfaction. He managed to remedy this with legs and paws in pneumatic drill mode, conducted a brief turf war with Goebbles six inches from my face and, just to make sure everyone shifted with the alacrity he expected, indulged in a quick bout of retching. His mission accomplished, he then settled down for a kip so we could all then listen to the birdies.

It had already been a disrupted night. At midnight, Goebbles had woken up, stretched and then started meowing to go out. I hopped out of bed, opened the window and off she went. At two in the morning she had arrived back, positioned herself on the garden bench about eighteen inches under the windowsill and mewed softly to come back inside.

I pulled the duvet up around my ears and tried to ignore her. It was a pleasant night, it would do her good to stay out and get a decent dose of fresh air. Goebbles paused in her gentle calls and I assumed that she had given up and gone hunting.

She hadn't. She started yowling; very persistently, very loudly and, as time went by, incredibly crossly. Cursing, I dragged myself back out of bed and flung the window open.

"Goebbles," I hissed at the dim shape now angrily sharpening her claws on the bench. "Will you shut up? You'll wake up the whole house."

The cat jumped up and purred happily as I closed the window and got back into bed. She then started noisily munching and slurping at her food bowl. I left her to it and went back to sleep, until Goebbles's midnight feast idea disagreed with her and she unexpectedly deposited the remains of her dinner, along with a large fur ball, in a pool of warm vomit onto my bare foot.

"You are such a rancid, manky, festering cat," I fumed, climbing out of bed and stalking to the bathroom to clean up.

"Is it actually possible for you to make any more noise?" came a voice from the gloom.

I promptly fell over one of the dogs who had decided to sleep on the floor and not in its bed and crashed sideways into the wardrobe. Regaining my balance I then stepped on an antler and swore loudly.

"Yes it actually is," confirmed the voice. "I know this is probably not the right time for this conversation, but if the animals slept in the hall, you would not now be stomping around at the crack of sparrow fart, with a stubbed toe and puke on your foot."

All the training guides had seemed to advocate keeping the bedroom as an animal free zone. Feeling that this was a tad unfair and obviously being far more experienced and knowledgeable in the matter than the established experts of our time, I had scotched this concept right from the start. How much more lovely would it be to have our little pack arranged sleepily around the room, ready to leap into action in an instant to defend us from all intruders?

John had had reservations about this but then he could also see the down side of two dogs and the cat being out of sight and up to no good on the other side of a closed door. Unfortunately, as I very quickly found out, the reason dog experts get their training books published is because they have a tendency to know their stuff, whereas I most certainly did not and ought to have bowed to higher intellects.

By this time it was far too late and both dogs and the cat were of the firm opinions that settling down with us in the evening was an established right. Being shut out was most certainly not an acceptable option. The one time we had belatedly tried to persuade them that sleeping in the hall was a preferable alternative, the error of our ways was immediately pointed out in a cacophony of howling, barking, scratching and shredding, as we lay in bed and tried to ignore the demolition of our house. The experiment had lasted about five minutes before we gave in, opened the door and the pack was reunited.

Nevertheless, we did set ground rules, the cat had her nest at the end of the bed and both dogs had their own bed, into which each would get, settle down and go to sleep, preferably with the following criteria; immediately, without snoring, without passing wind, without hassle until morning.

Inevitably the terrible trio had other ideas, which is why I was now limping round the house at four in the morning de-vomming my foot.

"I hope you haven't left lumps in the plug hole," said John, as I came back to bed.

"Don't be gross, of course I haven't, I flushed my foot."

"You did what?"

"Flushed it. Quickest and most hygienic way to clean. Put pukey foot in the toilet bowl and flush."

"But there is one of those bleach block things in the cistern."

"Oh, is there? Oh well, my foot is more hygienic than I thought then. Why is Monty on the bed chewing the duvet?"

"There are probably still a couple of tasty molecules of cat puke available. Seriously, did you really flush your foot?"

"Yes John, what is your problem with foot flushing exactly? It is just a more vigorous bidet."

"No, a bidet directs a gentle stream of water for purposes of achieving cleanliness of one's bits, you don't put feet in them either."

"Actually," I informed him. "The most common reason for which people use a bidet these days is to defrost the Christmas turkey."

"Good job we don't eat turkey then. I'd hate to be calling out a plumber at triple time on Christmas Day because you have decided to convert the bog into a bidet and flushed our lunch down it. I cannot believe we are having this conversation at half four in the morning."

We went back to sleep. Sure enough, when we came to get up a couple of hours later both dogs and the cat did their too-exhausted-to-get-out-of-bed routine as a result of the night's events. John and I left them to it and made breakfast.

Megan was the first to join us and sat in the kitchen scratching vigorously. She then shook herself, rubbed the side of her face on the wine rack and began using her back foot to scuff at her underside.

"She's itchy again," I commented.

Every year we went through this. She had been checked over by the vet, washed in the finest organic, chemical free, hand milled anti-scratch soaps and deflead regularly with top of the range, nothing-survives-this, fleas-and-ticks-are-so-toast treatments. Add in a diet free of just about every known dog allergen known to mankind and yet, from spring to autumn, she scratched away like a louse infested mongrel with mange.

She did, however, have a tendency to pick up grass mites, which lurked temporarily in her groin and armpit areas until we washed or brushed them off. Sure enough, as I crouched over an upturned Meg for the latest pit inspection, there they were – miniscule but aggravating. Time to roll out the secret weapon.

Entering 'itchy dog' into an Internet search engine a few weeks previously I had been intrigued by an organic treatment that should sort out the problem for good. I had discovered Neem Oil, derived from the seeds of the Neem tree. This was an evergreen Indian tree that had many beneficial qualities and that many people in India had in their back garden, providing staple ingredients for use in Ayurvedic medicine for centuries.

One such use was as an insect repellent. The oil was also anti-fungicidal, anti-bacterial and anti-inflammatory. I had persuaded John to order a bottle, expounding the many miracle properties with great gusto. It only needed to be used sparingly but we went for a litre, sure that it would become an essential part of our dog first aid kit. When it arrived we discovered that, in addition to its other antis, it was also seriously anti-social. In the quantities we came to use it would also last us about fifty years.

An olive brown oil, it had a pungent and long lasting smell. Its unusual aroma clung to your fingers more tenaciously than pig's kidneys but we quickly became fans of its efficacy.

"It's a bit like that moment when the redneck farmer goes to start pumping oil from the sump and there's a bit of a blockage," I described it to a friend one day. "And he is poking about wiggling pipes, trying to free up the flow when all of a sudden there's a bubbling and a green, bloated arm and a rotting head pop up to the surface. Then the credits roll and some crack forensics team descend on the farm."

"Really?"

"Yes, I'd imagine that's what his oil sump smells like; oily, sulphurish, greeny brownish gloop."

"You could do with working on your sales pitch for this oil."

Odour aside the stuff worked, we emulsified it and sprayed it on itchy Megan and it saw off the mites and soothed the sore patches where she had scratched the skin raw. Duly treated she went off to eat her kibble.

"Have you sorted out what you are wearing for tonight?" John asked, over toast.

"Yes, my dress is hanging up in the office."

After breakfast we went to check emails. An empty coat hanger swung from the doorframe as Megan circled and then made herself comfortable on the floor.

"MEG! Get off my dress. You are putting muff mites and neeminess all over it."

Megan looked up from a nest of taffeta and yawned.

"That will make for interesting dinner conversation," John said.

I turfed Megan off my dress and shook it out.

"I can't wear this now," I sniffed, as a potent waft of oily backwoods murder victim reached my nose.

"What? It took you about three weeks to decide on this outfit. We are going out at six." John looked panicked.

"I'll use my back up option," I said, glaring at Megan and reuniting my dress with its hanger.

"We won't be too late. Everyone has had their tea. Don't put up with any naughtiness, I've left my mobile number on the pin board."

"We'll be fine."

"If you could just let them have a pee around eight, but make sure you put the strong lead on Monty. And hang on tight to the handle in case he spots your cat."

"Honestly, we'll be fine, go and enjoy your evening."

"Give me a ring if you have any problems at all."

John and I were having a night out. The occasion was also a black tie event so it meant an opportunity to dress up. Our neighbour had offered to dog sit and now, as John was trying to edge me in the general direction of the waiting taxi, I was just finalising the basics.

"We will be back before the rally. If you could just put the lights out on the fish and cover the birds around eight as well. And help yourself to a glass of wine."

"Go, relax. I will probably take them over to mine, but don't worry about rushing back. Have a nice time."

In the taxi, I carried on fretting. The night car rally was due to come past the house around midnight, an annual event involving performance cars completing timed legs around the back lanes of Wales.

"I forgot to ask her to make sure the cat is in."

"Will you stop panicking," John said. "She has a cat too, I'm sure she will check on both."

In the end, we had a fantastic night. There were no frantic maydays to my phone, my full length gown was complimented all evening and we arrived home, pleasantly tipsy at about eleven thirty.

As John waved off the taxi driver, I picked my way over to our darkened house. The lights were still on next door. With a handful of silk devoré in one hand and my house key in the other I prodded at the keyhole.

"Hang on a second," John called. "Hadn't we better check which house…"

I opened the door a crack to totter over the threshold.

"…the dogs are in," finished John, as a large, muscled black form barged me out of the way, raced round the yard and then shot out of the gate for a nocturnal hurtle round the fields across the lane.

"Oopsh," I slurred.

John grabbed a bag of treats and set off in pursuit. I jammed a foot of evening gown into the top of my knickers and followed. Our neighbour, appearing in her doorway to welcome us home, sussed the situation immediately and headed off to fetch a torch.

Recall training with Monty was something we were trying to perfect and sessions were frequently implemented, but generally we now found that they were best conducted in daylight, not in our best evening wear and not when we had both consumed the best part of a bottle of wine and a couple of liqueurs each.

I positioned myself by the water trough that stood at the gate between the two fields across the lane from our house. John stumbled off into the darkness, following the blur of panting shadowiness that had just shot by us. Our neighbour stood at the gate to the lane and waved her torch in a series of arcs across the landscape.

A black shape raced up at speed, skirting the hedgerow and pausing briefly to sniff at the trough. I rattled a bag of treats and extended my arm towards his collar, cooing entreaties. Just as my fingertips made contact with fur and I began to relax, next door's torch beam scanned across our position and about a million halogen watts of daylight blinded me and spooked Monty into another mad dash into the dark.

"Will you turn the bloody sun out?" I yelled, completely

unreasonably, considering that our neighbour hadn't let Monty loose and was standing in a cold field near midnight, only trying to help.

The beam snapped off and she went home, clearly deciding that we could retrieve our own dog and stick my attitude where the torch didn't shine.

I felt guilty and embarrassed. Now I had an apology to make, but for now the pressing issue was Monty. We now had no one at the gate to the lane and were both painfully aware that the rally was due to come past at any time and that twenty plus kilos of mutt plastered to a driver's windscreen was not likely to do his time trials any favours.

Two gleaming eyes reflected the moonlight as they whizzed past me again.

"He's coming your way," I called in the direction of the whistling I could hear down the field.

"Really helpful," shot back an annoyed voice. "He's a black dog, in a black field, on a black night. Shut up, I'm listening for him."

"Only trying to help," I muttered to myself, realising how our neighbour must have felt.

The longest twenty minutes of our lives eventually resulted in a disembodied call from the dark yelling, "I've got him."

"Don't let go," I offered helpfully, hopping from foot to foot and shivering.

John and Monty homed into view, with our hot, happy dog panting and trotting along on a very short lead. John looked murderous but relieved.

"Before you start, yes I did praise him," John said, adopting the training method that, if you want your dog to exercise consistent recall, you do not exercise your right to string up your recalcitrant runaway by his dick when you finally get a hold of him.

Back in the warm house, with Megan sulking because she missed out on the night's events, we settled Monty down and attempted to shake off the beginnings of hypothermia with a couple of stiff brandies. Not ten minutes later we heard the first roars of the rally cars speeding past.

The next morning, instead of bouncing merrily out of bed at the crack of dawn, Monty refused to get out of his pit and adopted his best exhausted dog routine. I shot him the evils as I dragged myself into getting ready for work mode and realised, as I headed for the bathroom, that I had turned an ankle while plunging round the fields on his behalf.

Nature called eventually and Monty had to make a move, limping down to the front door with a sore paw, he had managed to tear a dew claw.

"Don't give me the woefuls, Mont," I said unsympathetically. "You're lucky you weren't flattened by the rally."

"I'll drop you off and get him checked out at the vet," John said as Monty tentatively licked at his sore claw and then whimpered.

I restored amicable relations with our neighbour with a bunch of flowers and some profuse apologies. A couple of days later the local weekly paper was issued, with a snippet of news somewhere in the middle proclaiming the night rally an uneventful success and thanking the public for their cooperation.

"Look at this," John pointed out the tiny column filler to me. "We could have been famous. The only thing stopping this being sensational front page headline news was about fifteen minutes of Monty time."

SCAREDY-POOCH

It was early summer and a very hot day. I decided that it was time for our first barbecue of the season. Dragging it from the side of the shed I discovered that it might have been an idea to have given it a little protection from the rigours of over-wintering outside. As I pulled it into the open a large chunk broke off in my hand and I found that the base was a lattice of rotten metal. It was totally unserviceable.

"Have we got one of those disposable barbecue things hanging around?" I asked, heading back into the house to report the demise of my cooking equipment.

"I think there might be one in the cupboard," John replied. "Why, what's wrong with the one outside?"

"It has a serious case of metal fatigue owing to the fact that you didn't put it in the shed and left it outside all winter."

"Excuse me," John countered. "I think you will find that I went to put it away but you decided you wanted to clean it off first."

"Oh yes, well, it's a good job we have a back up plan."

A few minutes later I had a little brick arrangement set up in the front yard and a disposable barbecue parked on top. 'Ready for cooking in twenty minutes,' I read from the wrapper, 'will provide cooking heat for up to an hour'.

In preparation I made potato salad and sprinkled seasoning on sausages and burgers. I marinated a couple of salmon steaks and threaded prawns onto kebab sticks. Then I dressed a bowl of rocket and green leaves. I collected the dogs' blankets from where they were draped over the car airing and shook them prior to bringing them inside. Monty promptly raced to the end of his tether and sat in the lane, trembling.

"Don't be such a wimp Monty," I called. "They're not going to hurt you."

The front half of Monty appeared back round the corner and decided to watch what I was doing.

I rooted sauces and mustards from the fridge and then I assembled barbecue tools and lit the sheet under the grill that would ignite the charcoal. Nothing happened. I used a couple more matches to light several different areas of the paper. The paper fizzled and burned away but did not set fire to the charcoal. I huffed back into the house and started clanking round the kitchen.

John came in to see what was up.

"You couldn't light that thing with a can of petrol and a blow torch," I grumbled, turning bottles out of the cleaning and storage rack. "Aha, found it." I brandished a quarter full bottle of barbecue lighter fluid. "Now we are in business."

I glugged a generous splash over the barbecue and tried again with the matches. A satisfactory whoosh and an unexplained rattling thud and flames started licking round the coals. Smoke rose as the fire took hold and the heat started to radiate outwards. I turned round to check what the dogs were doing. Megan, who had seen barbecues before and knew they entailed food and scraps, was sat close by sniffing the air and looking hopeful. The only sign of Monty was his lead hanging out of the kennel so I crouched down to peer in and see why he was under cover on such a lovely day.

Monty was squashed as far to the back of the kennel as he could possibly get. He was showing the whites of his eyes in the gloom and visibly trembling. I suddenly realised that the thud I could not place when I had lit the barbecue was him diving into the kennel with such urgency that he had collided with the back wall.

"Oh Monty," I said, extending my arm into the kennel to scratch his nose. "Not something else you are scared of? Don't be silly, it means food, wait and see."

I withdrew and went back to my cooking. Making a fuss would only reinforce his fear, he had to work out for himself that he was safe. Thinking back, there had been a slight hint that he had this issue. When I had lit a candle in memory of the anniversary of my grandmother's passing a month earlier Monty had been subdued and wary. His usual exuberance when I came home from work was absent and he had been uncomfortable in the lounge even once the candle had been extinguished. As soon as we had made the connection that he seemed scared I had put the candle out but he was on edge for a good hour afterwards.

I soon had the barbecue food underway. The smoke now contained hints of herbs and seasoning. To create more flavour I drizzled olive oil over the coals under the salmon and used tongs to turn sausages to gain even cover. Megan edged closer and the merest smidgeon of a twitching nose appeared in the doorway to the kennel. John assembled my salad plates and condiments on the kitchen table and the first of the cooked food made its way into a very low oven to keep warm. Burgers were topped with cheese and bread rolls were sliced.

Once all was ready I joined John for dinner. As usual, I had cooked far too much which meant doggy titbits were available. Megan sat by the table as John retrieved Monty, who by now had emerged from his hidey-hole to sit sniffing the air, albeit at a suitably suspicious distance from the barbecue. A satisfying meal later, for both humans and dogs, and we all relaxed in the lounge with the windows open wide to let in the evening breeze.

"Isn't it odd that they are so scared by different things? I mused. "Monty hates fabric and flames but is completely unbothered by noise. Megan freaks at noise but she practically had her nose in my barbecue."

"We don't know the early triggers for either of them really. They both arrived as unknown quantities, didn't they?" John said.

"It is nice having two dogs though," I said, sat on the floor cuddling Monty.

"It all started with you Smeggy, didn't it?" John stroked Megan, who was sat by his feet looking up at him adoringly. "Original nutty dog you are."

MEGAN'S STORY

There was a sudden commotion in the yard. It was towards the end of July 2010. John and I went to the front door late one afternoon. Upon investigation we found a scrawny border collie had tipped over our dustbin and was gobbling down potato peelings. Our next-door neighbour was standing in her doorway.

"Have you got a new dog?" John called.

"No, we have just shooed it out of the kitchen, it was raiding the cat's bowl and the cat is none too happy about it."

"Stop it, dog. Come out of it." John went over to stand the bin up and clear up the mess. The collie hurriedly snaffled a few more vegetable scraps, reluctant to lose this food supply, however unsuitable it was for it.

"Shoo, go home." The dog backed off but made no effort to leave the yard.

"I will go and ring the local farmers," said our neighbour, turning to go back inside her house. "Perhaps it has got loose and wandered off."

John had a closer look at the dog. It was very thin, very grubby, very smelly and had no collar on.

"Is it male or female?" I asked, happy for now to let John approach a dog which could be flea ridden or aggressive, or both.

"Female."

I fetched a bowl of water from the house.

"Are you a thirsty dog?" I said, putting it on the floor by the step. "Oh yes, you are, aren't you!" Grubby thin dog trotted over and lapped noisily, limping slightly. I pointed out the limping to John.

"Yes, I noticed, and she has a lot of scratches on her face too. Hopefully, she has just got herself lost, someone is probably looking for her."

Our neighbour reappeared to report that none of the local farmers were missing a dog or knew anyone who had. She had spoken to the police and had received the same response. It was getting late in the day but the animal charity she had rung could collect it if we could keep it until the next day. While she had been ringing around, John had contacted the local caravan park in case the dog was on holiday and had slipped her collar. No, no-one was going frantic over a missing pet.

"I am at work first thing, you could pop to the vet once you have dropped me off and see if she is micro-chipped," I suggested.

John had more pressing concerns. Grubby thin dog was heading back towards our bin. "Have we got anything we could give her to eat? She's ravenous."

Between us all, we managed to rustle up an unorthodox meal of sorts. I broke a couple of eggs and whisked them up, then defrosted a fish pie. Our neighbour brought round some meat scraps left over from her family's tea and we mixed it up with a sachet of beef cat food.

"She shouldn't really have cat food but it will do as a temporary measure. It's bound to be better for her than potato peelings," I said, giving John the bowl to put down for the dog. We then all watched as the food was consumed in seconds.

"If you are happy to take her to the vet tomorrow, she can sleep in our outside porch tonight," said our neighbour. "It's not heated but it's dry and secure. I hope someone is looking for her because the animal charity told me they are overflowing. If she is ill or has any behavioural issues and they can't find her owner or re-home her they may have to put her down."

We were happy with the sleeping arrangements for the dog. She could have fleas or mites, was certainly smelly, and we had nowhere other than in our general living area to keep her. It was also unknown whether she was housetrained. Leaving her in the yard was not an option; the weather forecast for that night was unseasonably cold and windy, it would also be risky in that we lived in sheep country. She might be a border collie but we had no idea whether she would worry sheep and get herself shot.

With grubby thin dog fed, watered and settled for the night in next-door's porch, John and I locked up and carried on our normal evening routine. Before going to bed I peeped out into the yard, a dim light glowed in the porch across the way and the door to it was closed to keep out the elements. The wind was getting up and the weather report had been right, it really was going to be a cold night. Stars twinkled in a cloudless sky and this meant the temperature would drop a lot further later on.

Goebbles had wanted to go out as we went to bed. She then meowed to come back through the window a couple of hours later which woke me up. Once I had let her back in I popped out to go to the bathroom. Returning to the bedroom I stopped as I heard a noise by the front door so I turned to check things out. Through the frosted glass I could see a shape on the doorstep – a sort of black heap. John was stirring in the bedroom, I knew that he would be easily roused and called if anything was amiss so I warily opened the door. The black heap was a grubby thin dog. She was curled up on the bare slate of our doorstep with her back to the wind that was whipping up her fur. She was fast asleep. Across the yard, the porch was still lit but now the door stood open.

"What are you doing there?" I whispered. The dog uncurled to look at me then put her nose back under her paws, sighed and went back to sleep. I went back to bed to find John awake.

"Where have you been, you've been gone ages?" he muttered.

"The dog is on the doorstep," I replied.

"You didn't go and fetch her?"

"No, she fetched herself. She must have let herself out of the porch."

"What is she doing?" John asked.

"Sleeping," I said.

We lay there listening to the wind rustling the trees and the clock ticking the cold night away.

"Perhaps she'll go back over to next-door, it must be freezing on that step," John whispered.

I agreed. "She has probably already gone."

A little while later we both gave up.

"Are you still awake?" John asked.

"Yes, are you?" I replied.

John sighed but didn't rise to pointing out the obvious.

"I'm going to check," I climbed out of bed and crept down the corridor to the front door. The black heap was still there. I opened the door and crouched down. The dog was still curled up but now shivering slightly.

"Stupid dog," I muttered.

I headed back to the bedroom and collected a couple of our tee shirts from the wash basket. Tucking them round the dog I tried to protect her from the worst of the wind. At least the night was staying dry. She did not get up so she was still mainly lying on cold slate, but it was the best I could do at four in the morning.

John was up first, as usual. "Good morning dog," I heard, followed by fussing with bowls as he offered water and the rest of the concoction we had come up with for her dinner the night before. "Bit stiff are we? That's what comes of sleeping here instead of in the porch."

I got ready for work while John found a length of rope to fashion into a makeshift lead. "Come on then dog," he said. "Let's see if you belong to anyone." He loaded her up onto the back seat of the car on an old blanket. "You had better not leave fleas all over my car."

John rang me later, at work. No microchip and still no progress on ownership with the police, dog warden or other vets.

Grubby thin dog had been registered as 'stray dog' with the vet and given the once over. She was underweight and had bleeding, scabbed pads on her paws which accounted for her limp. Her face was scratched but not infected and she had a scar on her tummy that in all likelihood meant she had been spayed. She had been subdued but tolerant of the vet's examination, although she had shown a reluctance to have her right hip touched. It was his opinion, considering the complete lack of anyone coming forward or reporting their dog missing, that she had probably been dumped.

"Did he look at that dip and scar on her nose?" I asked.

"He thinks it is possibly an injury from being hit with a stick. It could be that she has failed to come up to scratch as a sheepdog. Her hip is tender, she could have had a brush with a car while living rough, or she might have been kicked."

When I got home that night we tried to come up with a plan. We had to keep the dog for ten days before we could find her another home. As she had health issues and we had no idea what the reason might have been for dumping her, we had ruled out immediately handing her over to an animal charity if it meant that she could be put down.

Our neighbour was fine about the dog letting herself out of the porch to sleep on our doorstep. "It looks like she has chosen you," she smiled. "It is a bit soon for us to have another dog, we are all still a bit raw about losing our old girl."

We decided to check with the authorities daily for missing collies. The vet had given her a worming and a flea treatment and estimated her to be a year old at most, so she would stay at ours while the waiting period unfolded. John and I would absolutely refuse to become attached to her and would merely feed her up. We could assess her nature and let her wounds heal so that, if necessary, she could go to the animal charities with everything going for her in the re-homing stakes.

Ten days later John and I completely loved the dog. She had an accident indoors on her first night but otherwise proved to be housetrained. Muddy paw prints everywhere took some getting used to but she was friendly, loving and obedient. Why anyone would abandon this dog was a mystery. 'Stray dog' attended the vet to have her healing wounds checked and slowly put on weight as we filled her up with top of the range dog food. Once the waiting period was up we made final calls to vets, the dog warden, the local paper and the police. There had been other breeds lost but no border collies.

"What happens if someone tries to claim her now – if we were thinking of keeping her –which we are still thinking about – but, you know, if someone?"

The policeman was clear on the matter. We had done everything legally required to find her owner, we had allowed the correct period of grace for her to be reclaimed and we had registered our contact details with everyone we should have done. His advice – get her micro chipped, she was ours if we wanted her.

There was no real debate. We rang the vet to book an appointment. Arriving at the surgery we checked in.

"And what is 'stray dog' here for today?" asked the receptionist.

"Megan is here for her injections and microchip," we announced proudly.

The vet appeared, "Megan eh? Come on in then Megan." Ruffling her fur he smiled at her. "Looks like you have landed on your feet dog."

MEGAN MEETS THE LOCALS

We live in prime sheep farming country. Our woolly friends were everywhere in the fields around our house. Just because Megan was a border collie and the breed was renowned for its reliability as sheepdogs we could not afford to take any risks. We had no idea why she had been dumped so she stayed on a long tether whilst in the yard and on a long training lead while out on walks.

John introduced her to sheep by walking her on a short lead round the edge of the fields they were grazing in and initial impressions were favourable. She was obviously interested in them but there was no lunging behaviour or signs of aggression. We then progressed to allowing her off the lead in the field closest to our house where there were no livestock. She was quick to learn recall commands although John found that she always responded better to whistles, our confidence in her ability to return on demand grew daily.

The one problem she did seem to have was an issue with noise. If the jets performing low flying exercises in the hills roared over, she would bark and bounce around in manic circles until the sound reduced in volume. Late summer rumbles of thunder in the distance would have her leaping agitatedly about the yard, panting and stressing. On bringing her inside in anticipation of the imminent arrival of the storm, she would leave damp paw prints on the floor tiles, an indication of her distress. Even hearing fireworks going off in a programme on the television would galvanise her from deep sleep to frantic pacing in an instant.

In every other respect we found Megan to be a lovely dog. She had good table manners and would wait nicely at mealtimes until she was given the go ahead to tuck in, she was housetrained and knew most basic commands. While the cat was miffed at this new housemate to start with, Megan accepted the cat straight away, there was none of the mad chasing we later had to discourage with Monty. Likewise, the parrots posed no problem for her, she gave them a cursory sniff through the bars of the cages and then completely ignored them.

In fact, the only time she bothered with the birds was when one was seriously ill a few months after she arrived. Then she maintained a vigil under his cage, whimpering and watching when we had to feed him by syringe. She cried when he was loaded into a cage for the trips to the vet and when Percy sadly died Megan refused to leave her spot by his cage until we had shown her the body. Then, ever so gently, she had sniffed him and put up a paw, delicately to touch his feathers before backing off. It was only then that she had resumed her usual routine.

The dilemma of whether we could trust Megan to respect sheep was solved by Megan herself. One day John came back from taking her out, slightly flushed and breathless. All had been going well, he reported, until Megan heard bleating from a field of sheep two fields away. Suddenly slipping her collar she headed under the gate of the field she and John were in and raced across towards the flock. She squeezed herself under the next gate and John realised with horror that Megan was now in amongst the sheep, completely unsupervised.

He had made his way as fast as possible over to the field where Megan and the sheep were, all the while dreading what he would find. Sheep worrying was not a huge issue where we were as our location was reasonably isolated, but we both had seen television news reports of the carnage that can ensue when a dog is left to its own devices with a flock. We also knew that a farmer was totally within his rights to shoot any dog that he felt was out of control and being a danger to his livestock.

On reaching the gate he looked with trepidation into the field to find the entire flock gathered in a tight ball for his inspection about twenty feet in. Megan was lying in a typical collie herding position watching with her head between her paws. When a particularly stroppy ewe separated from the group and stamped her foot at Megan she crept forwards and faced off the sheep until it realised the error of its ways and retreated.

The flock numbered around fifty and it was impossible for Megan to see the far side of the gathering, but when she sensed a few sheep making a break for freedom she circled in a classic sheepdog collecting manoeuvre and neatly herded the runaways back into the group before dropping into a crouch once more and looking at John. She was executing textbook sheepdog behaviour, and we finally had our answer: regardless of the reason why Megan had been dumped, she had some experience in the field and was safe to be around sheep.

The next time John passed the time of day with the shepherd he mentioned what had happened.

"She's a fine looking dog," the shepherd had commented. "Young too from the looks of her."

"It seems that somewhere she has had some training," John said.

The shepherd rented the fields and had to travel several miles each day to do his daily checks. Sheep can go downhill fairly quickly for various reasons and can end up helpless on the deck. If they are discovered in good time it is possible to stand them up or treat their ailment but if the crows get to them first they can be doomed.

Crows are very intelligent but ruthless and will take the eyes of a downed sheep followed by attacking the back end. Quite often the poor animal is conscious during this attack, and a sheep that has been injured or killed by an onslaught from crows is not a pretty sight. Despite the occasional necessary cull there were lots of crows around the farm lands and a few sheep casualties beyond assistance had been discovered. Farmers and shepherds are generally pragmatic and unsentimental about their livelihood but finding an animal that has been blinded and virtually disembowelled while alive still has the capacity to invoke empathy for its suffering.

"Let her run with my flocks, if you are in the fields every day, you'd be doing me a favour keeping an eye on them. The dog will enjoy working them if she has been trained up."

And so Megan began to check on the sheep on her daily walks. She would begin by rounding them out of the field closest to the house so she could play. Then John or I would skirt the higher fields with Megan, checking on the occupants. On several occasions over the years it was Meg that alerted us to a sick or injured sheep or lamb, either by lying next to it and refusing to budge, or by separating out the sickly specimen for our inspection. We could then alert the shepherd and he was able to drive over to sort out the problem.

Sometimes the sheep was uninjured but had gone down and was unable to stand again. They bloat quickly which exacerbates their incapacity. Megan trotted ahead on her walks, returning every few minutes as she heard our call or whistle. If you called and she did not immediately appear you knew that she had found something. On homing into view you would see Megan sat looking attentively at a white mound on the ground, occasionally standing to wedge her nose under its bulk and trying to nudge it to its feet. Your pulse would quicken as you closed in, hoping that you had found it before the crows had.

As you arrived Meg would back off and sit waiting, giving you space to manhandle the ewe to its feet, watching and wagging her tail as it waddled off, farting a lot and bleating. Once the sheep had been seen successfully to re-join the flock Megan would present in a sitting position at your feet, looking up and hoping for a treat, she would then be commanded 'away' and the walk would continue.

The only spanner in the works with Megan as a sheepdog was her aversion to noise. She would totally lose any concentration and bounce in circles barking whenever anything loud like planes disturbed her working. As a pet dog with a sheepdog hobby this was not a problem, as a full time working dog it would have been unacceptable behaviour. We could only assume that this was the reason this lovely young collie had been abandoned.

FISH TANK MAINTENANCE, MONTY STYLE

"Right, you lot," I said, dumping the cleaning bucket, jug and paper towels in front of the little fish tank one Sunday afternoon. "Prepare to be cleaned out."

John had settled down with a beer to watch the rugby, Megan was sat outside surveying the yard and Monty was stretched out on the settee, fast asleep in the sunshine. The filter had been rattling which meant snails in the works. It also needed more frequent routine cleaning owing to the waste generated by the hundreds of baby guppy fish currently in residence. For the previous few weeks every time we looked through the glass there was another crop of microscopic fry, all born with robust good health and a total disinclination to adhere to the laws of nature and die off.

"It says here that only one in every hundred fry survives," John said, consulting one of our many manuals on fish keeping.

I stopped peering into the depths to remark, "Well, I can see absolutely loads of them, so if you multiply absolutely loads by one hundred there must have been…" My totally un-mathematical brain started over heating, "… Mega loads to start with."

John turned over a page. "Of the few that survive, most of those will be eaten by other fish in the tank and they will have to hide away until they are a decent size if they want to avoid being predated."

"Oh really?" I said, watching about five different lengths of baby guppies happily swimming around in the open with a shoal of varied adult fish. "We must have vegetarian fish then, either that or they all just want to feel the love. Baby gobbling would be bad karma."

John put the fish manual down and shot me an incredulous glance. "Feel the love? Bad karma? It is an aquarium not a flowery sixties hippy commune."

With that he went back to the rugby. I collected the cleaning brush and cotton buds from the storage cupboard under the tank and commenced operations. Turning the power off at the wall so I didn't run the risk of ending up more frazzled than usual I lifted the lid off and upended it onto the floor. Flicking the switch woke Monty up, he stretched, yawned and hopped off the settee to investigate. Ambling over, he sniffed at the lighting unit.

"Clear off Monty," I said, plonking the bucket between him and the light.

Monty head-butted the bucket out of the way and homed in again to lick the algae off the strip bulb.

"Monty. Pack it in, you are a dog. Dogs do not eat algae, it is not going to be good for you. Go away."

My hairy black helper backed off about a foot and sat, waiting to see what would happen next. I looked down at the water surface and sighed, one of my mature guppies was floating on the top, dead. Using the little tub we had for this occurrence, I scooped the deceased into the 'pot of doom' and put it on the windowsill in preparation for disposal. Disturbing the water meant all its guppy friends amassed in search of food. In the absence of any fish food being offered, flakes of their sadly deceased relative did just as well as my vegetarian theory was instantly scotched.

"That is gross fishies, show some respect," I muttered. Then to John, "We have a casualty."

"It probably died of exhaustion creating that latest lot in there," he responded.

A one bucket water change was usually enough to maintain optimum water quality levels. Filling the bucket with jugs full, carefully scanned for accidentally scooped fish, I looked down ready to empty the latest to find a large black head in the way. Monty had decided to assess the quality of the removed water himself and, from the vigorous lapping going on, he quite obviously assessed it as delicious.

Turfing an affronted head out of the bucket I took the filter apart and started to rinse the various sponges and components. Reaching for the tank cleaning brush I found that it was not where I had put it. Monty, clearly deciding that it would work much better with fewer bristles and a shorter handle, had retreated with it to the settee for purposes of remodelling.

"John," I huffed. "You are supposed to be pack leader. Will you tell Monty to stop nicking my tank stuff and winding me up?"

John took one eye off the rugby and cast it towards the Mont. "Oh Montiferous One, stop nicking the tank stuff and winding Helen up, there's a good chap."

I took both eyes off my bucket of water and filter gloop and glared at John. "Great, that should do it, thanks so much."

Retrieving the brush, I scrubbed snail eggs from the filter crevices and then set about reassembling all the parts. Monty had moved around to snooze in a sunny spot on the floor, or at least, that's what he was doing a good job of pretending to do. While John had been exercising his impressive pack leadership one of my filter sponges had mysteriously become eight sponges. Gathering the bits off the carpet, I considered squashing them all back into their holder, but settled on a new sponge with dark grumblings to Monty about our singular contribution to the annual profits bonus of our local pet superstore.

Finally the filter was replaced in the tank and a bucket of new water, treated to ensure chemical compatibility and temperature, was added to complete the process. I tidied up and turned the lights, heater and filter power back on. It was now time to dispose reverently of the sadly deceased former occupant and I turned to the windowsill to retrieve the pot of doom. Which was no longer there.

"Where is my dead guppy, oh pack leading one?" I queried.

"It was there a minute ago," replied John, engrossed in a possible try from our team.

"YES!" he yelled, as a large muscled Welshman dived over the try line with the ball.

"NO!" I screeched, as I spotted Monty lurking behind the coffee table with the pot of doom.

"Do you have a problem, darling?" said John.

"Yes, I do," I fumed. "Monty has eaten the dearly departed. How am I supposed to hold a ceremonial flushing when the corpse is motoring down Monty's gullet?"

"And am I correct in supposing that this is going to be all my fault?"

"Of course it is all your fault, you were supposed to be on doom watch."

John pondered for a second, then came up with a solution. "Tell you what, next time I take Monty out for a crap I will let you know where the turd is. You can go and fetch it and flush it down the bog. Ceremonial flushing by default, how's that?"

John got the look, big time.

THE SAGA OF THE
TROPICAL FISH

A few weeks before my birthday, John had started seeking ideas for my present. I promised to give it some thought and suggest some options. Being my upcoming fortieth, I think John was rather hoping I would come up with a nice necklace or a pretty ornament, but I had other ideas.

"Any clue yet what you want for your birthday?" he said one day, delivering my morning cup of tea.

"Yup, I rather fancy another parrot."

John nearly dropped my tea. This was before Megan and Monty, so at that time we only had Goebbles, Micky, Bobby and Percy (an Australian king parrot)

"No way! No more pets. Especially parrots."

I sat up in a huff. "What is the point of asking me what I want as a present if you are not even going to consider it?"

To be fair, John had a point, I had lost my beloved sulphur-crested and umbrella cockatoos in relatively quick succession in 2004 and 2006; one to cancer and one to post-operative infection complications, and the constant veterinary trips to the nearest avian vet three hours away by car and then their deaths had been completely emotionally devastating.

Not in the mood to accept the entirely rational refusal on John's part to consider another animal that required specialist insurance, specialist vets and caused untold upset when it died, every time he asked me what I wanted for my birthday, I resolutely stuck to "a parrot". I had, by doing this, backed myself into a corner. Thinking about it, I had Micky, Bobby and Percy, another parrot would divide my available attention to them. So, when John suggested a different option one night, my attention was grabbed.

"You know we can't have another bird, but if you are set on a pet, what do you think of some tropical fish?"

Ooh, tropical fish, the only area in the local pet superstore that I did not have a look around on a regular basis. I had not even thought of tropical fish. Fond memories flooded back from when I was about seven, of a goldfish won when they were still given out at fairs as prizes. This fish, along with my brother's, had pootled happily round a fishbowl for years, entrancing me with its little bug eyes and glinting orange colour. I mentally started siting a fish tank and we planned a visit to look at fish species the next day.

At the pet shop, we headed for the fish section and I was completely bowled over by all the colours, sizes and varieties. My eyes lit up and I beamed at John, tropical fish as a fortieth birthday present it was then. We went home with a book on fish husbandry and I started planning.

Siting the tank was not as easy as it looked, it had to be near a power source, but not near noise, so next to the television with all its sockets was out then. It could not be in sunlight or near direct heat, it had to be safe from being knocked over and water, apparently, weighed a ton, so there had to be space for a proper stand. Bunging it on the coffee table so I could view my fish from all angles was not an option.

Eventually, we came up with a location that matched all the necessary criteria and, on my birthday, we headed back to the pet shop to buy a tank. John walked over to a selection of compact thirty-eight litre tanks, I homed in rapidly on the sixty litre ones. Looking resigned as I pointed out the perfect model, John nabbed an assistant while I headed for the section with all the extras.

I had already decided I wanted a natural environment for my fish so I bypassed the neon grit, drowned pirates and sunken skulls in favour of subtlety. The tank came with a filter and heater so all

I needed was some gravel, a tasteful, decorative rock, some plants, a hidey-hole fake log for my fish, a bubble machine, some sand, a backing sheet that would let the fish think they were living in a reef, some bogwood and a little bag of natural pebbles.

John reappeared and peered into my groaning basket. "Where, exactly, are any bloody fish going to go?" he wanted to know.

Then I moved onto food, for both the fish and my plants; top of the range, enhanced with vitamins, minerals and special additives to help your fish glow with health and your plants bloom. Then, something you put in the water to help the water maturing process, and something to remove nasties from tap water. Finally, we picked up a kit to test the pH, nitrite, nitrate and ammonia levels and headed for the till.

An enjoyable afternoon passed as I laid out my tank décor in a happy fish *feng shui* pattern and added water. All up and running, my tank looked beautiful, the light softly lit the backdrop, the plants waved in the bubbles, all it needed was some fish and for that I had to wait a week. A week which went very, very, slowly.

Eventually, though, we were back at the pet shop, picking fish. Not wishing to overstock I came away with four white cloud mountain minnows and a pair of swordtails. Following all the instructions for adding them from their bag of shop water, they were soon swimming and enjoying their new home.

Next morning, I found that one of the minnows was less impressed than its mates with its new surroundings and had dropped dead. One of my plants also registered an objection to its new fishy friends by ceasing to wave in the bubbles and turning into a heap of black sludge overnight. The deceased was presented back to the shop and a replacement installed, sludgy plant was extracted and all seemed to go well as the tank settled. We were careful not to overfeed, I did regular water changes as per the manuals, and I loved having tropical fish.

Inevitably, the pet shop's tropical fish section became my second home. Over the next few months a Siamese fighting fish, a couple of corydoras, a couple of ghost glass catfish and a few neon tetras joined the tank. The plants grew bushy. I had carefully added up the length of the fish in the tank and had kept the number of fish centimetres well below the litre capacity of the tank, even allowing for any growing of the residents, so I knew I had room for the tiny, bulbous-eyed fish I was now looking at through the glass in one of the display aquaria. It was pale gold with a tapered appearance; obviously a bottom feeder, with all the cute visual characteristics of a tadpole mutated in a radioactive swamp. It became the last fish to colonise my tank.

I watched my little colony mature over the next few months as the plants continued to spread and grow. I loved turning the lights off in the lounge in the evening, letting the tank illuminate the room and watching the fish interact and explore their surroundings. We collected a library of books on fish types and how to keep them happy and I was diligent in my completion of a maintenance log so I knew when water changes and filter cleans were due.

All was well in fish world until my Siamese fighting fish suddenly turned into a pinecone. I had a sick fish, I was gutted. Back to the pet shop for anti-bacterial treatments, also Aloe Vera treatment to help my fish recover its health and vitality. The fighting fish promptly died and my neons went fluffy. I chucked a load of anti-fungal treatment in and hoped for the best.

In the meantime, my water chemistry tests had shown that, in no time at all, the readings had gone from perfectly normal to a toxic, acidic, chemical soup. Browsing the pet shop shelves, I came home loaded with pH adjuster, nitrite balancer and ammonia remover which, the labels assured me, would work together to restore my tank to crystal clear water health in no time. What actually happened was that the water turned over a weekend into a milky murk you couldn't see through.

Taking a sample to the pet shop, the assistant gloomily informed me that I had bacterial bloom, furthermore she was surprised the water hadn't dissolved my fish. Stop throwing every treatment under the sun into the water, do partial water changes every day and hopefully the tank's natural cycles would sort themselves out before all my fish decided enough was enough and snuffed it.

It took a month or so for the water to become totally clear again and for the chemistry to adjust to normal. I lost some fish but not as many as I feared. What I did discover, when I could finally see into the depths of the tank, was that my little bug-eyed radioactive swamp fish was now about four inches long. It was patently too big for the tank. After all we had gone through, all the trauma of fish funerals and the need to become experts in chemistry, there was only one course of action left.

"We will just have to get a bigger tank now, John!"

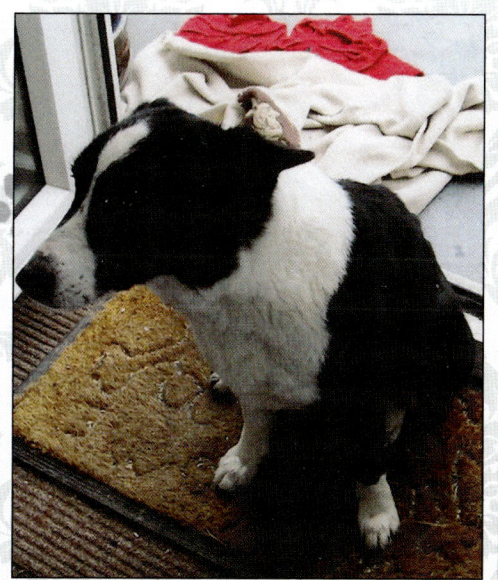

Megan's First Day

Odd looking Pup – Muttley

Big and handsome Monty

Muttley wants breakfast

Three months in, and still skinny

Megan with sick lamb and downed ewe

Why we needed a huge fish tank

Micky singing

Olly

Tufty fully feathered

Cross Goebbles

Hide and seek – can you spot Goebbles?

Huckleberry

Perry

Megan guarding sick Percy

Bobby

Megan's Stick

Out for a walk

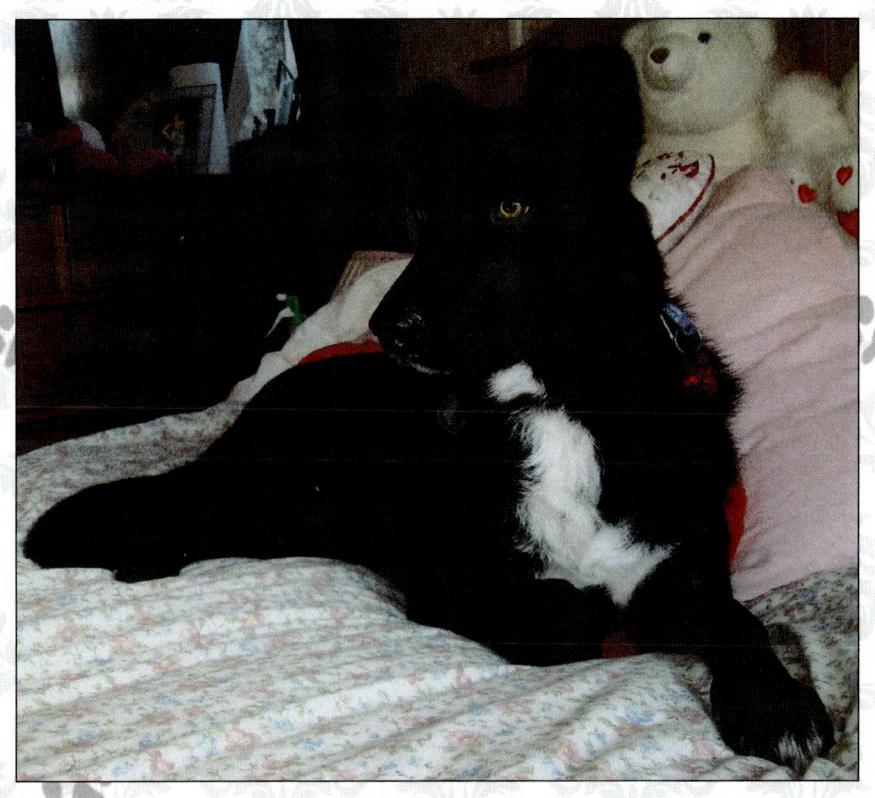

Regal Monty

Monty in the snow

All Together

TROPICAL FISH BEGIN TO TAKE OVER THE HOUSE

A bigger tank had never featured in John's original plan to have a few small, innocuous tropical fish in a small, innocuous tropical fish tank as a way of distracting me from the idea of another parrot. However, as he looked morosely through the glass at the tail of my golden plecostomus sticking out of one end of the six inch hidey-hole log and its head poking out of the other, he had to concede that I had a point.

"I thought fish only ever grew to the size of their surroundings," he muttered.

"It *is* growing to the size of its surroundings," I replied, trying to be helpful. "It will soon be the length of the tank, and if it gets much fatter, it will be the width. Plus, if you ever see it cleaning algae off the sides, it is practically the height of its surroundings."

John fixed me with a look. Presented with a *fait accompli* that we now had a rapidly growing fish that would soon take up the whole of the bottom of our tank we sat down to discuss the matter, then John outlined our new plan. We would buy a larger tank, set it up, transfer all the little fish into it, and sell the sixty litre with the smaller heater and filter, to offset the cost.

We would then be very careful, wouldn't we, to read the little labels attached to the fish descriptions that gave prices, care instructions and, most importantly, eventual maximum size? I was cross, I *had* read the size, but, never having the best visual acuity, had read 48cm as 4.8cm. So the fact that we had Moby Dick in our living room was now, apparently, all my fault.

Attempting to resolve the problem, I looked in the local papers. No fish tanks for sale. I went on eBay, and hit the jackpot. There were loads of tanks on offer, with everything we needed to expand in size. There were also tanks available from people obviously wishing to simplify their lives which came with their fish included.

"NO! NO! NO!" came the emphatic response when I called John through to look at one such offering.

"But it is cheaper to get a tank with fish. This person wants to get rid of their fish," I argued.

"Can't imagine why," retorted John, as Moby swam forward two inches and collided with the end of the tank.

This was an opportunity I couldn't resist. "I think you will find, darling one, that it was *you* who suggested tropical fish in the first place. I had never even thought about having tropical fish, my mind had not been crossed in the slightest by tropical fish, I wanted a parrot!"

John was undeterred. "We are not, repeat not, having any more bloody fish."

The impasse was solved by the little fish themselves. Sat in my favourite position, on a beanbag, looking into the tank later that evening, I spotted something. Or rather, several somethings. Swimming near the surface, in and out of the greenery were the tiniest fish. There had been fornication going on in fish world. Only a couple of millimetres long and translucent, half a dozen baby fish whizzed into sight and then shot under cover of the plants whenever a bigger fish swam nearby. But, it didn't end there. Now scrutinising every inch of the tank to try to obtain a rough headcount, I noticed movement on the floor too. Two miniscule corydoras catfish, about a centimetre long each, were scuttling over the gravel. Well camouflaged, you could only see them when they moved, or if you knew exactly where they were. I knew that I had a pair of swordtails and that they bore live young, as for the corys, that would explain the eggs that had been stuck to the side of the tank earlier in the month.

That now solved the problem in my mind, we could hardly shift our mini fish into a bigger tank without squashing or killing them. Even if we could net the middle swimming babies without a massacre, there was no way we could locate the young corys through the water. Moving the gravel without finding the fish first would definitely kill them. We headed to the pet shop next morning for fry food and advice. Our swordtails were easy to breed as long as the water quality was reasonable but the mortality rate for the babies was high, as other fish would pick them off.

When we pointed out that we also had baby corydoras, the assistant became more animated. "Ooh, you really must have a good tank set up to have baby corys. They are really quite hard to breed in a standard home aquarium. I have had corydoras for years and I have never managed to get babies. Well done!"

I looked suitably proud, John started looking a little queasy. We could hardly disrupt our little tank now, not when it was such a shining example of excellent fish husbandry, and the talk of the pet shop staff. However, we still had to put my golden plec into a bigger home, both for its own welfare but also now so that it would not flatten our rare and hard to breed fry. We could hardly put the poor thing in a new tank on its own, it would most definitely need some friends.

Thus it was that on my next birthday, a year and a bit since John had the Great Tropical Fish Idea, we found ourselves in a hired van heading home from the Midlands, having picked up the bargain one hundred and fifty litre tank we had found on eBay. We also had some large plastic tubs on board, containing mature tank water from our new purchase, but also containing the three silver dollars, two golden severums and the mottled black plecostomus that were included in the deal.

As we were using mature water and the gravel and fixtures were already in the tank, it didn't take long to set everything up once we arrived home. The little tank remained in its original location, the new monster tank went up against the wall behind the settee and the settee migrated about four feet into the middle of the lounge to accommodate it. Ignoring comments from John that it was like living at Seaworld, I fussed around arranging plants and a giant hidey-hole castle before we carefully transferred our new fishy friends into their existing home and my golden plec into its upgraded one.

The silver dollars were shimmering silver grey disc-shaped fish about fifteen centimetres long, the golden severums were about the same size but a beautiful deep gold orange colour with graceful fins. The mottled black plecostomus was roughly thirty centimetres in length with a black, grey swirl pattern. It dwarfed my little gold plec who suddenly looked very happy to have more swimming space, but all the fish seemed comfortable enough after their disrupted day and lazily began to swim around. I sat and watched them settle in while John headed to the kitchen for a large scotch and dry, he came back shortly afterwards with a glass of wine for me. I headed back and forth between my small tank with its little fish and all its babies and my new huge tank with its much larger occupants.

Finally, I joined John on the settee in our now slightly smaller lounge area and beamed at him adoringly. I still loved having tropical fish, but now I loved having big tropical fish too.

DÉJÀ VU ON THE FISH FRONT!

Sitting on the settee one morning I watched my two plecs having a territorial discussion over a section of gravel. It was about eighteen months after the arrival of the new monster tank and little golden plec obviously loved her new home. So much so, that she had rapidly grown in size and was now closing in on and being comparable with foot long black plec.

"You know John," I mused. "It's looking a bit crowded in plecworld."

John looked up from reading the papers. "Is it really? They're big fish now, I am sure they will sort it out between themselves."

A few days later I had a week's annual leave from work. Not going anywhere, we had decided to have a clear out and declutter. The second bedroom had been turned into an office to clear the lounge of all computer equipment and it needed a revamp. Deciding that we would file all our paperwork, statements and stuff we felt obliged to keep for years in case we suddenly needed access to a current account receipt from 1984, John suggested buying a filing cabinet. There was a local recycling shop in town so it was to there, on the first Saturday of my week off, that we found ourselves heading.

Our preferred style of shopping was to separate so John could inspect things carefully at his leisure and I could randomly whizz about having told him where I was intending to be at a given time. He would then come looking for me, invariably finding me somewhere completely different to my declared destination.

"Got lost did we?" John muttered as he homed in behind me.

I stopped gazing at my find and turned to face him. "Look at this! It is an amazing bargain."

He peered over my shoulder. "Would it be an amazing bargain filing cabinet by any chance? Oops no, silly me, it would appear to be an unbelievably bloody enormous amazing bargain fish tank."

Undeterred, I pointed out all the positive features. The tank was lovely, it was easily three hundred litres plus it came with the requisite stand, it was only twenty-five pounds and, furthermore, the label said that it did not leak.

John was not impressed. "What the hell is it going to say? 'Fish tank, leaks, will fill your home with water, fish shit and dead flopping fish, an absolute steal at twenty-five quid'."

I pushed my point. Being about five feet long it would mean that each plecostomus could do their High Noon impressions from each end of the tank and still have three feet of no man's land between them. It was a pain having a constricted lounge area so we could regain our living space, our *Zen* zone.

"Hang on a minute," said John. "Where are you proposing this thing goes then? That is, if we were considering it, which we are NOT!"

Way ahead of him, I was well prepared. "Hallway," I said, eyeing the tank and mentally planning its layout in terms of plants, rocks and fishy furniture.

"Right. I see, have you totally lost the plot? So, this tank is the best part of two feet wide, the hall is about five max and we are claiming back the *Zen* of our lounge by plonking the Welsh Water Board back up reservoir in the middle of our main access route to the rest of our house?"

I shot a look at John that indicated that he was being a spanner in my works again.

"Ok, plan B, kitchen. We don't need a massive kitchen table, we can get one that extends when we need it. The tank will go against the wall between the fridge and the veg cabinet. The new kitchen table can go in front of the tank. We can turn the main strip light off and have nice romantic meals by the light of the tank, gazing into each other's eyes and chatting, while watching our fish…"

"Crapping," finished John. "We do not need this monstrosity in our house."

On the way home, we stopped off at our local garden centre. While John sought out the compost we had come to buy, I inevitably ended up in the tropical fish section and promptly became transfixed by a huge and very sad looking eight inch fish in a tank on its own.

Quizzing the staff I found out that it was an oscar, an Amazonian fish that starts life about the size of a fifty pence piece and grows, in record time, to something that if it were a food fish, you could fry up and feed a family of ten on. It had been given to the garden centre as it had outgrown its tank. The oscar is known as the dog of the fish world as they can become relatively tame and feed from your hand. I watched it swimming up and down and felt for its poor, abandoned existence. It was just an unwanted dog with scales and fins, I asked how big a tank it should live in and was told a three hundred litre was ideal.

At this moment John appeared. "I thought you said you would be looking at seedlings?" He glanced past me at the oscar and sighed.

I put my case. "It is meant to be John, by pure chance we have seen a three hundred litre tank today. We have also, purely coincidentally, come across a poor unwanted fish that needs a three hundred litre tank today."

John interjected, "Not if you had been in the seedling section, we wouldn't."

I continued, "Our plecs need more bottom space and I knew there had to be a reason the severums died for no reason, it is karma in the great scheme of the universe, fish out fish in, this oscar is meant to be ours."

And so, this is how our kitchen became home to a fish tank which, admittedly, looked a lot smaller in the shop than it did in our house. Our plecs grew to full size and had room to spare, and the oscar was duly collected a couple of weeks later and immediately made itself at home, rearranging my carefully designed tank by shoving everything around with its nose and mulching all the plants.

At our next romantic meal by fish tank illumination, we looked lovingly at each other while trying to ignore golden plec cleaning the side of the glass and trailing about a foot of fish poo. Sharing 'us' time we discussed life, the universe, and the fact that under NO CIRCUMSTANCES WHATSOEVER were we going to get any larger in the fish tank department. Serving pudding, as John watched the oscar trying to destroy the temperature gauge, I smiled. It just had to be said, I still loved having tropical fish but now I loved having huge fish. It was almost on a par with having a parrot.

FISH FUNERALS: TO FLUSH OR NOT TO FLUSH?

As anyone who has tropical fish knows, they have an annoying habit of being perfectly fine one day and perfectly dead the next. From the moment our aquatic friends settled in I made it clear that any dead fish would be entitled to the same rights to a decent send-off that we would extend to our other pets.

"We need to discuss what to do with any dead fish," I had declared very early on in our fish keeping odyssey.

John was characteristically pragmatic. "We take it out, check that it is definitely dead and then chuck it in the green recycling bin," he said. "Although, from the look on your face I take it you have other ideas?"

"Indeed I do," I retorted. "We will need to hold fish funerals, ceremonial flushings."

"Oh, here we go," John was all ears. "Enlighten me."

I had the funerary rites all mapped out. Once the deceased had been scooped into the pot of doom, it would rest in its little tub of water so that we could, as John had said, check that it was definitely dead.

"You're sure you don't want to try the kiss of life at this point?" John appeared to be failing to grasp the gravity of the discussion.

"Then there are some essential formalities," I continued. "First of all, no one is allowed to use the loo for an hour or so."

"What? Why on earth not?"

"Because John, it would be most unseemly to have the deceased racing a log to the septic tank."

Warming to my theme I outlined the rest of the fish funeral process. With decorum and dignity the ex-fish was to be tipped down the toilet and flushed. The lid was to be lowered in a suitably reverent fashion and a candle placed on top.

John could not resist interrupting. "Are you serious?"

"Yes. I have already put tea lights and matches in the bathroom cabinet. Once the candle is lit, we just need to bless the fish with suitable good wishes as we send it on its final journey round the U-bend. This will conclude the funeral service."

"And we do this for every dead fish?"

"Well hopefully we won't have too many, but yes, if a fish dies it gets a funeral."

"And what if one of us needs the loo during the down time?" John sought clarification on an important point.

"There are plenty of bushes in the garden," I clarified.

"No way! I am not taking a leak in the garden so that half an inch of dead minnow can have peace and quiet in the pipe work."

A compromise was reached, fish funerals would still go ahead but the candle would go on the bathroom windowsill and the facilities would be reopened for general use five minutes after the flushing. This system worked well for the residents of the little tank, it did however, require some adaptation as we progressed to ever larger fish.

One of the golden severums had died. We had acquired it along with our middle sized tank and it had been fully grown then. Its previous owner had had it for years so we liked to think that its time had come and that it had simply died of old age.

"It looks perfectly healthy apart from the fact that it is dead," I said, sadly extracting it from the tank with a net and transferring it to a bucket of water.

Leaving it for the requisite time to decide whether it was going to stay dead John moved the bucket to the bathroom, out of the way of the cat, and we headed into town to go shopping.

With the weekly shop completed I steered us towards the supermarket café.

"Let's go for coffee and cake before we go home," I said. "We have a funeral to plan."

"This funeral is not as easy as the others though, is it?" John remarked, as we moved from the till and claimed a table.

I was thoughtful as I stirred sugar into my latte. "You know, I don't think it is going to be flushable."

John nodded as he agreed with me. "I think you are right, but it can't stay in a bucket on the bathroom floor for ever."

Prodding my cake with my fork, I pondered, "There's no desperate rush to get rid of it though, it will stay fresh for a while and it was just so impressive."

At this juncture the old lady on the table next door seemed to stop listening to her husband in favour of eavesdropping on our conversation.

"Perhaps it would be a double flusher?"

"No," John commented. "Even a double flush and a poke with the loo brush wouldn't get that to go down. Then you'd have to fish it out and we would be back where we started."

I munched my cake and then had an idea. "You don't think it would flush even if we dropped it in narrow end first? You can quickly do a double flush and I can add a bucket of water?"

"Nope, it would block the bog and I would just end up having to take the U-bend to bits."

The lady on the next table dropped her spoon.

"If it's too big to flush we will just have to bury it in the garden then," I concluded. "But it will have to be reasonably deep, I will be cross if the cat digs it up and I see her playing with it."

The eavesdropper was now looking across with undisguised horror. Suddenly realising that we had not mentioned that we were talking about a fish at any point in our conversation, it occurred to me that our little chat could have been completely misconstrued by our nosy neighbour. Having finished our coffee and cake we were now ready to go but I could not resist one last mischievous comment.

"Burying it is then John, but I do want to take a photo to remember it by first."

ALL ABOUT GOEBBLES

Monty rapidly proved to be a dustbin on legs. He stopped draining water bowls relatively early on as the vet was proved right and a plentiful and continuous supply soon taught him that he did not need to guzzle it all up in case no more was forthcoming. Food, however, was another matter. Granted, he did eventually learn to graze his breakfast and tea rather than wolf it all down in one go, but any other food was fair game for immediate and total scoffing. This meant that an unattended kitchen provided unlimited temptations, anything left unattended by the cat constituted another source of contraband.

Goebbles was fed in the bedroom, which she had adopted as her main relaxing area. When we first acquired Monty, Goebbles's food and water bowls were kept on the floor, just inside the bedroom door. Within a couple of weeks of regularly hearing the bowls being shoved around the floor and cleaned of every last molecule of cat food as Monty barged his way through the door, the bowls were removed to the high windowsill.

There were a couple of reasons for this. Firstly, Monty lived up to his two-by-four plank brain by completely failing to learn that Goebbles could more than stand her ground and demonstrated her annoyance at seeing her dinner disappearing down Monty's gullet by swiping him forcefully around the face with her extremely sharp claws. Secondly, Goebbles was on a daily steroid to control her bladder tumour and occasionally the naughty puss ate her food but left her tablet, licked clean and gleaming white, in the bottom of the bowl. On a couple of occasions we just rescued the bowl in time as Monty homed in to investigate. The thought of Monty on steroids gave us the heebie-jeebies.

We'd had Goebbles for over five years by the time Monty came to us. After a decent period of mourning for our previous cat, Pest, who had finally died at the ripe old age of seventeen after a brief illness, I had broached the idea of a replacement cat. I had started with a subtle and sensitive approach.

"It has been two years since Pestie snuffed it, when are we getting another cat?"

John replied with equal subtlety. "Forget it. We aren't."

This was not the response I wanted. I expounded upon how we had an environment entirely suitable for a cat; we were away from a main road, the barns around us provided plenty of mice hunting, there was a lovely sun-trap in front of our lounge window ideal for cat sunbathing. Furthermore, there were hundreds of unwanted cats seeking homes. It was selfish not to give one a home. John appreciated our cat friendly location, he agreed it was unlikely our cat would get run over because there was not going to be any cat. The barn mice were no doubt quite happy with a break from the risk of being torn limb from limb and the sun-trap was going to be kitted out with a couple of sun chairs so that we could enjoy it without the huffing and spitting of an angry puss, cross that we were blocking her rays.

"It is a farm," I retorted. "You can't have a farm without a cat."

"The farm has been without a cat for the past two years. It has survived. We do not want another cat." John was adamant.

I disputed the 'we' with all the reasoned arguments that I could come up with. Admittedly, Pest's last illness had been expensive and her death sudden and upsetting. She had been buried by us, wrapped in her favourite blanket, in a little plot by our kitchen window and her grave was topped by a piece of slate engraved with her name and age. She had been with John since turning up as a tiny kitten, I had come into his life when she was about a year old. She had had a wonderful life and a 'good innings' as they say. We had mourned and remembered, photos had been framed and displayed, Pest was never going to be forgotten but now though, it was high time we considered getting another cat.

"Do you think 'Goebbles' is a nice name for a cat?" I asked one day.

"I think 'Goebbles' is a bloody ridiculous name for a cat! Why are you naming a cat we have no intention of getting?"

"Just pondering, you know, I've always wanted to call a cat 'Goebbles'."

John replied, "You need to work on your spelling."

"How is 'Goebbles' a silly name for a cat but 'Pest' wasn't? And this is the female spelling if you must know. We wouldn't want a tomcat."

John sighed. "I don't know if it is worrying that I know where you are going with this. Let me guess, 'Goebbles' the female cat is 'Goebbles' because she has no balls?"

"Aha! You have it exactly. Just like the wartime song. Don't you think it is amazing that you can read my mind with the barest minimum of information?" I smiled across at him.

"Oh, amazing isn't the word, darling. In the grand scheme of things though, the song wasn't really about cats, was it?"

And so the cat conversation was placed on hold once more. A couple of weeks later John made a trip down to visit his mum on the south coast. Whereas normally I would have gone too, we hadn't been able to sort out a parrot sitter. Also, we were short staffed at work so I had been called in off my holiday. Waving John off with an instruction to ring me as soon as he arrived I headed into work for the afternoon. We had been starting to prepare for a stock take and had in excess of fifty thousand units to ensure were correctly coded so, by the time I reached home again later, I was tired and stressed. I also hated being on my own so decided to cheer myself up with a glass of wine.

The bottle of wine John had stocked me up with was particularly delicious so I freely imbibed while making myself some dinner. Looking through the kitchen window while waiting for the timer to signal serving time, I was horrified to see an enormous rat sat on the feeding tray of my bird-feeding station in the back garden. No more than fifteen feet from the window, it sat stuffing its face and then, to rub it in, paused for a leisurely clean of its whiskers. I opened the window and lobbed a couple of spuds at it. Completely unconcerned by the incoming missiles, it ignored me and brazenly carried on munching. We so, so needed a cat.

Purely on the grounds that I could not have rodents the size of the average family hatchback making free with the food I was putting out for our little wild birds, I took it upon myself to ring a local animal sanctuary to make tentative enquiries about the availability of cats that needed re-homing. What I would then do would be to present this new information to John when he arrived home.

John hated rats, the only good rat was a dead rat in his opinion. Any options I could present that would convert our scavenging rat into this condition would surely be welcomed. However, I also wanted to be responsible about this; I wanted information about proven mousers and ratters, everyone always wanted the cute kitten so I opted for asking about older cats. It did not have to be particularly good looking, there must be a cat that had been bypassed by people looking for an adoptee.

Topping up my glass of wine I animatedly described the rat to the lady on the phone, she mentioned that the sanctuary did have a cat that might meet our requirements. 'Bubbles' was a ten year old female cat, had been with the sanctuary for quite some time and as far as she knew was an excellent mouser. I finished the phone call having carefully logged all the facts to relay to John on his return. It had not escaped me that 'Bubbles' was similar to my ideal cat name of 'Goebbles' so, if John agreed to the rat killing cat, it would be simple and stress free to change the cat's name. Thrilled with my evening's detective work I headed off to bed.

I woke up the next morning with a headache and an empty wine bottle. Arriving at work my mobile rang. A male voice boomed in my ear. "I'm on the way in with your cat. Are you at work yet?"

"Erm, cat?"

"Yes, you agreed to give Bubbles a home, your place sounds ideal. We ask for a donation for adoption. Edge of town you work, isn't it? Be there in ten minutes."

Oh crap! Now I was in trouble.

The cat was duly delivered to me at work, I was relieved of ten pounds, and I found myself peering at a manky looking specimen with droopy whiskers and very short legs huddled in a carrier. My staff made a quick trip over to the supermarket for an emergency litter tray, litter and cat food, then the new arrival spent the day in my office while I prayed my boss did not make an impromptu visit, also that the cat did not decide to pee over my office computer equipment.

The staff found having an illicit cat in their midst infinitely more entertaining than preparing for a stock take and took every opportunity to request things from the office. It was a very long day. Eventually, having persuaded a friendly taxi driver to transport me and my unexpectedly acquired cat, I reached home. The cat promptly shot behind the washing basket in the bathroom and refused to come out. Then the phone rang. Uh oh.

John's mellow tones came through the receiver. "Hello sweetheart, have you had a good day? I'll be back lunchtime tomorrow."

"Oh, hi John! Um that's lovely, can't wait."

"Are you ok? You sound a bit ... odd."

"No, I am fine. Are you fine too? There was just this massive rat on the bird feeder outside. Well, it was huge, so I have sort of invested in an organic rat reducing machine. I was just assessing its features when you rang."

"YOU HAVE GOT A CAT, HAVEN'T YOU?!"

I tried to dig myself out of a hole. "Sort of."

"Cut the bull, do we now have a cat or not?"

"Erm, well, you do say that the only good rat is a dead rat, and this was the most enormous rat I have ever seen, putting its nasty rat diseases all over the bird feeder."

"CAT?" John was now sounding less mellow.

"Yes well, we do actually now have an excellent rat catching cat."

John arrived home the next day as promised. The cat had flatly refused to emerge from the bathroom since her arrival the previous night so I had positioned a litter tray, food and water bowls on the bathroom floor, with a fleecy blanket behind the washing basket for her to sleep on. Coming through the door, I could see John taking a furtive look around for our new arrival.

"Would you like a coffee?" I soothed.

"Where is this cat then?" John asked, completely un-soothed.

"She is in the bathroom, she won't come out. Look behind the wash basket."

John stalked into the bathroom and shut the door. I sneaked up to the door and heard the signs of freshening up after a five hour drive home.

Then a pause.

Then, "Hello cat."

The door opened and John eyed me with his best look, he then headed down to the bedroom to change. "Come on cat," he said.

Bubbles, now Goebbles, trotted out of the bathroom and followed him, taking up a new position under the bed. I had some grovelling to do but the cat was here to stay.

THE AMAZING RAT KILLING CAT SETTLES IN

Cats have a tendency to disappear if they are not confined to quarters for a reasonable length of time. We had been advised that a month was ideal. The new arrival would have time to make indoors its own and establish it as a new territory, so when the time came to let the cat outside there was less chance of our recently adopted pet clearing off into the sunset or moving in somewhere else.

Our previous cat, Pest, had been independent pretty much to the end, disappearing outside to toilet and then arriving back at regular intervals for food, or to snooze in a sunny spot on the settee. She had been a lovely cat but never what you might call a cuddly one. Essentially a farm cat since she had turned up as a kitten, she had patrolled the barns and exterminated lurking mice with ruthless efficiency.

It had not been uncommon to hear a crunching and scuffling under the bedroom window as dawn broke, only for sleepy investigation to reveal the grim scene of Pest in the process of dispatching and then eating an adult rabbit. All that would be left when she had finished with her prey would be the little fluffy tail which she would then toss around and play with until, distended and full, she yowled to come in to sleep off her unfortunate meal.

Pest mellowed over the years as she progressed into old age but you still lived with her on her terms. If she wanted attention she would hop up and tread your lap before curling into a tight little ball for a nap. She would purr contentedly as you stroked her and would occasionally stretch, uncurl and expose her tummy for a rub, eyes closed as she lazily treaded the air with her front paws. She could be very affectionate in her own aloof way.

If, however, you deigned to pick her up because you wanted to cuddle her, most of the time she would wriggle free and stalk off to groom her ruffled fur back into shape, casting a haughty look over her shoulder as she went.

We could go on holiday for a week or two, come back, and find that our cat-sitting neighbours had probably only seen her about three or four times for feeding. The stack of cat food we had left with them would be virtually untouched but Pest would then come running out of one of the barns, hurtling across the yard to rub round our ankles, vocalizing her pleasure at our return with nonstop meowing.

She would be sleek, muscular and shining with health and we just knew that the local rodent population would be drastically depleted. The only problem we ever had with Pest was an ongoing battle with tapeworms arising from her wild diet, which led to an almost obsessive ticking off of dates on the calendar as we logged the next due date for worming.

So, this was the benchmark our new cat was up against; Pest, the queen of the barns, the prettiest, haughtiest, fastest most independent pet-farm-cat ever. But the best mouser, ratter and all round rodent killer was now planted in our back garden in restful repose so I set about converting John to the charms of cat number two.

I had set up a litter tray in the bathroom. This, in John's opinion, did not constitute a charm of cat number two, in any way, shape or form.

"I hate litter trays. They are disgusting and unhygienic," he declared.

"Not as disgusting and unhygienic as not having one," I countered, busy with woodchip cat litter and fitting the domed roof to the base so the cat could have some privacy. "Besides, I have put loads of litter in. Goebbles can dig a hole, bury her poo and then all we have to do is…"

"We? What do you mean 'we'? *You* acquired a cat that we now have to encourage to crap in the house for a month. Any and every excretion, from whatever end or orifice of this cat, is your responsibility. *Capiche*?"

"No problem at all John," I smiled, then I had a thought. I queried, "Um, does that include cat vom?"

"Is vomit an excretion?"

"I suppose it is."

"And does it generally get excreted from an end or orifice?"

"I suppose it does."

"Then yes."

"Although actually," I suggested hopefully. "It could be called an expulsion rather than an excretion."

John was having none of it. "Tomayto, tomahto. No trying to wriggle out of it on technicalities. Any substance or deposit that was originally inside the cat, and for whatever reason is now outside the cat, is your responsibility to clear up, okay?"

Having to admit that the boundaries on cat litter maintenance had been firmly established and hoping that Goebbles would not prove to have a bilious nature I moved on to the charms of her appearance. From her hiding space in the bathroom, she had decamped on day two to the bedroom where she took up residence under the bed, emerging only to eat or use the litter tray.

Crouching to communicate with our new pet as she skulked amidst old board games that last saw the light in the early nineties did not do John's back any good so we made it a priority to entice her out. This was achieved by about day four when she crept out, took a look at the duvet, hopped up and lay down to clean under-the-bed dust off her whiskers.

"Isn't it lovely to have another tabby cat like Pestie in the house?" I commented.

"She may be a tabby, but that is where the similarity ends,"

John replied. "She has got no legs and she looks like a barrel." To illustrate his point, he waved an arm at a framed picture of Pest, sitting halfway up a tree looking serene and athletic. "She has also got droopy whiskers and looks miserable."

"Of course she looks bloody miserable." I leapt into action to defend Goebbles's corner. "You have made disparaging comments about her legs, her figure and brought attention to her whiskers. To top it off, you are comparing her with another female of the species. Bad move."

It did turn out however, that the reason for Goebbles's unhappy appearance had less to do with an unwanted comparison with her slinky predecessor and everything to do with the fact that she had raging toothache. Obviously a portly cat who enjoyed her food, it was alarming when she suddenly refused to eat. A trip to the vet revealed that she had gingivitis and about a million rotten teeth that needed removing, and so it was that we found ourselves picking up a groggy cat a few days later, with a prescription for antibiotics and a care sheet for a cat that now had significantly less rat killing equipment than when I had brought her home.

This fact was not lost on John. "What is she going to do now? Suck the rats to death?"

Painful teeth removed and sore gums treated, Goebbles recovered quickly and regained her appetite. As she settled in she began to explore the house and spent many hours on our high windowsills looking out over the garden and fields. Being still on house arrest I tried to make things comfortable for her in her enforced confinement. I put a cat bed on the windowsill and the cat made it a place to curl up in the sun and watch the world go by. Little birds on the feeding table would cause an animated tail swishing.

The rat which, by now, John had also seen brazenly sneaking through the garden produced a fixed cat stare as she followed its path. She seemed less bothered by her month indoors than John and I, who soon discovered that her use of the cat litter tray could permeate the entire house with a nauseating odour within seconds. Finally, however, the month was up. Assuming that Goebbles was now happy to stay in her new home, we flung open the front door one April morning, expecting our cabin fevered cat to bounce merrily forth to investigate her new territory and put paid to her rodent nemesis.

Except that she didn't. It was a fine spring with several days of warm sunny weather, which meant that we could have the door and several windows open for prolonged periods. Goebbles was happy to sit in the open door or look out of the window but she made absolutely no effort whatsoever to leave the house.

"Slight technical hitch in the rat killing stakes, isn't there darling?" commented John, as a hairy specimen scuttled along the barn wall one day and the cat sat cleaning her face on the doormat in the open doorway. "I think this has been a house cat."

"Can't have been a house cat, she came with excellent rodent killing credentials," I retorted.

"Perhaps her previous owners had a house infestation but this cat is about as farm savvy as a house brick."

I was affronted. I took to sitting on our doorstep and wheedling Goebbles to join me with treats and cuddles. After about three months she would actually sit outside on the step with me, but if I moved she would run back inside. Meanwhile, our rat friends decided the neighbourhood was the ideal safe and friendly place to raise a family and brought their numerous offspring out for early evening ambles. In the absence of any risk whatsoever of our excellent rat killing cat catching an ailing rodent, John took to browsing the local farmers' co-op and returning with tubs bristling with hazard symbols, labelled with such rat friendly titles as *'kill 'em dead'* and *'ex rat no rat'*.

When we heard scuttling in the roof space and we knew that the rats had gone for a desirable loft living environment, he flung open the loft hatch and lobbed about a ton of *'kill-your-rat-humanely-so-it-doesn't-stink-your-house-out-while-rotting'* granules in the general direction of the occupants while casting a disapproving look at the cat. In the end, the rodent control we needed had nothing to do with Goebbles and everything to do with John. She did eventually start exploring her surroundings but it took about six months for her to become comfortable outdoors. I had to agree with John's assessment of a house cat.

Once she did gain her bearings however, she was only too happy to make her mark on the rodent population control issue. She proved adept at catching and dispatching mice. The only problem was that her preferred method was to bring the mouse in sometime during the afternoon, let it go, and then resume hunting at a far more appropriate time. A time when all concerned could appreciate her skill and dedication to the task in question. We very soon found that our excellent rat catching cat invariably found this time to be around three in the morning.

AND NOT FORGETTING MICKY

"*I'm a good boy! I'm a good, good boy!*" Micky was marching up and down the back of the settee, flashing pin prick angry orange eyes and stopping every now and then to chomp a hole in the throw and glare evilly at me.

"I don't think so parrot." I stood a few feet away, nursing my hand and fumbling for a tissue to stop the blood that was running free from three deep bites.

I had made a rare miscalculation predicting the onset of his four times yearly 'Amazon rage' and was now paying the price. Now I had to get him back into his cage where he would spend the next few days venting his frustration on corks and pieces of wood instead of me. In his current state he was dangerous. He was able to fly and if he went for my head he could cause real damage.

When in his normal mood he spent hours on my shoulder preening or snoozing and stepped readily onto my hand to be placed back in his cage, where he would accept a walnut as a reward. He rolled onto his back and lay upside down for a cuddle or climbed down my leg to explore the floor of our lounge, doing his best to scuttle as fast as possible around to the far side of the coffee table where he could sneak a quick bite of the wooden base.

"Bad bird," I would admonish, as he reappeared with a chunk of table leg in his beak.

Micky would transfer the splinter to his foot and look up at me. "*Hello Micky. I'm a gooood boy,*" drawing out the vowel for emphasis.

For forty-eight weeks of the year Micky was a lovely, playful good-natured Amazon parrot. You could play with him, kiss him, preen what few feathers he did have and let him sit on your shoulders without any worries whatsoever. The other four weeks were a completely different matter as he turned hormonal or went through a moult. Then he ceased to be a parrot and instead became a creature spawned from the fiery dark matter of hell.

Over the years I had learned to read the signs of this transformation and prepared accordingly. He stayed in his cage with plenty of things he could destroy; it was originally my cockatoo's cage so more than big enough for a period of incarceration. Fingers, faces and anything that could have large bleeding chunks ripped out of it were kept firmly out of beak reach.

It would take about a week and then one morning, lunging, snapping killer parrot from hell would be gone and little Micky would be back. It was as if Micky himself recognised the symptoms.

When he wanted to come out and play he positioned himself by the door and cooed, "*Come on then, come on mate.*"

This happened most evenings when I returned from work and headed into the lounge to say hello. In spawn mode he never said it at all, no matter how close to the cage you happened to be until one day a little voice would wheedle "*Come on Micky*" and you knew he was once more safe to be around.

All very good in theory but this time I had got it wrong and evil spawn bird was gnashing his beak at me on the wrong side of the mesh. I hadn't really been paying attention and couldn't remember him saying '*Come on then*' before I let him out so now I was in trouble. I pulled my sleeve down over my hand and bent one of the floppier cushions round my arm. Micky paused in stomping along the settee and stretched his wings, fixing me with a look.

"*Whatcha doin?*" he wanted to know.

"Nothing chick," I smiled while thinking to myself, 'It's only a little beak, just get the featherless fiend in the cage, what's a little blood between friends?'

"Birdie want a walnut?" I cajoled, holding out a half shell.

Micky flashed his eyes, whipped the nut from my grasp and

flung it halfway across the room. He then flapped and took off, launching himself at my face. Birdie most certainly did not want a walnut, birdie wanted eyeballs.

I brought up my cushion-wrapped arm to intercept him, and as he landed he started chewing his way through the cover. Stuffing him unceremoniously through the open door of the cage I turned him onto the floor and beat a hasty retreat. Thwarted and exceedingly cross, Micky threw his toys around in a fit of rage until I posted some pieces of apple branch through the bars whereupon he proceeded to reduce them to matchwood.

Only then was I free to inspect the damage to my hand. "That bloody bird is going to be a kebab one of these days," I grumped, as John sought out the surgical spirit.

"What's up with him?"

"He's hormonal and I didn't see it coming. He has gone all unreasonable, unpredictable and downright bad tempered. You can't do a thing with him. Evil parrot."

"Well, look on the bright side," John soothed as he applied plasters. "At least you only get it a few times a year. I have to put up with that once a …"

"Don't even go there." I retrieved my mended hand and glared.

MICKY'S STORY

It was summer 2006, Olly had died and I was completely devastated. He was a beautiful umbrella cockatoo and I had been given him as a fifteen-week-old chick for my eighteenth birthday.

He'd had to have an operation a couple of months before and seemed to be making a good recovery. Then he took a turn for the worse and developed an internal infection that was proving difficult to cure. Our nearest avian vet was a three hour drive away and Olly had made several trips for tests and treatment including some residential stays. Prognosis was positive but I was well aware that birds hide symptoms of illness very well. By the time they look ill they can be extremely ill and then you can already be at a disadvantage with regard to battling whatever is wrong with them.

Nevertheless, our avian vet was among the best there was and my daily phone calls for updates on his condition during his latest hospitalisation were met by reports of a slow but steady progress. He was putting on weight, eating and charming the nurses with his sweet nature. His blood tests were showing continued improvement, he was on the mend.

One morning in July I rang in for my daily check. The nurse who took the call seemed hesitant and said the vet wanted to speak to me. I wasn't unduly worried, perhaps he just wanted to go over a change in treatment.

Then the vet came on the line, "Hello Helen, I was just going to give you a call." There was a pause, "I am really sorry to tell you this, but I'm afraid Olly died about twenty minutes ago."

I was completely shocked and the next few minutes passed in a blur of questions and information. Olly'd had his morning medication as normal and had seemed perky and well. The night nurses were in the process of handing over to the day shift and Olly was entertaining them with his repertoire of chortles as they had coffee. He had been given his breakfast and was in the process of eating a walnut (his favourite food) when he suddenly keeled over and fell from his perch. By the time the staff had crossed the room to him, it was too late, he was dead. Everyone was horrified and deeply upset.

The vet was baffled, I gave permission for a detailed post-mortem to try and find a cause. The practice would then arrange for an individual cremation and I could bring the ashes home in a week or so. Frustratingly, nothing came back from the examination to explain his death; tissue samples, organs, bloods were all normal. It was just one of those things but the end result was still that I had lost my beautiful Olly after nineteen years, was sad beyond belief, and there was a huge parrot-sized hole in my life.

About a month later we had a German friend staying over, the weather wasn't brilliant so one day we decided to take her to the local animal park. Amongst the animals were unwanted exotic pets and former exhibits from larger zoos. You could buy bags of food and feed the residents; it was small but friendly and an ideal way to spend a couple of hours.

We ambled around, feeding monkeys and watching the antics of the meerkats in their colony. A huge snake was on display, wrapped around a handler as he explained facts about the species. Guinea pigs and rabbits entertained children in the petting section and various pens and enclosures held notices giving information about their occupants. As usual John adopted a planned approach to viewing, heading round the paths in an organised fashion, while I haphazardly dragged our guest from pen to pen, revisiting those with maximum hand feeding opportunities, and following no real path.

As we neared the end of our tour John said, "Did you see the bald parrot?"

"What?" I was all ears. "What bald parrot? Where?"

John gave directions. Within seconds, I was scuttling back through the mini zoo and soon found myself standing in front of a very large cage. Inside at eye level, on a perch that led into a little shelter, was a blue fronted Amazon parrot. It had a feathered head, wings and tail – the rest of it was completely bald. A sign hanging on the wire warned, 'My name is Micky – Beware, I bite!'

"Hello Micky," I said, thrilled to be talking to a parrot again, even if it did look oven ready. "Would you like a peanut?"

The little bird cocked his head and then sidled along the perch towards me. Very slowly he extended his neck and gently took the monkey nut from me. He then headed back to his shelter and began to eat. I was smitten.

John and Anne showed up. "Vot iss wrong vith ziss bird?" queried Anne, peering into the cage. "It is nicht gut for it to be looking like this, vair iss its fur?"

She spotted the sign, "Ha, I am thinking zis parrot iss nicht so freundlich, ja?"

The parrot seemed perfectly friendly to me but the park was due to close and John was trying to edge us towards the exit.

While John made dinner back at the house with Anne, I took the chance to sneak off and make a telephone call. Before long I had a potted history of Micky's life in note form in front of me. He was twenty-eight years old and for twenty-six of those years he had been with an owner who loved him to pieces. Unfortunately, owing to health reasons he had to be given up and had then gone to a new home. This had obviously not worked out and Micky had wound up at the zoo with a new reputation for viciousness and no feathers.

Yes, he could be a lovely bird. No, they wouldn't consider re-homing him because he had caused some serious bite injuries to the staff, one even needed stitches. He was perfectly healthy despite his appearance, it was just that he had an attitude and a bad temper and was unpredictably moody. I was pondering all this when John came to find me.

"What are you doing in here? Why are you not entertaining our guest?"

"I was just ringing the zoo. You know, to check on the bald parrot."

"And is the parrot okay?"

"It is fine, but I think it would be more fine with us. Look." I showed John and now Anne, who had appeared by his side, the advertisement for the attraction in the local paper that I had used to find the phone number. "'Adopt an animal', it says it here."

John sighed, "I think that means you set up a direct debit, send them money each month, and a random meerkat sends you a card at Christmas and on your birthday. I really don't think it entails visiting the place, spotting the first waif you come across and then pestering them to let you move it in."

He picked up my notes, "Let's see – 'bad temper', 'needed stitches', 'vicious', 'serious bites', great credentials for your potential adoptee, it is an ASBO parrot!"

"Vot is ziss 'asbo'?" Anne was interested.

"It means it is misunderstood, it just needs to be loved." I grabbed my notes back.

"I will remind you of that next time the little ASBO urchins are nicking stuff from the shop," John said as the timer began chiming in the kitchen. "Tea is ready, I am going to dish up."

After dinner we all relaxed in the lounge. I upended the empty wine bottle and gave John a meaningful look. He took the hint and went to find another. While he was out of the room Anne looked over at me.

"I am thinking that you vill not be forgetting ziss parrot. It vill soon be in ziss house, ja?"

Over the next two weeks I contacted the owners a couple more times. I enquired again about the possibility of re-homing Micky, outlining my experience with parrots and the fact that I had kept birds since I was twelve years old.

I told them about Olly and how I now had a huge parrot-sized hole in my life. They commiserated but pointed out that if I took on Micky I would soon have huge, beak-sized holes in my person. I was undeterred, something about this little bald bird had touched my heart. Eventually they decided to give me the benefit of the doubt, with some essential provisos.

He was a lovely bird and deserved another chance as a pet parrot, but he was not to be messed around. I could take him home but if I felt that I could not handle him, or cope with his moods then he was to be returned to the zoo. Under no circumstances was he to be passed on to another stranger and end up with more disruption in his life. I was also taking him with full disclosure from the zoo, he bit and he bit hard. I had been warned.

I spent the August bank holiday weekend thoroughly scrubbing and disinfecting Olly's cage. It was then decked out with new toys and perches more suitable for a smaller occupant. On collection day I commandeered the assistance of a work colleague as John was away for the day, loaded up a carrier and set off to fetch Micky. Tempting him into the transit cage with a peanut I made a final list of food likes and dislikes with the zoo, made an adoption donation and then headed home. It had all gone very smoothly and I promised to send photos and updates as he settled in.

Back in my kitchen, we held the door to the carrier up to the door of the big cage and coaxed Micky to swap. He promptly sidled between the doors and climbed onto the top of the cage where he assessed us at eye level.

"*Hello Micky,*" he said.

"Hello Micky," we quavered in unison.

"*I'm a good boy,*" he stated.

"Are you?"

"*I'm a good good bird.*"

I took a step forward, Micky cocked his head to one side and let out a wolf whistle. Then he stood up on his legs, in a fair impression of a parrot on tiptoe and let loose a long, musical but indecipherable tune. While he was serenading us I put my hand in the cage below him and picked up a selection of nuts.

Micky cut off his warble and looked down.

"*Hellooo*," he said in a deep, slightly naughty chortle.

I put one arm up to him, using the hand with the nuts to tempt him forward. He stepped neatly onto my wrist.

"*Come on then*," he ordered.

I introduced him to his new home and let him step off onto a perch; he took a peanut and looked around curiously. I withdrew my arm and shut the door as he finished eating and began climbing down to investigate the rest of the food on offer.

As we made a coffee and watched, Micky took a quick look at the bowl with the parrot mix and nuts in and then moved across to the fruit. I knew he was partial to apple but had filled the bowl with a selection of everything we had given Olly; peas, sweetcorn, apple, orange, pear, grape, pomegranate, banana, celery tops and carrot. He sampled, interspersing his tasting with liberal doses of '*Hello Micky*', before finally he climbed back up to his top perch and wiped his beak.

Clenching his foot into a ball and pulling it up into his tummy, which would have been the equivalent of tucking it into his feathers if he had any, he looked out at us.

"*I'm a good good boy*," he assured us, and went to sleep.

A couple of days later John and I were on our way home from a visit to our avian vet. Micky had been booked in for a new bird check, an essential formality to rule out any diseases he might need to be treated for before he was allowed to come into contact with our other birds.

We had seen the same vet who had treated Olly. We gave Micky's history as far as we knew it and he gave him the once over. Apart from his total lack of feathers anywhere but on his head, wings and tail, he seemed to be in good health. He had pulled his feathers so often that it was likely that his dermal papillae were permanently damaged, which meant that they would never grow back but if we could live with a parrot that had a passing resemblance to an oven ready *poussin* then there was no problem. Twenty-eight was verging on middle aged for an Amazon but he could easily live to fifty plus; he was a healthy weight, his beak, feet and eyes indicated good condition and a faeces sample had come back clear of parasites and infection. Micky was ready to become a fully-fledged member of the household.

As we brought him out through the waiting room Micky spotted a couple of dogs waiting for their appointments.

"*Yip, yip, yip,*" he barked. "*Grrr yip, yip, grrrr.*"

We hadn't known it before that moment but our bald parrot was a terrier in disguise. The vet laughed, "You've probably taken on a handful but it looks like he's a character. Enjoy him. And don't take this the wrong way but I really hope we don't see you again."

Then he waved us and our barking parrot off on our long journey home.

THERE IS ONLY ONE 'F' IN TUFTY

"Here we go again," John emerged from the office and was brandishing something official looking at me. "Have you seen the latest heating bill? We could power a substation with what we spend on keeping that parrot warm."

"The chick turns purple if it drops below fifty," I responded, glancing at Micky who was sat on his perch, eyes half closed and burbling contentedly to himself in the 'chatty old man' series of phrases that we had yet to decipher. He sounded very much like someone sat alone, muttering at the news and putting the world to rights but his individual comments were hard to make out.

"What about the fact that I turn purple seeing the size of this bill?"

"It will be fine, we managed with Tufty."

John smiled, "We did, didn't we?"

It was not the first time that we had to keep our house warm for a bald bird. A long time before, a beautiful, gentle, sweet-natured cockatoo had come into our lives.

It was a treat to make the two hour journey to the nearest big town for a shopping trip. A few times a year we would drive through the hills and mountains and make a day of it; shopping, a spot of lunch and a look around a town that was renowned for its Tudor architecture.

It also had a big pet shop with a 'pets for sale' section upstairs and it was inevitable that I would check on the animals each time I visited. One time in 1992 there was a pretty little medium sulphur-crested cockatoo in a large cage. I said 'hello' and it pushed its head against the bars so I could scratch it, then it put up a foot and ever so gently took my preening finger in its grip and mumbled my nail with a careful beak.

I wasn't expecting ever to see this bird again but when I made a return trip by train with my mother a couple of months later we popped into the pet shop for provisions. The cockatoo was still upstairs and put up its crest in recognition when it saw me. Once more I tickled it around the head and once more it returned the favour by preening my finger. This time though, I noticed that it had a chewed patch on one shoulder, nothing major – just a few shredded feathers and a couple of missing ones.

Christmas shopping was the next reason to visit but now the bird, though as friendly as ever, had two chewed shoulders and a substantial bald patch on one. I asked the pet shop owner about it. Yes it was a shame about the feather picking, but it was going to a new home soon so all would be well. Sure enough, when we next visited the little bird had gone.

It was June 1993 when we next found ourselves heading inland. We picked up pet food and I popped upstairs for a quick look, not expecting to see anything of interest. In a large cage sat a parrot – a medium sulphur-crested cockatoo – its chest and wings almost completely denuded apart from a few shredded strands of down. Hunched over, it was using a foot to pull its once beautiful yellow crest feathers down so that it could chew them too. The pet shop owner was nearby, tidying.

"Bit of a state, isn't it," he conceded.

I moved over to the cage and the bird put up what remained of its crest in greeting and poked a foot through the bars towards me. As I watched it preen my fingernail I realised with horror that this was the cockatoo I had been visiting.

"What happened to it?" I asked the owner.

He looked upset, the people that had bought it had taken it to be a mascot in a kiddies' nursery. The children, being young, had teased it and the new owners had eventually returned it to the shop in its current condition. The fact that the bird was still so friendly after being poked with crayons was a testament to its good nature.

The pet shop owner shrugged sadly and moved a few feet away. I scratched the bird under its chin and watched as it closed its eyes in enjoyment of a tender touch. Then I turned to John, fuming at the idiocy of someone who would buy a parrot as a nursery decoration and declared to the bird, to John and to the entire upper floor, "I don't care what it costs, I am not leaving this shop without this parrot!"

John raised his eyebrows, "I wouldn't take up poker if I were you."

With instructions to me to keep quiet, John commenced haggling.

We left the store about half an hour later with a medium sulphur-crested cockatoo peeking out from a carry box. We also left with its cage and equipment, which John had managed to persuade the owner to give us free.

I called the bird 'Tufty'. She proved to be the gentlest, calmest, sweetest parrot I had ever owned. Despite her early treatment, never in the eleven years she was mine did she ever bite. She was only about three when I came to own her, she loved being near Olly and would sit on your shoulder and go to sleep. She would dance on her stand and quickly learned a repertoire of whistles and phrases. We gave her toys and varied her diet and she came out most evenings for a wander around the floor or furniture.

This was a bird who had every right to be angry at the world but who remained serenely good natured. She was terrified of children but even then showed no aggression, she merely retreated and trembled. With adults she couldn't have been more engaging and friendly and if, on the rare occasion, she was not in the mood to be handled she would softly take your finger or hand in her beak and gently push it away.

It took eight years to break her feather picking habit. We

regularly changed her toys and provided vitamin supplements. There was no physical cause the vet could ascertain, it was purely as a result of psychological upset. Even when she was nearly fully feathered again, you would sometimes catch her with her head under a wing, sleeping, apart from her beak mumbling at a bit of down.

And then she did it, she stopped feather picking and developed into a beautiful example of a healthy medium sulphur-crested cockatoo; snow white apart from yellow colouring on the undersides of her wings and tail and a yellow crest that she would fan upwards into a gorgeous sunshine crown. She even began to accept children in the vicinity, as long as they were quiet and moved slowly around her. She was fourteen years old and in the prime of her life. We looked forward to many more years of her being the happy, healthy bird she was entitled to be.

But sometimes, things are just not meant to happen that way.

"Bit wheezy are you Tufts?" I queried one day at the end of September 2004. "Better get you checked out."

I was cleaning her out and had just heard the merest whisper of hoarseness in Tufty's breathing. It was there and then it wasn't. It was only because I had my head so close to her face that I heard it at all. Nevertheless, birds hide any signs of illness to avoid being predated in the wild so arrangements were made to take her to our avian vet the next day.

She gave that little wheeze a couple more times that day but as we loaded her into the car next morning she was singing her heart out, climbing round her carry cage and looking the picture of health.

"Going to make me look silly, are you Tufty? Do you know how much it costs to cart you down to Cardiff on a wild goose chase?"

"*Hello Tufty*," said Tufty before starting whistling again.

The vet was upbeat but cautious, "It is probably just a bit of respiratory irritation, but we'll take some bloods and do an x-ray just to rule out anything else."

Luckily we had insurance so we could agree to the vet's recommendations. Being a specialized vet, even the initial consultation where they go 'yup, it's a parrot' costs more. When they start talking about x-rays it also means expensive anaesthesia suitable to a bird's fragile respiratory system, before long you are into second mortgage territory. Moral of the story – get a parrot – get insurance.

We came back to the surgery a couple of hours later. Tufty had recovered well and the vet was ready to see us. He did not look quite as upbeat as before.

"We have found a couple of shadows on Tufty's x-rays," he started. "There is one in her throat and one on her chest wall near her heart. I have taken a scraping of the one in her throat, I was hoping it would be an abscess but as there is a second shadow, it could be something a bit more sinister."

"*Hello bird*," chirped Tufty happily.

Shell-shocked, we took our leave and left for home with Tufty singing in her carrier. We were due to go on holiday abroad the next day so my birds were being dropped to my parents' house. We paid the interim bill and took a copy to forward to the insurance company. It wasn't until I got home that I noticed that it referred to 'Tuffty'.

From Bulgaria I rang in daily; my birds were fine, Tufts was wheezing a little more obviously now but looked perfectly well. The vet had sent a message that he wanted 'Tuffty' back for more tests so my dad had taken her to Cardiff for me. Then, when I rang the day before our flight home there was a pause in the information. It was not good news, the throat mass was a tumour which meant the one on the chest wall probably was too. The vet had repeated the x-rays and both shadows had grown. My dad paid the second bill, and did I know they were spelling it 'Tuffty'?

"Yes," I said. "Do me a favour will you? Let them know there is only one 'F' in Tufty."

"Will do," said my dad, his voice strained.

I relayed the information to John and we spent the last night of the holiday in sombre reflection. Arriving home we made arrangements to collect the birds but before we could do so I became ill. Blood tests revealed I had somehow picked up glandular fever, probably from the recycled air on the flight, my spleen was enlarged and my liver was out of whack. Consulting with the vet, he said that many viruses could affect birds too so it was probably better for Tufty to remain with my parents for now.

When I visited a week later I was shocked at my beautiful bird's deterioration. It was late October, she was noticeably thinner and the wheezing now echoed with every breath. I checked with the vet who had been in constant contact. She had painkillers and drops to reduce the symptoms but I had been in denial, I knew she had growths but people lived for years with cancer, this all seemed too quick.

"We are talking days, a couple of weeks at most," the vet told me. "Birds go downhill fast, but we are doing everything we can to make sure she is comfortable. If she stops eating or drinking that's the biggest worry."

I came off the phone and got Tufty out. She was ecstatic to see me, raising her crest and rubbing her face on my neck. She had an odd smell to her, a sick smell that she breathed over me from the evil thing that was killing her. I put her on her stand and we did 'Horsey, Horsey'.

'Horsey, horsey, don't you stop,
Just let your feet go clippety, clippety clop,
When your tail goes swish, and your wheels go round,
Giddy Up! We're homeward bound.'

As I sang, she stomped her feet to the clippety clop, danced to the swishing, bobbed her head to the wheels going round, then finally spread her wings and gave a call with her neck stretched to the ceiling for the homeward bound.

She would normally then want to do it all again, but this time she was exhausted.

A couple of days later I rang the vet again. We had an appointment but I wanted to bring it forward. Tufty was not eating or drinking much now and while she didn't seem to be showing pain, one eye had started to shrink back into her head and her balance was affected.

"I think this is it," I said to the vet.

"Give her as many cuddles as you can today, we will see you tomorrow."

That night Tufty cried.

In the early hours I woke to hear a mournful calling from downstairs. I went to investigate, Tufty was awake and rubbing her blind side on the cage bars. She was making a noise I had never heard before. I took her out and up into my bed, cupping her head in my hand. She rested if my hand was there and cried if it wasn't. In the dark hours before dawn I cradled my dying parrot and cried with her.

We made our appointment with time to spare. John and I were moist-eyed and strained, then the vet came in and gently looked Tufty over.

"I'm so sorry," he said. "But there is nothing more I can do for Tufty."

"Yes there is," I said, through tears I was biting back so as not to stress out Tufts. "There is one more thing."

The vet nodded and produced a syringe. He found a little chest muscle and injected the overdose. Almost immediately Tufty slumped in my hands.

"She's very weak," he observed.

My brave, gentle parrot's breathing slowed and then stopped. The vet tested for an eye reflex and then stood up.

"She's gone," he said.

I brought Tufty up to my face and rested her body against it, then kissed her. Whispering into the feathers she had finally grown in full abundance I murmured my goodbyes.

"Giddy up Tufty, you're homeward bound."

Then the tears came and I completely lost it.

The final bills came through and were settled. The 'F' had been removed. Tufts was laid to rest in my parents' garden with a gravestone that gave her name and the message 'homeward bound', engraved on slate by my dad. When the initial horror and shock of her death had abated John and I chatted about her life and antics.

"I am glad they took that extra 'F' out of the paperwork," I said. "It seemed silly but it was wrong."

John smiled at our memories, "You are right, there was definitely only ever one f'in Tufty."

ALPHA FEMALE IN CONTROL

It was the longest day of the year. This meant that not only was it light until gone ten thirty at night but also that dawn broke just before four in the morning. Monty, being an adaptable dog, altered his circadian rhythms accordingly. He woke up at the first hints of light and settled into some vigorous butt cleaning, while Megan snored and John and I lay still so that he did not realise we were awake.

Our plan did not work. Finely attuned to the surroundings about him Monty soon ascertained that we were trying to con him and presented at the side of the bed, patting it with a paw.

"Go back to bed," John muttered.

There was a sense of Monty backing up then a thump and a pained 'oomph' from John. "Not this bloody bed," he huffed. "YOUR bed."

I sniggered in the half-light, "Don't be mean, puppy wants a cuddle."

"Does he really?" John was unsympathetic to the puppy's needs for a hug in view of the fact that all twenty plus kilos of puppy had just landed unannounced on his midriff. "Get on the case with cuddling him then."

With that John tugged the duvet back and Monty was rolled into the middle of the bed.

"Shift over then," I said, needing space. Goebbles was curled up by my left shoulder, and with Monty now burrowing into me from my right I felt like the filling in a pet sandwich.

"Shift over? What do you mean 'shift over'? You've had ninety per cent of the bed all night, where exactly do you expect me to shift to?" John was being unreasonable.

I maintained a dignified reasonableness, "What rot! Move! There's three of us and one of you, we need wiggle room. And by the way, some duvet would be nice."

The early hour had turned John into a parrot, "'Some duvet would be nice'. Are you winding me up? You've been wrapped up like a cocoon all night."

Ignoring this I claimed back what I felt was a fair and proportional portion of the duvet and we all settled back down for the last hour of sleep. About twenty minutes later I started squirming.

"Now what's the matter with you?" John wanted to know.

"I'm too hot. Do you want some duvet back?"

This latest exchange woke Monty up again and he decided to complete the rest of his morning ablutions. Starting with nibbling his paws he then gave his butt the once over again before grooming his hindquarters and finally turning his attentions to his groin. After some energetic slurping he stood up, shook himself and then plopped back down for a good prolonged scratch.

"I assume you have been defleaing this mutt," a voice came from the other side of the bed.

"No, I thought you'd been doing it," I said.

"What?"

"Only joking, is it getting up time yet?"

John sighed, "I take it that means you would like a cup of tea?"

Before I could answer Monty stood up again but this time he stayed up. Standing at the foot of the bed he coughed slightly then retched.

"What's up Monty, got some fur in your throat?" John asked.

Monty coughed again then turned and snuffled up to my shoulder. I put out a hand to stroke him as he stood next to me, a dark shadow outlined against the dim light behind the curtain. He then retched once more.

"No chucking up on the duvet Monty. It's *verboten*," I muttered, starting to feel a bit nervous. "Get down if you are feeling sick."

Too late, all of a sudden Monty arched his back gave a series of quick 'aaaarck' sounds and deposited a slimy pile of hairy bile about four inches from my head.

"Urgh, you are such a gross dog," I complained, hurtling out of bed at lightning speed.

"Oh, don't be mean, puppy feels pukey," John commented. "But since you are up, you may as well make me a coffee."

Later on, with the duvet in the washing machine I finished getting ready for work. As John prepared to drop me off in town he said, "You have remembered that I am out tonight, haven't you?"

I had remembered, John would do the afternoon walk before leaving and I would arrange a taxi home. Any problems with this plan and John would leave a text for me to pick up when I turned my phone on after locking up. I could then spend an enjoyable evening as alpha female, bonding with my pack.

The working day passed uneventfully and it came to six o'clock. My phone beeped as soon as I turned it on with a message from John, 'Monty did not have a crap on his afternoon walk'.

"Uh oh." I thought to myself as the taxi motored out of town.

I arrived home and let myself in to find the house ponged like an overflowing septic tank. Casting a look around I was relieved to find that Monty had not had an accident but he was assailed by a case of wind that threatened to strip the wallpaper. Dumping my bags I took both dogs out, only to find Monty decided that the need for an imminent turtle was overpowered by the more immediate need to eat next door's cat.

"Clear off Kitty," I called, clinging on to the lead as Monty lunged and bounded in her direction. "Monty! Pack it in and have a crap."

It was then that Monty lost interest in the cat in favour of something far more interesting. As the cat disappeared into the barn he noticed the veritable smorgasbord of sheep poo left in the yard by the farmer having our woolly friends in for essential maintenance during the afternoon. The whole expanse of ground in front of the house was dotted with runny poo, lumpy poo, dry poo and even poo with random bits of sheep attached that merited immediate investigation.

"You didn't text me about this, did you John?" I grumbled to myself, as both Monty and Megan selected tasty poo morsels and started munching. As I dragged both dogs away from their impromptu buffet I began mentally drafting a letter to the head office of our local pet supermarket.

'Dear sirs ... May I respectfully make a suggestion that could benefit your annual turnover ... never mind this 'gold standard lamb with hand polished rice and veggies grown on the verdant Himalayan up-slopes' cobblers ... market a dog food filled with sheep shit and you're made... Yours etc. ... Owner of Monty.'

I left the dogs outside while I made my dinner. In preparation for keeping them occupied I had bought them both a new chew each while on my lunch break.

"Who're lucky pooches then?" I cooed, unwrapping the chews and handing them out. "Now you enjoy the sunshine, I'm going to make my tea."

It wasn't long before I heard growling and scuffling outside. I popped my head out the door to find the dogs in a face off over their chews. With my best glare I instructed them to desist. A few minutes later they were at it again, it was clear that Megan wanted Monty's chew while Monty wanted Megan's and a little bit of a doggy discussion on the matter was in full swing.

"Look you two, what is your problem?" I snapped. "Both these chews are exactly the same." I herded Megan to the doorstep, "So you have yours here." I called Monty over to the kennel, "And you have yours here, and let's be nice, all right?"

I made to go back into the kitchen as both dogs sat where I had put them, watching me. At the door I issued a parting shot, "The same, okay? Both chews are exactly the same, no difference, understand?" Satisfied that my mediation had restored amicable relations I went back to cooking. Within a very short space of time the latest round of snarly barking could be heard clearly in the kitchen.

I gave up and stomped onto the doorstep bellowing, "ENOUGH! GET IN THE HOUSE NOW, OR I SWEAR I AM GOING TO STRING YOU UP!"

I was treated to the best 'yeah, you and whose army?' look from the pooches as next door legged it out of her allotment and scuttled indoors.

I retrieved the dogs and dished up just before eight o'clock. Monty came to lie at my feet and looked lovingly up at me. Not to be outdone Megan assumed the position on my other side. Just as I was about to tuck in Monty let rip with another flatulent emission. Megan sniffed the air and then added her own pungent contribution and then both dogs synchronised in an appreciative inspection of their back ends.

Sighing, I stuck my dinner back in the still warm oven and took them both out for their evening constitutional. As I savoured the longest summer evening of the year, watching the sun still glinting its golden rays over the fields behind the house and contemplating my dinner slowly drying to a crisp, Megan and Monty conducted a leisurely inspection of every blade of grass and tufted weed in the garden before finally deciding to get down to business. They then headed back into the house ready to settle down for the evening. Just another average day in pooch world was drawing to a close.

TRIPE, TRAINING AND FACIALS

I was owed some time from work so one day I had an early finish. Before coming home I had insisted on stopping at the pet shop for dog treats.

"And do we need dog treats?" John queried.

"I just want to check, there might be a treat we haven't tried yet, the dogs will have missed me."

"They last saw you at nine this morning, it is now three o'clock, they are hardly likely to be in mourning yet."

I persisted, "The shop is on the way, I'll only be two minutes." As I hopped out of the car I added, "I will just have a quick look at the tropical fish while I am in there."

"Aha. Now we come down to it," John called after me. "No more fish, although you could ask them if they want to take about fifty million guppies off our hands."

I made my way to the fish department but the store had just had a delivery so all the tank lights were dimmed. Foiled, I headed for dog treats instead. Nothing much caught my eye, most of the brands and varieties we already had at home anyway, but then I spotted something we hadn't tried. Dried tripe, now this looked interesting, and the happy dog on the packaging was positively drooling in excitement. It was on a three for two offer and on this basis I grabbed three packs before going to pay. There was also a queue, so I took the opportunity to browse the offers at the till point.

"What is that?" John wanted to know as I got back into the car.

"It is a giant tennis ball, John," I replied happily, plonking my prize on the back seat along with two of the tripe packets.

"I suppose I should be grateful that it is not a fish but we have rubber balls, plastic balls and enough tennis balls at home to stock Wimbledon. Why do we need a giant tennis ball?"

"It was lonely."

"Sorry," John paused in reversing out of the parking bay to eye me. "It was what?"

"Lonely. It was reduced at the counter as end of line; the size was being discontinued because it didn't sell very well. This is the last one, we are giving it a good home."

John cast his eye onto the back seat, "I would imagine it didn't sell because it's the size of something you normally see on the end of a chain, wrecking buildings. And will soon be on the end of Monty, wrecking our house."

Shaking his head, John drove home while I read out the health benefits of dried tripe and examined the contents through the clear packaging.

"Have you ever smelled tripe?" John asked.

"It must be quite nice, people can eat it too," I replied.

"It is vaguely passable if it's been braised for about three weeks with two tons of onions, but it smells pretty objectionable otherwise."

I brandished the pack, "This dog looks enthusiastic about it."

"They are hardly likely to put a picture of a dog honking its guts up, are they?"

We arrived home and I put the packets of dried tripe on the kitchen shelf and the new huge tennis ball in the toy pile. I greeted a happy Megan and then Monty, who acted as though he had not seen me for weeks. Both dogs then bounced into the kitchen and started sniffing. While Megan tested the air, Monty stood up on his back legs and firmly placed both front paws on the units, nose straining in the general direction of the shelf where the tripe was.

"See," John said. "I told you, tripe permeates. They can even smell it through heat sealed plastic. I hope you have put them out of his reach."

"They are up on the shelf, any higher and we will be putting them in the loft," I replied. Megan headed off down to the office to sit with John while I decided to distract Monty from hunting down the latest possible swipe-able contraband. Getting him to sit in front of me I instigated our welcome home routine.

"Paw," I said holding up my right hand. Monty obligingly put his left paw in my palm. "Good boy, other paw," I extended my left hand and Monty put up his right foot. "Good boy." I praised, pointing at my ear which Monty quickly licked then sat back waiting.

"You are such a good dog," I beamed. "Now cuddle." This was Monty's cue to move forward and put his head on my shoulder while I put my arms around him. It was normally a sweet moment of trust and love between us. Monty duly moved forward, sat and wagged his tail. He cocked his head and looked at me, making eye contact with his huge amber eyes and panting happily – he then paused for a tiny moment before sneezing the biggest, stringiest wodge of dog phlegm straight into my adoring face.

A few seconds later John appeared in the doorway, "What are you going bananas about now?" Followed by, "Why have you got an alien on your face?"

I glared, getting the impression that this all seemed rather too humorous, "Monty flobbed me!"

"Well, you are always smearing gunk on your face, it's probably good for your skin."

I was miffed, "I do not 'smear gunk' on my face John, I occasionally use face masks infused with revitalising aromatherapy oils and soothing moisturisers, but last time I looked none of the ingredients listed featured the contents of Monty's sinuses."

"Must be all those whiffy tripe molecules milling about, making him sneeze. Besides, you are always looking for moneymaking opportunities no one else has thought of. What about it – 'Acme Monty Face Masks – marketed shortly'?"

"Don't think they will catch on somehow," I grumbled, grabbing a tissue and wiping furiously.

After dinner I decided that Monty needed to redeem himself. I had recently bought a dog magazine that had a very helpful article on teaching recall. Quite whether the article had been written with a dog who had the concentration levels of a microbe in mind was another matter entirely, but I was prepared to give it a go.

The advice was to commence training in a secure environment and to kneel down on your dog's level. Once you had the undivided attention of your dog you were to perfect the call with a clap and outstretched arms. With a bit of luck you would be rewarded with the arrival of your dog in front of you, at which point you would reinforce the good behaviour with treats and praise.

"Come on Monty, training time," I said.

Monty hopped off the settee and stood in the lounge doorway. I went almost to the end of our very long hallway and secreted a bag of tripe treats on the stand by the bedroom. Then I crouched down and commenced training.

"Come here," I commanded, at the same time clapping once and flinging my arms wide.

Monty turned and disappeared back into the lounge, by the time I arrived after him he was ensconced back on the settee and John was laughing.

"Let's try again, shall we mutt?" I fixed Monty with my best trainer-in-authority look.

With a reluctant Monty once more persuaded to sit in the hall I resumed my position and repeated my recall routine. "Come here," I called with a clap and my most enthusiastic tone. It suddenly sank in to the canine grey cells what I wanted and Monty legged it in my general direction.

"Now we are getting somewhere," I thought to myself.

What the article had failed to mention however, was that

Monty's idea of a recall response involved taking off in a flying leap towards me from around eight feet away. I had also made myself comfortable on a loose rug on a tiled floor that I had recently polished. When Monty came into land on me – all splayed feet and slobber – I found that we promptly continued his journey along the ground, as the rug did nought to sixty in a matter of seconds towards the bedroom door.

Monty, who had obviously been labouring under the impression that he was going to be subjected to more of this boring training lark, was thrilled by this exciting new game. As it inevitably resulted in a collision that rattled my teeth, put a door-sized dent in the back of my head, and led to an unseemly sprawl on the deck, he was quivering with glee as he untangled himself and stood over me. I found myself on my back, looking up at parts of the Mont that you are generally not supposed to view from about four inches away.

"I think that is probably illegal," John smirked, appearing to investigate the commotion. "What sort of magazine did you find this training in?"

Squirming out from under Monty I moaned about my bumped head, "I'm at work tomorrow, what if I have concussion? I would have to have this as my absence-from-work conversation with my boss."

"Don't worry, I'll ring in for you," John said. *"I'm sorry Helen cannot make work today but whilst wearing a face full of flying dog she slid into our bedroom door and bumped her head."*

MONTY HAS A SMASHING TIME

A combination of poor weather and the shepherd doing sheep treatments in the yard is always dreaded as it means Monty is indoors and bored, which results in cabin fever. While Megan takes the opportunity to curl up and snooze, Monty invariably gets up to no good. As a resourceful pooch he has a tendency to create his own entertainment that usually starts with a failure to have a crap on either the morning or afternoon walk. This means every time he drops a stinky one, looks at his back end, or whimpers, one of us has to leap into action to take him outside and stand in the peeing down rain in case he decides to drop one in the hallway.

One such afternoon he decided that it was completely acceptable to wind us up by appearing with random items from the wash basket and distributing them around the lounge. Trying to ignore him, he then vigorously killed the underwear with the same rat-killing shake he applied to farmyard rodents. Working on the principle that a reaction would constitute positive reinforcement we studiously refused to respond as he despatched more smalls; however, he then disappeared and an ominous dragging noise resulted in him shuffling backwards into the room with the entire wash basket in tow, crunching happily on its wicker rim.

Imminent destruction of household furniture merited intervention, so the washing was gathered up and the basket shut in the bathroom; game one foiled.

Monty slunk off in disgust, only to come bounding back gleefully a minute later with the cat basket in his mouth, which he proceeded to disembowel all over the floor. Knowing that Goebbles was around somewhere I headed off to check on her. She was standing on the bed, bristling and doing a fair impression of a bottle brush, spitting her indignation at the sudden lack of sleeping equipment. Realising that Monty had probably whipped the basket out from under the cat while she was curled up in it, I attempted to mollify Goebbles with strokes and a filthy look at the large black head that had appeared in the doorway. Turfing Monty out, I closed the door so the cat could resume sleeping in peace and headed for the lounge once more.

I then settled down with the papers and everything else I needed not to have to get off the settee for the next hour. Monty had other ideas. Sidling over on the pretext of having his head stroked he made a lightning fast lunge and promptly swiped the cordless phone from next to me. Bouncing around out of grabbing reach he issued his best *'You want it, you come and get it'* growl. Retrieval involved a pincer movement by John and me as Monty slunk at speed behind the settee. Cornering him, we homed in, wheedling with treats, phone in our sights. While we congratulated ourselves on retrieving the phone with only minimal amounts of slobber damage, Monty upped the ante.

"Where has my bloody mobile gone?" I asked, only to find Monty perfectly happy with the swap and making off down the hall in a blur of wagging tail and skidding paws.

Thrilled with the attention this exciting new game got him, he dropped my mobile on the rug and backed off a couple of paces, tail still waving but now assessing my next move with a gleam in his eye. I ambled towards him, pretending to be engrossed in examining the hall ornaments and completely uninterested in my phone.

"You all right there, Monty?" I smiled, dead heading the aspidistra.

Monty dropped to a sit, eyeing me. I made it to a reasonable lunging distance and found something incredibly interesting to look at through the window.

"Ooh, look at this Monty."

Completely unconvinced by my subterfuge Monty cocked his head and slowly plonked a large foot on my phone. The phone beeped alarmingly, I wafted an aspidistra leaf at him as a distraction and made a dive. The Mont clawed my mobile towards him and grabbed it with his mouth in a speed of light movement that proves that the average domestic dog has reflexes that outshine mine about tenfold. I resorted to plan B.

Declaring that it was only a phone and he could have it if he wanted, I retreated to the kitchen with as much nonchalance as I could muster and rattled the treat box. Megan appeared in a flash and was soon tucking into paddywack. Monty's head and my phone appeared round the doorframe. The rest of Monty stayed in the hall ready to leg it.

"Mmmmm," I said, peering into the box of treats. "Yummy yum yum."

The rest of Monty made it into the kitchen and slobbered drool, via my phone, onto the tiles. Megan decided it was Christmas as I used her as a lure and gave her a second titbit. Unable to resist any further Monty dumped my mobile on the floor and presented in a sitting position, paw waving at me. Ignoring the ominous crack as my mobile hit the floor tiles, I duly rewarded Monty while John, who was waiting for this moment, grabbed it and whisked it out of the way. Examining it afterwards, I was relieved to see that it appeared to be intact, if a little slimy and wet. It was only when I went to send a text later that I found the 'o' had failed to survive the battle of the phone.

Exhausted by his latest round of naughtiness, and with the yard still full of sheep Monty decided a snooze was in order. I resumed my space on the settee and all electronic devices were relegated to the highest shelf available. John settled into the recliner and turned on the television, Megan nabbed the armchair and Monty chose that moment to prove that weight is all in the mind and a twenty plus kilo pooch could be a lap dog if he wanted to be.

Later, John went out for the evening. He was going to a get together which was a good hour's drive away. It would be a late return but he promised to ring me before he started for home. I planned a relaxing night catching up on bills and paperwork, followed by a long soak in the bath and a couple of glasses of wine while I watched a film.

To start with I made dinner. Washing up afterwards, I had my hands in the sink when I heard a series of crunchy crashing noises.

"Monty! What are you wrecking now?" I called down the hall.

Wiping my hands, I headed to investigate. No sign of Monty but complete devastation in the hallway. Along the tops of the bookcases, well out of reach of marauding paws, I had built up a display of decorative eggs. Some were enamelled, some porcelain and some were fashioned from the real eggs of various sized birds, including quail, hen, goose and ostrich. The latter were individual and beautiful and had been birthday and Christmas gifts over the years to me from John and my family. I dusted them carefully and never failed to appreciate their intricate decoration.

Now most of them lay in shattered destruction on the floor, shards of shell and china surrounded by a scattering of crystals and semi-precious stones.

Monty was in the office, sitting in the dark. I put the light on and glared at him.

"Well done Monty, you've excelled yourself this time," I said.

As I stepped towards him, he started crying and flattened himself as far as he could against the computer stand. I stopped to look at him. His ears were flat to his head and his eyes were rimmed white as he hunched over in misery.

He carried on whimpering as I came closer and was now actively trying to burrow under the desk. It was then that I realised that I still had the towel in my hand from when I came out of the kitchen.

Horrified, I put the towel out of his sight and crouched down to his level, showing him my empty hands. Touching his flank I felt him shaking with fear.

"Oh Monty, they're only decorations. I'm not going to hurt you. Let me see your feet, I want to check you haven't got any splinters."

With the offending towel gone, Monty slowly crept out and I pulled him towards me. His feet were fine and I sat on the office floor cuddling him until he calmed and his ears and eyes returned to normal.

"Finally I took hold of his face and kissed his nose. "Look dog, I am not going to hurt you, John is not going to hurt you, no-one is ever going to hurt you again, okay?"

Then, as I looked over the top of his head at the glinting remnants in the hall I nuzzled his fur and muttered, "What's a few hundred quid's damage between mates, eh?"

In detective mode a few minutes later I managed to work out what had happened. We had been having some Internet connection problems in the office so John had extended a phone cable to the main inbox to the house. Despite the fact that this cable was firmly secured where it ran under the mats and was then attached by ties to the wall until it ran behind the bookcases, somehow Monty had managed to detach it from the wall and excavate it from under the carpet. As he careered about his business in typical bouncy fashion he must have caught himself up in it and tugged it free. It then swept my eggs off the top of the bookcase in a tsunami of cascading shells as it whipped from one end of the shelf to the other.

Later that evening John rang, "On my way, everything all right your end?"

"Safe trip home," I replied. "Any idea where the house insurance policy is?"

"Why? What's he done now?"

I bristled with protective feelings for our traumatised pooch. "Assumptions! Why does it always have to be Monty's fault? A tree could have landed on the roof, or I might have dropped a ring down the loo, or I could have tipped my phone into the fish tank or …"

"Like I said, what's he done now?"

"He's smashed my egg collection."

There was a long sigh from the other end of the line but when I told of Monty's reaction John's attitude was the same as mine. They were only ornaments; as long as Monty was fine that was the main thing.

The next day, all the broken and damaged eggs were gathered with all the pieces we could find in a box in the office. We estimated the loss to be around four hundred pounds, with a couple irreplaceable as they had been unique designs.

As John morosely searched eBay for similar replacements, I came through from the lounge with an article I had found on the cost of keeping a dog over the period of its lifetime.

"Look here," I waved the paper. "It says it could cost up to twenty thousand pounds to keep Megan and Monty if they live to about fifteen."

John glanced away from the computer. "Over fifteen years I can cope, but I would really rather Monty didn't try to cram the whole sum into the first eighteen months of having him!"

GOEBBLES COMES FOR A WALK

"Your turn."

It was somewhere around four in the morning and whimpering was coming from the darkness. John prodded me with an elbow.

"Oi! Your turn."

"But I did the last one," I mumbled.

"And I did the two before that. Your turn. Are you going to get your rear into gear before he craps all over the bedroom?"

The whimpering was sounding more urgent so I hopped out of bed, attached Monty's collar and lead and headed for the yard. Megan put her paws over her nose in the gloom and tried to ignore the latest disruption to her sleep. Despite the cries to go out Monty still found the time to select his spot as I gazed up at the starlit sky, tinged in the east with the merest hint of rose in this pre-dawn hour.

My sense of wonder at the beauty of the eternal cosmos was then interrupted by a series of flatulent squirting noises from the shape crouched near me in the grass. Monty hopped a couple of paces forward, still in a crouching position, and then let loose again before standing, yawning and looking from me to the house.

"Are you done?" I asked him, as he yawned once more. "Tired are we? That's what comes of being up all night pebble-dashing the yard."

I let Monty have a drink and then settled him back into bed.

Usually a dog bouncing with health, Monty had developed a dose of the trots and just over an hour later he was whimpering once again. John gave up and got up. It had been the ultimate test of Monty's housetraining and with all credit to him he had whimpered diligently every time he needed to go out during the night. It was just that he had needed to go out five times in total and we were all now exhausted.

As it had been a particularly violent attack I rang the vet for advice.

"Had he been ill for long?"

"No, he'd been fine until one in the morning."

"Was there any indication of blood or mucus in the faeces?"

"No, it just looked like very runny poo."

"Was he vomiting too?"

"No, just squitting for Britain."

"Did he need worming? Or had he just been wormed?"

"No and no."

"Was he drinking water? And was his tummy soft?"

"Yes and yes."

"What is his normal diet? And has there been any change recently?"

"His food, Meg's food and any food he can get his chops around really. Um, does the random dead rotting thing he scoffed in the field yesterday count as a change?"

"Aha. Did the dead thing look like it had been recently shot or poisoned?"

"No, it looked like it was last alive in the stone age."

"I think we have solved the problem. Typical lab, he has given himself a tummy upset by eating nasties he shouldn't. Give him plain boiled rice and chicken for twenty-four hours, let him rest and drink water and pop in for a probiotic, which will help restore his gut flora. If he doesn't get better bring him in."

So the morning after the night before, on the vet's advice, Monty was going to have a duvet day. Because he was exhausted by lack of sleep and was now on the 'rice and boiled chicken' diet as opposed to the 'sheep poo and random dead things in the field' diet, he curled up on his bed and looked at us with a woeful expression.

I decided to make the most of the opportunity for a walk without the usual chaos involved with taking Monty and set off with Megan. Meg generally came back when you wanted her to, didn't spend the whole hour trying to trip you up and you could take your eyes off her for a few seconds to admire the scenery without her eating something disgusting or charging off and almost pulling you over. As we reached the gate I paused for a moment to take in the view down the valley to the sea, which was sparkling in the sun and reflecting the deep azure of a summer sky. Meg sat at my feet like a good dog and waited patiently for my next move.

As I opened the gate a persistent meowing caught my attention. Goebbles had left her position under the bedroom window and was plodding through the garden towards me. Evidently pleased to see that we did not have Monty in tow she had decided to join us on the walk. This was something Goebbles had done occasionally before we had Monty; wandering next to me in the closest field to the house while Megan ambled ahead to check on her sheep, skirting its boundary to return home when we ventured further and began to climb the hill. She had crossed to the reed beds, stalked hiding toads and jumped the stream to keep her paws dry and mud free.

"Coming with us are you puss?" I asked, watching as she squeezed through the fence. Casting a doubtful look at the grassy field I admired her enthusiasm but had my reservations over her ability. She was old and recent wet weather and a lack of livestock meant that the grass was long and lush.

"You would be better off staying here," I told her, popping her back over the fence into the garden. Goebbles gave me a cross stare and wriggled through the mesh again, presenting at my side and huffing.

Never the slinkiest of cats, the daily steroid she was taking for her bladder tumour had turned her into what is most accurately described as a hairy slug. However, she had clearly decided that portliness and stumpy little legs were no discouragement so off we went. Megan bounded around as usual until I threw the ball for her to find and she shot off in pursuit. I ambled along with Goebbles trotting at my side, keeping the pace slow and steady and stopping frequently. The cat forged valiantly through the greenery, swatting at the butterflies and bugs she disturbed and scratching around the dark roots. We made it slowly to the middle of the field and then Goebbles decided that she'd had enough; the novelty of the verdant pasture had worn off so she plonked herself down, refused to continue and started meowing.

I wandered on with Megan, calling suitable encouragement to the sluggy one but she wasn't having it. Meowing turned into indignant yowling as the local red kite homed into view and started circling hopefully.

I returned to Goebbles and crouched down, the cat started purring and nudged my hand with her head. I gave her a stroke and backed off a couple of paces, she instantly switched off the purring and meowed angrily. Approaching her again, the meowing was once more replaced by a purr. Megan ran over with the ball to see what was causing this interruption to her walk so I told her.

"Goebbs knew better Meg. She didn't listen, is now knackered and is having a sit in." Megan lay down in the grass next to the cat and waited. "So now Megan, I think Goebbles is hoping I will carry her because if I move away, she does this…" I stepped away and Goebbles yowled her annoyance as the kite continued its attentive circles above.

Exasperated, I picked up the cat and we carried on. She made herself comfortable on my shoulder, purring loudly in my ear and showing her satisfaction with the inflight facilities by settling down to enjoy the view and vigorously treading her claws on my neck. At the far side of the field I turned her off onto a grassy bank where, rejuvenated and relaxed from her journey, she decided to shoot straight up the nearest tree. Sharpening claws that she had blunted on my nasty tough neck she sat in the fork of a branch and watched me throwing Megan's ball.

She was in reach and amenable as I approached to fetch her down prior to returning home. But then I froze as I spotted a hairy caterpillar on the trunk, right in the middle of my cat retrieval route. In my teens I had developed an abiding horror of caterpillars and ever since, with a passion, have hated them.

Backing off to a safe distance of about fifteen feet I commenced negotiations, "Get out of the tree Goebbles."

The cat was entirely happy with her elevated vantage point and showed no inclination to shift.

"Now would be good Goebbs."

In my mind the caterpillar was growing and now my skin was crawling as I contemplated all its mates wriggling through the undergrowth around me. I stomped my foot as I felt a creeping on my leg and my forehead was clammy as I looked down. It was only a blade of rye grass touching my skin but the bug had inflamed my phobic imagination and now even the breeze rustling my sleeve against my upper arm freaked me out.

I backed out a few more feet so that there was nothing above my head but sky, well clear of the overhanging branches loaded with their crawling inhabitants just waiting to drop on my head and burrow under my hair.

"Come down from that bloody tree NOW cat, or you are kite food."

The hairy slug started washing her face while the caterpillar bristled menacingly at me. With the impasse going nowhere and my blood pressure rising I decided to head slowly for home with Megan. Affronted by this abandonment Goebbles paused in her ablutions and glared. With an annoyed meow she finally scrambled down, past my tufted nemesis and trotted after us.

In the middle of the field I reprised my role carrying a hot, grumpy, tired cat, depositing her on the doorstep before inspecting every inch of my skin and clothes and heading to find John.

"Hello," he smiled. "Did you have a nice relaxing Monty free walk?"

I put my hands on my hips, "You have got to be joking! I ended up being a transport system for Goebbles who came with us and then refused to move out of the middle of the field. I couldn't leave her because the kite was planning to eat her. Having flown Air Me outbound she then climbed a tree with a ten-foot caterpillar on it, which then sent out wriggle vibes to all its mates to come and get me. Goebbles then flew Air Me inbound and just look at the state of my neck."

I paused for breath, "I hope Monty is feeling better because it's a lot less eventful taking him out than I thought."

LOST IN TRANSLATION

John is able to whistle. He can project a series of peeps and whistles over the distance of the field using nothing more than a pursed mouth and air. This is his preferred method of controlling the dogs while out on walks. Megan, being a part-trained sheepdog, is obviously well used to whistle commands and, most of the time, will react and respond quickly and obediently, dropping into a collie crouch while waiting to be told what to do next. Monty, who had been used to not responding to any command of any description, was slower on the uptake but was gradually learning to pay attention.

I, on the other hand, have never been able to whistle. I had given it a go but the ineffectual results I came out with were never going to command any dog. I also seemed to have a destructive effect on the two dog whistles John bought me, both of which lasted about ten minutes before inexplicably falling to pieces. This meant that I was restricted to the time honoured method of calling commands. Taking both dogs out together had its own challenges. Furthermore, it had not always been straightforward, even in the early days when we just had Megan.

One evening in midsummer 2011, I had taken Meg out for an extra run, as her afternoon walk had been shorter than normal owing to the excessive heat. On reaching the gate we found that the field was full of sheep. Megan sat, waiting.

"Away Meg," I murmured.

Megan headed off in a wide run to the right, gathering the sheep and herding them across the crossing point of the stream towards the adjacent field.

"Good girl," I called. Followed by, "Here Meg."

Meg raced back across the field to within about fifty feet and then dropped into a crouch, head on her paws, waiting for her next command. I called her to me and she sat at my feet. Looking across the sunlit grass I noticed a couple of figures about two fields away, checking on something at the next farm. It was one of those totally still evenings where the birdsong could be heard all around, every sound seemed magnified and the late sun gave an almost gilded look to the rays falling across the grass. It was an evening where you stood, breathed, listened and felt glad to be alive.

Megan soon felt so glad to be alive that she did not feel inclined to sit all evening admiring the scenery and prodded me with a foot. I catapulted the ball I had brought out for her.

"Find it."

She raced off and ferreted about in the reeds until she located the ball and reappeared.

"Bring the ball," I called.

Megan ran up and dropped it about twenty feet away. Using the catapult to emphasise my point I waved my arm in a circle and gave the command, "Round, round, round." She picked the ball up and circled me in a fast wide curve.

"Lie down."

Meg hit the deck, fixing me with a collie stare and waiting. I looked beyond her to see that the distant figures had paused in their activities and seemed to be watching us. I walked over to her, retrieved the ball and put it back in the catapult.

Hurling it with all the force I could muster I said, "Away and find it."

Meg shot off in search mode and then headed back in my direction, with it in her mouth. Suitably proud of our excellent performance I collected the ball off her, pretended to throw it and commanded, "Away." Once more she ran off until I called her name and raised my arm to show her the prize still in my hand. She immediately came back towards me in a low slinking creep, never taking her eyes off me. Our little collie was amazing – and was that an appreciative nod I could see the distant observers giving our performance?

Then two sheep meandered up from the culvert they had been grazing in when Megan had initially cleared the rest of their friends from the field. With her eyes fixed firmly on me and the ball, Meg did not notice them. Flushed with the success of my command over her I lobbed the ball once more, in the opposite direction to the sheep.

"Away and find."

Off she went, grabbed her find and then noticed the interloping ewes. With a look across at me, she dumped the ball and zoomed off in a classic wide arc to the right. The sheep scuttled down into the culvert again, then promptly reappeared with Megan right behind them. Evidently she wanted them to head off like nice obedient sheep and re-join their mates in the next field but these two were having none of it.

Separating, they skirted around the oak tree. One hid whilst the other wandered off in the general direction of the hedge. Quite clearly, Megan wanted them both together so she could round them up in a mini flock; she retrieved the wanderer and set about fetching the one out from behind the oak. What followed was a version of round the mulberry bush as the ewe circled the tree with Meg in pursuit. I decided to call her back and leave the sheep to it.

"Here Meg," I called, as she reversed tack and skulked round the oak to meet the sheep face on, totally ignoring me in the process.

"Megan, come here," I tried again as two white behinds and one black and white one disappeared into the culvert.

"Here, Here, Here girl!" I yelled, as two white faces and one black and white one ambled back into view and disappeared behind the tree again.

Giving it one last go I stomped into the middle of the field and shouted again, "Here Megan. Now Megan!"

The sheep started grazing while Meg diverted her attention

momentarily to me waving the catapult and angrily going red in the face. Obviously deciding that I did not really mean it she dropped into a crouch and faced the sheep again.

I'd had enough.

"MEGAN! WILL YOU LEAVE THOSE F*****G SHEEP ALONE!" I bellowed, with all the menace I could manage.

It was then that I found out just what a still evening it was and how far sound would travel given the right atmospherics on a beautiful summer evening. The two distant figures had been watching the whole proceedings, obviously finding the goings on in my field decidedly more entertaining than those in theirs.

One turned to the other and said, in spoken tones that reached me as clearly as if he had been standing next to me, "I think what she meant was 'Come by, dog'."

STILL LOST
IN TRANSLATION

As our tender loving care of Monty paid dividends he put on weight steadily. He filled out as he grew into a healthy adolescent and we monitored his progress with weigh-ins at the local pet store and on vet visits. As we approached the first anniversary of him coming to live with us he reached a sturdy fifty-five pounds.

Approximately two ounces was given over to his brain while the rest was pure, rippling muscle power. He honed his impressive physique twice daily as he towed me or John around the fields in his quest for new things to eat. While he had made huge progress in training, working on his ability to walk nicely to heel and not to cannon off like a turbo-powered freightliner every time we opened the gate was an ongoing issue.

By nature of the fact that I was at work a lot of the time, I did not go out quite as often as John did with Monty so my control over him slightly lagged behind. I made it my mission to address this. I decided to take him out separately from Megan so I could give him the full benefit of all the valuable training nuggets I was gleaning from the Internet. Monty needed to see me as his pack superior; this would mean authority and command on my part and a modicum of paying attention on his.

Each evening I also scrutinised our training books for tips and hints on control outdoors. I would then attempt to apply my new found knowledge to Monty. Before leaving the house I crouched down to his level for a little chat.

"Ok Monty, it's going to be like this. We are going out for a nice stroll. You will walk calmly next to me and listen to what I am telling you. We will then enjoy the countryside and I won't end up yelling at you for an hour. We are a team, it is not done for one half of the team to try to kill the other. Got it?"

As Monty sat absorbing every word with rapt and devoted attention, John appeared from the office.

"Very motivational," he commented. "But are you taking him for a walk or teaching him a degree in English?"

"Me and my mutt are bonding," I replied, stroking the Mont's head. "A bonding session with your dog means greater mutual respect."

"Where did you get that from? DodgyDogAdvice.com? I will remind you of this when you've spent the next hour bonding with the pasture."

Ignoring John, I prepared Monty's lead and harness. Leaving Megan at home I headed out armed with treats and a positive attitude.

At the gate to the lane I commenced being authoritative and commanding.

"Wait," I said sharply.

While I shut the gate Monty commenced paying attention, unfortunately just not to me. I clung to the gatepost for dear life to avoid being dragged off my feet and down the lane as he spotted a crow about three miles away that needed immediate investigation.

"Sit. Sit. Sit." I shouted, working on the principle that reiteration might just sink in faster. "Sit!"

The crow in the distance flew off but now there was a heap of fox scat about ten feet beyond the end of the maximum length of the lead that had Monty's attention. He needed to sniff, scoff and pee on it *now* and I was just not moving fast enough. Bracing himself in his expensive, patented proven anti-pull training harness, he tugged me forcefully into the field.

I leaned backwards to curb Monty's momentum and issued my next command, a loud, "Pack it in yanking the lead, Monty."

Monty appeared to have totally forgotten that he had bonded with me in a mutually respectful fashion and charged off at a tangent in pursuit of the delights of the hedgerow.

Following up my previous instruction, with growing annoyance I called, "Will you stop running off?"

Monty developed an instant case of sudden and acute deafness and it was at this point that the neighbouring farmer found what I was doing far more interesting than trying to work out what was wrong with his tractor. Taking stock, I stopped still and refused to move until Monty ceased hauling away at the end of his lead. When he presented himself back at my side I knelt and looked him straight in the eye.

"What part of our little chat did you not understand, dog? We are not strolling, you are not listening and I am yelling again."

Monty cocked his head and yawned. It was then that I remembered John's comment. Perhaps I was being too wordy. Deciding my approach was too complicated I reviewed my technique. Too many commands were just confusing Monty; starting with 'pack it in yanking the lead' and then 'will you stop running off' would be expecting him to respond to the equivalent of 'blah, blah, blah'. To crack this training business what I needed to do was meld both commands into one clear unambiguous instruction.

I stood up and we set off again. Skirting the field I let Monty play but whenever he showed signs of dislocating my shoulder and surfing me face first through the pasture I firmly planted my feet and bellowed confidently down the valley, "Stop Yanking Off."

The poor neighbouring farmer seemed to be having no luck with fixing his tractor and climbed into the cab to open a flask of tea and watch our training. Glad that one of us was making progress, I was happy to share my new found breakthrough and practiced my instruction in a variety of tones and decibel levels as I encouraged Monty to become a calm participant in our walk. Eventually, we headed home and I cheerfully informed John that our bonding session had been a success.

Next morning, John delivered me a cup of tea and attached Monty's lead, ready to take him out for his first constitutional of the day. Just at this moment, the postman popped the letters through the box and both dogs made to hurtle off to investigate.

John whistled Meg and as Monty made to tug the handle of the lead out of John's hand I commanded, "Stop yanking off."

"I beg your pardon," John looked over his shoulder.

"It's my new command to get Monty's attention. You were right, I needed to be more concise," I replied.

"'Stop yanking off?'"

"Yes, it worked quite well yesterday, we made good progress. Even the farmer was impressed."

"So you have been walking round the fields yelling 'stop yanking off'?" John said, grinning.

"As I said."

"And did he?" John seemed to be finding something very amusing.

"Did he what?" I sensed I was in the dark here.

"Did he stop yanking? Was he using both paws or only one?" John was going purple trying not to laugh now. "You do realise that you have been concisely telling Monty and probably, knowing you, the whole county, to stop pleasuring himself?"

As I stuck my head back under the duvet, John looked down at Monty, shaking his head and chortling, "Come on pooch, do you want to go out for a pee? Looks like you have more fun in the fields than I thought."

THERE'S AN EARWIG IN MY FISH TANK

"We need to work on my time management," I announced one morning, after the usual chaos of getting up and ready meant that, once again, we left the house with the barest minimum of leeway in guaranteeing my arrival at work on time.

"Do you?"

John was reluctant to be dragged into any discussions on tardiness when he had been up for the best part of an hour longer than me, feeding and cleaning an assortment of animals while I savoured every last possible minute in bed.

"What I am going to do, as from tomorrow, is get up as soon as I wake up. Then I can help with the chores and everything won't be the usual mad rush."

"There is no problem with finishing the chores, all you need to do is get up on time and try spending less than half a day in the bathroom." He glanced across at me, "And looking at your watch every few seconds is not going to get us there any faster."

The next morning I was true to my word and implemented my new regime by bouncing out of bed early. Monty and Meg were thrilled and milled around me, dropping toys at my feet. Grabbing a ball I chased them into the lounge, round the coffee table and then back into the hall where I threw the ball for them to fetch.

Both dogs shot off in pursuit before presenting back in the lounge for more, but this time they both brought tug toys with them. I held one of the toys until Megan took one end and Monty the other and then left them to it as they hauled each other around the lounge growling and barking. John was busy uncovering Micky.

"*Hello mate*," chortled the parrot.

I went to the cage, "Morning, chick."

Micky fluffed his head feathers and sidled up for a scratch. "*I'm a good bird*," he told me, using a foot to scratch one side of his head while I tickled under his chin and kissed his beak.

"Excuse me," John needed space to put the covers away and change the base paper.

"Get you out later, chick," I told Micky, moving away to pick up the throw and cushions that the dogs had turned onto the floor in their search for the ball earlier.

"What are you doing?" John queried, as he came back with filled food bowls.

"I am tidying, John. I am helpfully assisting in the morning routine so that we might actually leave the house on time today."

"Not being funny, but there is nothing wrong with my time management. What you are doing is getting in my way, winding the dogs up and at this rate, going to be getting into the bathroom even later than normal. It is your time management that goes tits up every morning."

With what I hoped was my best affronted 'only trying to help' look I headed off to the bathroom, momentarily making a sneaky pit stop in the kitchen. I was not speedy enough.

"This is not the bathroom," John pointed out as he stood the kettle back in its cradle and switched it on.

"Just quickly checking Facebook, I need to send a birthday message."

John cast a meaningful look at the cuckoo clock and then a peeved look at me. I got the hint.

Concluding my ablutions in double quick time I dressed, brushed my wet hair and started ferreting around in the pot I kept in the hall for the hair slide I was sure I had tidied away the night before. It wasn't there which led to random stomping around the house on my part and deep sighing on John's.

"What now?"

"I have lost my grip."

"Oh, you lost that a long time ago, darling. Are you nearly ready to go?"

"I will be when I find my grip and my other shoe."

"There is a matching pair of shoes by the door," John chivvied.

"I can't wear those, they are wrong for this outfit. I won't be a minute. Monty! What have you done with my shoe?"

As the dogs sat watching me shuffling along the hall on my knees, checking under the hall stands for my missing footwear, John gave up and headed out to start the car and to assess the latest engine warning lights the dashboard array would inevitably decide to flash up for the day. I joined him a couple of minutes later.

"I thought those were the shoes you couldn't possibly wear with that outfit?" he observed, putting the car into reverse.

I ignored him then remembered something, "Hang on, stop, I forgot to feed my big fish." Opening the door, I hopped out as John leaned his elbow on the windowsill and began to rub his temples.

"Won't be a tick."

Back in the kitchen, I lifted the access lid off the big fish tank and began dispensing flakes. The fish amassed and churned the water surface as they tucked into their breakfast. I was about to replace the lid when I spotted something. A scuttling interloper charged across the corrugated plastic sheeting.

"What are you doing in there? If you fall in, you will be fish food."

Consumed with concern for the imminent watery demise of the tank's squatter I ignored the annoyed beeping from outside and tried to coax it onto the end of a fork. The squatter was obviously quite happy where it was and did not wish to be evicted, scurrying into a corner and hiding behind the lighting cable.

A yell floated in from the yard, "You are going to be late. GET A BLOODY MOVE ON!"

I gave up on the rescue attempt, poked a fish flake behind the cable with the plastic handle of the fork and replaced the lid.

"You are on your own mate, here's some lunch, I'll check on you tonight."

As I climbed back into the car John managed to make his point by simultaneously glaring at his watch and the cockpit clock in disbelief.

"How long does it take to chuck a pinch of flakes at a handful of fish? Your new time management plan needs some serious refinement." He jammed the car back into gear and we set off.

"There is an earwig in my fish tank," I said serenely, as we hurtled down the lane.

"An earwig?"

"Yes, an earwig. I was trying to rescue it, I would have been on time otherwise."

"And what is it doing now?"

"Settling in, I think. I've given it a fish flake, it seems quite happy." I busied myself with putting in my hair grip that I had found on the floor as I left the house for the second time, bracing myself as John made the most of the empty road and national speed limit to try and make up some time.

"'There's an earwig in her fish tank'," John muttered to himself as we reached work, only two minutes late. "Only in this household can that be normal."

I hopped out of the car, "See you later, got to dash, running late." I waved a kiss and called after the car as John pulled away, "Look after my earwig for me."

LITTLE BIRDS

The Budgies;
I used an elbow to lever Monty's paws off the windowsill and gave him a filthy look. He dropped to the floor but maintained his focus on the budgies' cage, from which I was trying to retrieve their food and water bowls.

The budgies fluttered and chirped as Monty hopped around my feet in a state of excitement; he loved the budgies, in a sort of *'you're so fluttery, I want to chew on you and find out what you are made of'* way. This is why their cage is on a high windowsill and any dog/bird interaction is closely monitored.

The budgies had arrived the summer before Monty, heralding my new plan to introduce the wider populace to the wonders of pet keeping. As a child my family had bred pet birds as a mini hobby. Every chick was finger tame and friendly, going to thoroughly vetted new homes to become much-loved pets to children and adults alike. Our reputation for good natured and healthy baby budgies spread through the little village we lived in and we relished the chance to follow the progression of tiny bald chicks taking their first peeps in the nest boxes, to seeing off a whistling baby in a brand new cage with a proud new owner.

So, it was with interest that I was now listening to a friend on the other end of the phone one June evening. She was telling me about her budgies and we had been chatting for a while about the pleasures of rearing chicks.

"Would you like a couple?" she asked.

I covered the receiver with my hand and looked at John.

"Do you like budgies?" I whispered.

"Yes, I suppose so," he replied, engrossed in his book. "They are quite cute."

I went back to my phone conversation.

"Yes please," I said.

John put his book down.

"I have about eight chicks to choose from," said my friend. "But they are still very young, I'm not sure of the sexes."

"No problem," I replied, with all the wisdom of a seasoned budgie breeder from thirty years ago. "Adults have blue ceres if they are boys and brown if they are girls. Babies have blue ceres if they are girls and purple if boys. It will be easy to pick a pair."

John waved his book at me.

"What are you doing now?" he mouthed.

"Budgies," I mouthed back and then made arrangements to visit our friend in a couple of days' time.

I came off the phone in a gleeful mood.

John crossed his arms, "Well?"

"Budgies," I said happily.

"Yes, I got the 'budgies' bit. What about them? Because it sounds awfully like we appear to be having some?"

"Not some, two." I gave him an accusing look. "You said you liked budgies?"

"I do, I also quite like the South American Condor and the Wandering Albatross but it is a bloody good job she's not bred those as well!"

I outlined our plan. We would collect the budgie pair and settle them into the large cage we had fortuitously ended up with after my dad's budgie had sadly passed away. As long as they seemed compatible, at a later date we would offer them nesting facilities and see if they bred. Budgie breeding was an enjoyable and rewarding hobby that I was keen to restart and that John, I was sure, would love too.

"Our hand tame babies were really in demand," I enthused.

"Were they?" John responded.

"And I know ours will be too," I continued.

"Will they?"

"People used to ring us up from all over the village."

"Did they?"

"Yes, we had a waiting list."

"Did you?"

"A little, finger tame, fluffy baby budgie going to sleep with its nest mates on your hand is the cutest, most adorable thing ever," I pushed.

"Is it?" said John.

A few days later we were on our way home with our newest pets. Our friend had a large indoor aviary that her newly fledged chicks occupied. I had carefully picked a purple and a blue cered bird. They were the prettiest little things; one was slightly smaller in mottled blotches of lemon and bluey green, the other was one shade of khaki green with a bold chest and classic wing markings. They chattered away as I fussed about with greens, food and swinging bell toys. I named the female 'Perry' in honour of her dearly departed predecessor and the male 'Huckleberry' because he looked like one and promised to give updates on our new venture to our friend as they happened.

Our new additions grew and matured, flew around the room, scattered millet and budgie seed husks everywhere and made the most of their extensive toy supply.

A few months later John assessed the situation.

"The budgies are tossing themselves off again," he commented one night, as ecstatic warbling drowned out the television and both birds made energetic use of the stimulation properties of their perches. "So, what do we need to buy to get our nesting operation under way?"

"Um, two females," I muttered, exceptionally quietly.

"But?"

"It's not a completely fool proof system," I explained sheepishly. "Our girl with the blue cere must have been a little bit older, so the purple cere she had as a baby boy had already started turning into the blue one he'd have as an adult."

"Clear as mud."

"But all we need are two females and…"

"No way," John said. "We are most definitely not having a rerun of the fish situation. If you think it's turning into the Australian outback round here, you've got another thing coming."

So the grand plan for the budgie breeding programme ground to a shuddering halt. Both Perry and Huckleberry were happy with a lads-only bachelor pad arrangement, warbling and chortling at high volume through anything we wanted to listen to or watch on the radio or television. They dealt with the lack of ladies in their lives by using their perches for a little light relief, usually throughout the time we had guests.

"What are the budgies doing, Auntie Helen?" asked a small niece one day.

My brother's family were visiting my parents for the weekend and had dropped by to see the menagerie.

"Um well, they're… actually, they are… erm," I spluttered.

"Scratching an itch," said my brother tactfully.

"They are very itchy, aren't they daddy?" commented enthralled small niece.

B obby and Percy;
We bought Percy during the void created by Tufty's loss. I never tried to replace a pet, I just loved having pets in my life. Being a strong believer in 'it is meant to be', when the advertisement in our local paper seeking a home for an Australian king parrot came up just as I was sadly contemplating our empty cage, I was hooked.

Percy was installed and he was absolutely beautiful. The male has stunning crimson plumage with glossy, deep green wings tinged with pistachio emerald stripes. His beak is red, edged with black and the long tail is an oil-on-water shade of dark green black, hiding a subtle rainbow. The female is green headed and breasted but otherwise resembles the male. Both birds are medium-sized parakeets, good natured and musical.

Bobby came along shortly afterwards from the same owner. The male ring necked parakeet is noisy, bolshie and full of attitude. The sexes are similar in colour: long tailed, pale green with the male having a deep red beak and a rose ring around the back of his neck. In their native countries both species are rated as pest status and, despite their beauty, subject to periodic culling.

These birds flew together and whistled to each other from their large cages. Whilst they were not particularly tame in terms of coming onto your hand, they would come up to the bars to talk to you at close quarters; Bobby strident and quick to move, Percy softer, calmer and more gentle.

Bobby loved to annoy the dogs with his piercing calls and had a bite that could chew through steel, as I found to my cost on several occasions when he refused to return to his cage and had to be captured by hand. He flung regurgitated food up the walls and could shower you from several feet away while taking a bath in his cage. Every morning, he would allow you to put his fruit bowl back in its holder before flashing his eyes, grabbing it and flinging it with a clang onto the floor of the cage. This trick only ever applied to his fruit bowl, never his seed or water containers, and trying to wedge it more firmly would be met with an enthusiastic chomp from an annoyed beak.

For several years all was well and I never failed to appreciate the wonder of a beautiful bird in flight. In their own way the parakeets made their mark on our lives, their beguiling characters overcoming the less tactile relationship I had with them. So, it was no less upsetting when things went wrong.

It was just a little thing. The first few times I hardly registered what I had seen. Percy climbed back up to his perch from where he had been foraging round the cage floor but, as he made to move his foot from the cage bars to the perch, there had been the merest hint of unsteadiness.

And then he was back in position, chortling happily. I crossed to the cage, "What's up Percy? Are you all right?"

As I looked him over, he whistled softly to me and sidled up to the bars.

Then he fluffed up his feathers, ground his beak contentedly, closed his eyes and went to sleep. All looked perfect. He looked perfect. Except that he was sleeping on both feet when he always slept on one.

The next morning he seemed fine. He ate and drank normally and climbed down to retrieve food that had dropped from the bowl during his enthusiastic morning investigations. But, as he headed back up to his perch once more it happened again. His head knew where he wanted his feet but his feet were not cooperating.

I caught him up in a towel and had a look at him. He might have lost a tiny bit of weight but that wouldn't do him any harm, he'd been getting a little bit pudgy. One foot didn't seem to grip my finger quite as strongly as the other, but there was nothing wrong with the grip of his beak as he energetically chewed the end of my thumb through the towel.

We made arrangements to visit our avian vet for a check-up. Bloods were taken and Percy was given a thorough examination.

The vet thought that it was possible that Percy had caught his leg while climbing the bars and had pulled a muscle. He was happy with his diet, although he advised us to cut down a little on the nuts he was so fond of. While we waited for the test results to come back we moved the perches downwards in Percy's cage and placed his food and water bowls on a lower level. This reduced the climbing he would need to do and would aid any healing process.

The vet gave us the results over the phone. The usual suspects that could cause unsteadiness such as zinc and lead poisoning came back negative. His bloodwork was reasonable but he was showing a nine percent level of monocytes, when it should be less than one percent in a healthy bird. This could be an indication of a battle against aspergillosis, avian tuberculosis or chlamydia.

Percy's biochemistry results showed raised levels of creatinase, bile acids and cholesterol, which might show a liver problem. We drew up a plan. To rule out chlamydia the vet needed three days of faecal samples, he also needed Percy back to conduct an endoscopy. During this operation he could inspect the air sacs and liver to check for the other possibilities thrown up by the results. Once more, we were pleased that we had insurance; in birds these were expensive procedures.

The endoscopy showed nothing of note. Percy was still unsteady as we brought him home again and waited for the faecal test results. He had lost more weight so the vet provided a formula to be administered by syringe feeding to keep his essential nutrition stable.

We wished that he had just been a bit clumsy and had caught his foot in the bars.

Two days after we brought him home I was in the process of settling him for the night. I had given the nightly syringe feed and cleaned the excess from around Percy's beak with a piece of damp cotton wool. He sat on the base of the cage on a soft bed of tissue with a low perch within reach if he wanted to try climbing up. He had fresh water and food, with rationed nuts, and he watched me as I put blankets around the cage to keep out draughts and give him a dark and peaceful haven.

He was due to go back to the vet the next morning so I

crouched down and told him to get a good night's sleep ahead of his journey.

And then he came over to see me. On wobbly legs that barely supported him, he reached the bars and gripped them with his beak to steady himself. Then he sang. His old musical, beautiful singing, full of soft melodic notes that I had not heard since he became ill. I listened, entranced, as he warbled just for me and then settled back against the side of the cage and closed his eyes.

"Night, night Percy," I whispered, as I lowered the blanket.

I headed down to watch television with John.

"Percy must be feeling a bit better," I said. "He sang to me."

I made myself comfortable then paused, lost in thought, "He's either feeling better, or it could have been his swan song."

Next morning I was up early to uncover the cages. Percy was still asleep against the cage side, fluffed up, eyes closed. I opened the door and used a fingertip to stroke his head.

"Wakey wakey Perce. It's vet day again."

He was cold.

With care I lifted him out and cradled him against my chest. The other birds were uncharacteristically subdued as I took him down to the bedroom.

"It was his swan song," I said.

John looked at us sadly, "Oh sweetheart, I'm so sorry."

We let the other birds see the body. Megan, who had maintained a vigil for days under Percy's cage, resumed her position and refused to shift.

Showing her Percy now, she sniffed him gently all over, nudged him softly with her nose and then carefully raised a paw to touch his feathers. Only then did she issue a little whimper and leave her watch.

I rang the vet to let him know what had happened and to cancel our appointment. As Percy had been under continuing treatment there was only a need for a basic post-mortem examination in terms of satisfying the insurance policy. Our vet was apologetic as he commiserated with me on the phone; we still hadn't really found the root cause of Percy's illness. Avian medicine is a developing area and it was frustrating when this sort of thing happened.

"Would it help?" I asked, "If you could do a full post-mortem?"

I could tell that this would be the option the vet would want to take, but he did not want to be insensitive or intrusive on our upset state.

"Every full examination we do teaches us a little bit more," he replied. "There are still cases that are inconclusive, but we are learning all the time. Avian autopsies never used to include the head in the UK…" he tailed off. "Of course, it would mean that Percy would not be – particularly, um, presentable – to be returned to you, but we would treat him with the greatest respect."

"Do the full autopsy," I said. "If you could ensure he gets an individual cremation afterwards and let us know if you learn anything."

"Of course," he said. "And thank you."

So Percy made his final trip to the vet and a week or so later came home again in a tiny casket.

Our vet rang us up to thank us again and give us his findings. Examination of the body had thrown up the results we already knew about. It was not until they looked inside his head that they found the answers we sought.

"There was evidence of an old bleed inside the skull," he revealed. "But crucially, we found a much larger new bleed too. Percy'd had a series of strokes. I hope you don't mind, but I took some pictures for reference."

I didn't mind at all. A basic post-mortem would not have shown this sort of revelation and Percy may just have contributed, in some tiny way, to the development of avian veterinary treatment that would stop someone else feeling like we did.

Not bad for a little bird with a beautiful song.

GOEBBLES RECLAIMS HER HOUSE

I flattened myself against the side of the hall as a small brown, furry shape streaked past me, closely followed by a large slavering, black one.

"Sorry, you two, was I in your way?"

From the bedroom came a crashing and yowling, "Monty. Stop trying to eat the cat!" I yelled after them.

The commotion continued unabated so I unpeeled myself from the wall and went to investigate. Goebbles had cornered Monty between the bed and the bookcase and was energetically swatting him around the face with her paws.

"All right," I sighed. "Goebbles, stop trying to kill Monty."

The cat backed off and jumped up onto the windowsill. I called Monty to me to see what damage he had sustained. Goebbles had looked like she meant it this time. Once more, I was surprised to find no evidence of scratches; she had been whacking his nose with her claws sheathed.

When we had first brought Monty home he had made a favourable impression on everyone except the cat. He seemed ecstatic to have a new home, his favoured methods of making friends with his pack companions were energetically and enthusiastically applied and generally his boisterous approach was well received and tolerated. Except that is, by the cat. Goebbles, being elderly and grumpy, with very short legs and a tendency to podginess, was out of sorts at the prospect of being chased around the house by this hairy new whirlwind.

Therefore, she set up court in the bedroom where she could uncurl and hop quickly onto the high windowsill from the bed if necessary, and where she could snooze in peace for the rest of the time. Monty however, being a gregarious sort of chap, decided very early on that making friends with the cat was a top priority and that this cat lurking in the bedroom scenario was an unacceptable situation that needed resolving. From the outset he set about turning the cat into his new best friend with unbounded gusto and dedication.

First off he had adopted the direct approach; by diving onto his reluctant new mate from as far away as he could feasibly leap and trying to chomp her face off. He then backed up this sure fire winner by cramming his nose into any available genital regions and homing in for a good old friendly slurp. Goebbles firmly used to send him packing with a face full of claws.

Realising that his methods were not working Monty had followed up with a tactical refinement of technique. He took to dropping onto his front paws, with his backside in the air, showing a grin full of gleaming, pearly white teeth and bellowing 'WOOOOFF', followed by swiftly turning to stuff his own nether regions into Goebbles's face and wiggling frantically.

The cat remained singularly unimpressed despite Monty trying on numerous occasions to win her over and perfected a look that would turn most dogs to stone. This impasse in cat-dog friendship negotiations remained in force for the best part of eighteen months as Monty continued to develop creative ways to bond with his feline mate.

One afternoon I was folding washing in the bedroom. Goebbles, curled up in her cat nest, was fast asleep on the bed when Monty padded in, sniffed gently at the edge of the cat bed then backed off, sat, and watched me.

I was impressed that, for once, he had not instigated a turf war with the cat and told him so, at which point he made a sudden lunge for the edge of the bed, grabbed the cat nest in his teeth and whipped it out from under Goebbles in one lightning move. Still with the nest in his mouth, he then launched himself onto the bed and gave it a vigorous *'you are such a dead rat'* head shake before collapsing in a heap next to a cat, who was now positively quivering with affronted rage.

As a party trick it beat the tablecloth from under the dinner service routine hands down and I couldn't help giggling. Monty showed all the empathic vibes of a breezeblock and settled down next to the cat for a snooze, failing completely to feel the death rays that Goebbles was spitting in his direction. The cat removed herself to the windowsill to plot her next move as Monty sighed and began snoring.

Then, with a *'you've messed with me and now you are going to get it'* glance at the sleeping dog, Goebbles hopped down onto the bed, and with gossamer tread sneaked towards him. With a final haughty pause she took her revenge, putting her face close to his and letting loose with an almighty "*MEEOWWW.*" Monty's eyes snapped open and he leapt about a foot upwards, staring around him in confusion as Goebbles, with an alacrity that belied her years, cleared off back to the windowsill and started nonchalantly cleaning her whiskers.

While Goebbles was happy to stay in the bedroom and go in and out of the house via the window we could close the door and give her peace and quiet to snooze. Any interaction between her and Monty could be supervised as they worked on their friendship. Eventually though, there came a point where the cat clearly decided she was missing out on life at the other end of the house and it was high time she reclaimed her territory. This meant that their madcap Tom and Jerry routine now had no limits.

We intervened on behalf of the cat when we felt things were getting out of hand, then we realised that she could more than hold her own and it was Monty that needed protecting. Finally, when it was clear that there was no real violent intent from either of them, we left them to it and they sorted things out relatively amicably and with only minimal damage to the house. Goebbles accepted a certain amount of chasing but would freeze Monty in his tracks with a hiss when she had had enough.

Her self-imposed exile finally came to a permanent end towards the end of summer 2014. We left all interior doors open and became used once again to Goebbles snoozing in the sun in the lounge with the dogs going freely in and out. It was a nightly routine to move down to the bedroom to watch television once the parrots were covered for the night. If, for any reason, this routine was disrupted you would find Monty and Goebbles had given up waiting for the rest of us, they could be found on the bedspread curled up together, fast asleep as best friends.

BALL TRAINING
(INDOOR ROUNDERS)

"Monty needs to learn to fetch balls," I announced one morning. "I am going to start a training regime."

"Jolly good," I could tell John was suitably impressed.

Retrieving a ball was something that Megan was great at and had picked up quickly, so I saw no reason why the Mont should not learn too. It would make his walks more stimulating and it would complete another level in his ongoing training. If he returned to you with a ball so that you could throw it for him once more it would also form part of reinforcing his recall skills, at which he was still completely hopeless.

To avoid excessive ball losses in the field, I decided to gently introduce the idea indoors in a carefully controlled fashion. To gain interest I also purchased the bounciest of bouncy balls I could find.

"Right Monty. Let's go," I called him out of the lounge that evening.

"Wait just one second," John wanted to query the finer details of my training session. "Why aren't you doing this in the yard?"

"Because we will end up losing the ball in the long grass and next-door are cooking in their kitchen so Monty will end up paying attention to them and not to me." I had it all worked out. "Besides, I have bought an extra bouncy ball so I won't need to throw it very hard. Watch."

With that I threw the ball downwards onto the kitchen tiles. It promptly shot back up into the air, hit the ceiling, then the floor again and then ricocheted sideways, colliding with the side of the microwave before whizzing through the air about six feet off the ground and nearly taking John's face off.

"Oh, I can tell I am really, really going to enjoy this one! What's the damn thing made of – flubber?"

Admittedly, the bounciest of bouncy balls was a lot more bouncy than even I had anticipated, although I was not about to let John know this. Retrieving the ball from under the large fish tank I commenced operations. What resulted on our first night's training session was essentially indoor rounders. Apart from the kitchen, which was now out of bounds as John was making tea, no part of the rest of the house was off limits. The furniture became part of our pitch as Monty took to this new game with gusto.

I let Monty have a sniff of the ball and gave a demonstration of its characteristics by dropping it in front of him. It promptly bounced up past his head and settled on the windowsill, which led him to plant his paws on the sill to try and find where it had gone.

"Good start Mont. Now that I have your interest we are going to play 'fetch the ball'. It is going to be fun."

"It is going to be expensive, more like," a voice floated out from the kitchen.

Megan ambled over to see what we were up to. "Are you going to show him what's what Meg?" I asked. "Go on then, find it."

I tossed the new ball down the hall. Megan cast a glance in its direction as it disappeared through the lounge door then ferreted about in the toy pile until she found the tennis ball she was used to finding in the fields. She dropped the tennis ball at my feet and then wandered off, clearly uninspired, to snooze on her armchair.

"Part of the team has gone to sit on the bench Monty. Never mind, it's like this." Crouching down and holding the ball in front of his nose I outlined the rules, "I throw this and you fetch it. You then come back to me by the quickest way possible and we do it all again. Extra brownie points if you have to hunt it down."

As a practice run I had Monty sit and watch the ball in my hand. With the minimum of force I rolled it behind the vacuum cleaner which was standing against the wall about four feet away. "Fetch it," I urged, pointing in the direction of the now hidden ball.

Monty snuffled round the base of the vacuum and then used one foot to claw the ball free. He then stood looking at me with the ball between his feet. While he did not actually return it to me, I took this as a positive start and was suitably enthusiastic.

"Good boy, we'll call that 1st post. Now we will make it a bit harder."

I stood halfway down the hall and lobbed the ball; Monty paused for a fraction of a second and then took off in pursuit. His quarry bounced into one of the grooves between the floor tiles and shot into the lounge at an angle, landing on the settee.

"Yes!" I yelled. "You've made 2nd post, go for it Mont."

As Monty hurtled through and over 2nd post he decided that, however urgent the need to bring back the ball and make me happy, there was always time to wreck the furniture. Even though the ball was a lurid neon green and completely visible, it was now written into the rules of indoor rounders that turfing all the cushions onto the floor was essential. Eventually, he grabbed the ball in his mouth and, with a flick of his head, flung it off the settee. It landed on the coffee table, bounced off and settled on Megan who started an indignant growling and huffing.

"3rd post Monty. Well done, extra points if you get out of there alive."

Monty paused, panting and eager to continue, but wary of 3rd post's capacity to eat him. Megan obliged by standing up on the chair and shaking herself, then settling down again. The ball rolled off her and onto the floor; with lightning reflexes Monty grabbed it and then hurtled back towards me.

"Almost home, come on Monty," I leapt up and down at the end of the hall urging him on. As he bounded onto the hall rug I called, "And you have made 4th post, you are going to be such a top-scoring dog."

A slight hitch occurred when Monty's momentum propelled

4th post along the floor under him. With the ball in his mouth and the rug rucked up underneath, top-scoring dog skidded straight into me in my adopted position as deep fielder.

I took the ball from him. "Hooyeahh! Hut! Hut! Hut!" I yelled, waving the ball above my head. Monty bounded around my feet and jumped up and down in glee trying to reach my hand.

"Come on Monty, let's go and tell John what a clever boy you are."

As I made for the kitchen John beat me to it and his head poked out the door. "It is an hour before their bedtime, is it really absolutely necessary to wind Monty up so much?"

Monty, still quivering with excitement, charged at John and planted his paws on his chest, lunging at the tasty looking wooden spoon he was holding in search of food. John sighed, "And what's all this 'Hut! Hut! Hutting!' about?"

I adopted a knowledgeable tone, "We are playing rounders. Rounders is basically baseball across the pond and as I am fielding, I am entitled to 'Hut!'"

John adopted an even more knowledgeable tone. "I think you will find that you have the wrong game actually, that happens in American football, not baseball."

I gave John a gesture. "Charming," he said. "And I think that would probably get you a telling off from the referee in both games."

He looked at Monty, "I take it you enjoyed ball retrieving Mont?" Monty, still hyped with excitement, panted and wagged his tail.

"He got the idea pretty much straight away," I declared proudly. "A couple more sessions and we will have two retrievers."

John surveyed the hall rug and the remnants of the settee before going back to his cooking. "A couple more sessions and we will have no house left. Dinner will be ten minutes, any chance you can rebuild the lounge while I dish up?"

ME MASTER, YOU DOG

I was head of the pack again one night. Arriving home I started off with my best 'Me Master, You Dog' look as I sidled through the door and then used my handbag to fend off eight paws and two tongues.

"Right dogs," I stated masterfully. "I have a splitting headache. This means you need to be on your best behaviour so it doesn't get any worse."

Megan took me at my word and lay down to watch me with the same look she reserved for ailing sheep. Monty cleared off to aerate my welly boot and turn the lounge into a war zone. Along with my own tea I decided to rustle up a mince, carrot and potato casserole for the dogs. Reappearing to watch the preparation of this provided a very temporary distraction for Monty from chewing holes in my boot. Then, unimpressed with the fact that it then had to cool down before serving and equally unimpressed with the fact that I put it to cool on top of the large fish tank, which remained for the moment out of his reach, he set off to hassle the cat.

Sitting down after dinner in the hope of watching a little television and reading what remained of the paper, I discovered that Monty appeared to be under the impression that the session of 'indoor rounders' from the other night should now form part of the ongoing evening routine. A large paw appeared and clawed the papers off my knee and the bounciest of bouncy balls dropped into my lap. Megan, obviously unwilling to reprise her role as 3rd post, disappeared behind John's recliner in search of a bit of peace and quiet, indicating to Monty with an emphatic series of grumbles and growls that she was not playing.

Sighing, I tried to fob off the Mont by feebly rolling the ball across the floor. One large, black head swivelled to follow it as it stopped all of five feet away, then it was quite clearly decided that I needed a little motivational encouragement. Monty springing onto my lap followed retrieval, as the ball was dumped next to me and two massive paws started digging vigorously at my sweatshirt. As befitted being alpha female I pushed him off and firmly re-established my pack leader status, whereupon he clamped his jaws round my sleeve and proceeded to drag me off the settee.

"All right, all right, I'm playing, let go."

Thinking I could get away with a quick but intense burst of activity, I lobbed the ball down the hallway. Monty hurtled off in pursuit. Just as I was pondering how quickly a dog could achieve terminal velocity the ball decided not to play fair. An unexpected ricochet off the bookcase sent it careering into the steamer on the other side of the hall, which promptly fell over. Monty performed a perfect leap over this new hurdle without slowing momentum but came into land on his water bowl, which, being lightweight stainless steel, shot along the floor disgorging its contents until it met the leading edge of the doormat and tipped up.

At this point, Megan appeared in the lounge doorway to investigate all the commotion. Having made her opinion on the rounders issue abundantly clear to Monty earlier, she was not expecting him, by now slithering along wet floor tiles at a fair rate of knots, to appear in her face and flatten her up against the armchair. A brief but energetic discussion on doggy behavioural etiquette ensued and Monty called time on playtime while he still had a face.

Massaging my temples I mopped up, refilled the upturned water bowl, tidied up the general devastation and started preparations for bedtime. With the parrots covered and fish tank lights turned off, I moved on down to watch television in the bedroom.

Before I could relax however, the dogs needed to have their last toilet break. It was dark, I have a vivid imagination, I was on my own and the weather was windy and wet so I planned a speedy excursion into the garden before locking up. Expecting Megan and Monty to have the same attitude towards the howling night as I had, I did not take a torch.

The tree branches around me waved and creaked spookily in the gloom as I nervously scanned the blackness of the abyss beyond the garden for hardy ghouls fancying a bit of soggy haunting. And then a disembodied call echoed through the night; Goebbles had decided that it would be a jolly jape to lurk just out of reach of Monty and meow a lot in the undergrowth to wind him up.

As Megan finished up her business and disappeared back into the warm house, Monty took flight, dragging me unceremoniously over the graves of our long deceased cat and recently deceased fish. I clung onto the lead for dear life but it was a training lead so easily long enough to wind round every tree and bush in the pitch-black garden. Monty refused to backtrack so, as every ghost in the near vicinity was scared back into the ether by the crashing and crunching coming from the herbaceous borders, I had no option but to follow his path and unravel him.

Eventually I located Monty, reeled the lead in to a length of about a foot and hauled him out of the garden and into the house, whereupon he promptly started whimpering that he needed to go out for a pee. I stood on the step and gave him access to the fifteen feet in front of the door with strict instructions to get on with it or tie a knot in it.

With my head now pounding and my fingers needing several thorns tweezing from them after my impromptu scramble over the greenery, I decided to run a bath. I made it as hot, bubbly and scented as I could and closed the bathroom door on the three furry faces in front of me. I then thought better of it and opened it again. Sinking into the water, I basked in the steamy atmosphere and finally felt my throbbing temples begin to relax. Using my foot I turned the tap on to add more hot water and shut my eyes.

I registered Monty's arrival in the room and then his departure after a quick inspection of the toilet bowl but I was too relaxed in my aromatherapy heaven to move. I had been liberal with some expensive foaming oils and now practiced some breathing exercises to see off this headache for good. Inhaling deeply, I found myself combining the calming action not with restorative aromas but with the unexpected pong of foetid bowels. Monty's visit had included his calling card of a silent-but-deadly that no amount of lavender and eucalyptus could compete with and which brought my spa session to a putrid finish.

Once in the bedroom, I set up the dogs' beds and then arranged cushions so I could relax and unwind.

"Right, it's bedtime," I said. "Settle down and don't mess with me, pooches."

Megan instantly hopped onto Monty's bed and made herself comfortable. Monty, a bit bemused but not wanting to upset her again, settled on hers. This was most unacceptable to Meg and she issued a long growl in Monty's direction. In the interests of his continuing health Monty speedily vacated Megan's bed and decided that Goebbles's cosy nest would do just as well.

Unfortunately, Goebbles happened to be in it at the time. Entirely disinclined to sleep wearing a huge black dog, the cat relocated herself to my pillow, where she bristled indignantly as Monty shook her cat nest to kill it first before lying down with a sigh.

I had, by now, had enough. I stood in the middle of the bedroom and politely suggested to everyone concerned that if they didn't want to be sleeping in the yard then they had better get into the correct beds, pronto. With much huffing Megan shifted, Monty reclaimed his and the cat hopped onto the windowsill to assess the situation on her own terms. Satisfied that my pack leader status was now being well and truly given the respect it deserved, I settled back on the cushions with the TV remote control.

I woke up the next morning to find myself surrounded by a carpet of sleeping animals. Monty was sprawled lengthways next to me, snoring in my ear; Megan was curled up by my feet and Goebbles was stretched out by my shoulder with her tail extended across my face. As pack leader, I was squashed into the remaining couple of square feet of bed.

THE BATTLE PLANS OF GENERAL COW

Being, for once, out of bed first I made tea and coffee and swished the curtains open one late autumn morning.

"Bullocks!" I huffed.

"What's the matter darling, is the weather not to your liking this morning?" came John's response.

I turned away from looking at the row of huge, shaggy black heads peering over the garden fence to glare at John.

"The weather is fine actually, but the sheep have turned into bullocks."

John started humming the theme tune to the X-files while moving round to stand next to me at the window. "So they have, clever sheep eh?"

Watching one of the bullocks turn around so it could use our fragile fence to scratch an itch on its substantial back end I muttered, "Where did they come from?"

John grinned, "Well, there was a mummy cow and a daddy bull and they had a special cow cuddle."

Using one eye to fix John with a peevish look while keeping the other on our fence, which was slowly moving back and forth and creaking ominously as the other cattle decided it was a great idea to scratch itches too, I marched off to the other windows of the house. The lounge and kitchen overlooked the fields too and it soon became clear that there were cattle everywhere.

John joined me, "It was dark when you came home last night

and I forgot to tell you. The sheep have gone for now, it is time for us to have some new farm friends."

I was not impressed, how was I supposed to take the dogs into the fields with about a hundred tons of hairy, stomping beef stock? John had already spoken to the farmer, and apparently it would be fine. Welsh Blacks were a mellow breed, they were already used to dogs. Once they got to know us they would ignore us and we could carry on as normal. Great, I worried, it would be what they did while they were getting to know us that was bothering me.

John tried to soothe with some helpful cow facts designed to defend the corner of our new friends. "They are curious creatures, but they are usually friendly. If you lie down in the field they will come and stand around you."

"The field is full of crap, I am not about to test that theory. Plus, I don't think that experiment happened while attached to an excitable mad dog, with another collie bouncing around the place."

I carried on, had he not seen all the stories in the papers over the years about people walking on footpaths through fields; minding their own business, with and without dogs, when they were stampeded into a mush by herds of rampaging, rabid, bellowing cows?

These tales invariably started with versions of the following; *'The cows always looked so friendly', 'I'd walked the fields for years with my dog and then they suddenly turned on me', 'I had no idea they could run so fast', 'They came out of nowhere and charged me'.* They then invariably finished with a forlorn statement by the unfortunate squished one and a long list of broken and crushed bones and internal organs that they, and their dogs, were hopefully expected slowly to recover from. Case proved against the malevolent beasts that had taken over the fields surrounding us.

It was clear however, that the cattle were here to stay and I would have to get used to them. They did have a tendency to move as a herd between fields so there was usually one that was free when I took the dogs out. I would then exercise Megan and Monty in this one field with a frenetic system of ball throwing and chasing that wore them out but ensured we stayed well away from the cattle.

Cow Whisperer John, on the other hand, made it his mission to prove his point by ambling around the edge of the fields in which the cattle were grazing, dogs in tow, with no problems whatsoever.

The main issue he did encounter, in the wake of the farmer helpfully swapping our woolly mates for our shaggy new ones, was the fields rapidly becoming a veritable smorgasbord of cow pats, of variable consistency and copious size. Megan would home in and take a delicate couple of laps, as if sampling a particularly fine wine. Monty, on the other hand, careered at speed from pat to pat, gobbling and slurping as if downing shots.

One morning in November, I was out in one field with the dogs, firmly keeping a wary eye on the herd in the field next door, evilly swishing their tails, gnashing and watching me from the other side of the fence, when the farmer turned up to dispense feed. Megan abandoned me to shoot off and sit by his feet while Monty dragged me over to the fence.

"Fine mornin', been in the field with the cows yet?" queried the farmer.

"Err, no, not yet actually, um, I've sort of been staying away from them."

"Tsk, they will be fine with you. See, they're ignoring Meg."

Aware of the fact that Megan was ignoring *me* in favour of looking attentively at the farmer and Monty was trying to haul me off my feet, I was quite pleased when John appeared from the house to pass the time of day. Megan diverted her loving attention to John; Monty changed hauling direction and now tried to pull me to the gate John was leaning on.

"Strong young dog you've got there," the farmer observed, stating the obvious as I braced my feet and leaned backwards.

He finished up offloading hay and made to go, with an expansive wave towards the munching cows, "You will be fine with them, they're okay. Not like my friend, his bull sneaked up and gored him. Didn't even hear him coming! But then that bull is a mean old bugger, don't worry about this lot."

Reading between the lines on a lot of the horror stories about stampeding cattle, I began to see some common denominators, the cows usually had calves or there was a bull in the field. The farmer had divided his cattle into a field of bullocks across the road and the cows were in the nearest fields to us. They did not, however, have any calves, so after another month of avoiding them I resolved one day in December to brave the herd.

Heading out with Megan and the Mont, we began our usual playtime in the field closest to the house. The cattle were amassed, chewing the latest lot of hay, in the entrance to the adjacent field. As we moved around in the general direction of their gate I tried to see their swivelling stares as the gentle curiosity of a peaceable animal, their swishing tails as the equivalent of a dog wagging its tail. The cows were pleased to see me. I tried to persuade myself they were not looking at me as something soft to clean their muddy hooves on.

I shortened Monty's lead and called Megan to a close walk and we slowly headed towards and then past the gate. The cows watched but stayed put. As we three homed to within about five metres one ambled forwards a couple of paces and swished a little more vigorously but we walked on and were soon heading for the reed beds. Casting a wary look over my shoulder, fully expecting to see a cow breathing down my neck and pawing the ground, I was relieved to see that they didn't seem at all bothered by my presence and had carried on with their bovine business amongst themselves.

Playing in the reeds was followed by a relaxing wander up the hill, along the hedgerow with all its rabbit holes, to the marshy area at the top. A quick check on the neighbouring sheep, which meant a quiet sit on Megan's part and a lunging pull on Monty's, followed by moving across the top of the hill to the vantage point. This allowed a fantastic view of the sea in the far distance in one direction, the distant mountains in another, and finally, the cows all gathering menacingly in the gateway and glaring at me.

I rang home for advice, "I have been cut off by marauding interlopers, need help."

"What are you on about?" came the reply.

"The cows won't let me back into the field."

A long sigh ensued from John, "All you have to do is have Monty on a short lead, Megan with you, and just move slowly past them. They will either ignore you or move out of the way."

About ten minutes later, my phone rang. "Are you back in the field yet?"

I was miffed, "No, I am *not* back in the field. I am actually at the top of the vantage point field, waiting for General Cow to make her next move. She has mustered the troops. I am going to head down to the reeds to try to find another way through the fence." Rather getting the impression that John was finding all this vaguely funny I rang off.

Reaching the reed beds again I examined the fence. Everywhere in the entire acreage of fields we walked there were holes and gaps, that is, apart from this section of fence where it was secure enough to hold back a ten ton rhino. Furthermore, my hiding place had been discovered and each time I peeped round the reeds, having whispered to Meg and Monty to maintain cover, General Cow had plodded closer.

Enough was enough, I was not going to be outwitted by a beef burger on legs. Finding a lower point of the fence I climbed over and called the dogs. What I would do would be to grab a pooch and lift them over the fence and we would then make a break for home. The only problems with my plan were that both dogs weighed a ton, had no idea what they were meant to be doing, and refused to cooperate. I had no choice but to ring home again.

"Let me get this straight, you are one side of the fence, the dogs are the other and you want rescuing from a cow?" John seemed astounded and not very sympathetic, which wound me up.

"Well technically, I am actually safe and it is the dogs that need rescuing but yes."

About five minutes later John appeared. Both dogs were sat observing General Cow and looking bored, I was quivering on the safe side of the fence looking relieved. John headed towards us shaking his head and looking incredulous, he took control of Monty's lead and summoned Megan, while I scrambled back over the fence. Slowly, we all did exactly what he had told us to do in the first place and headed back to the gate past the herd. Large black heads followed us but the cows stayed still, chewing cud. Making it home, I had the feeling that I would probably not be allowed to forget the Great Cow Rescue.

After my brush with General Cow I rapidly came to the conclusion that communication in the field was an issue. Although both John and I took a mobile phone with us when we went out, for safety and security in the face of an accident, there was invariably patchy signal or no signal at all for most of the routes we walked. It was virtually guaranteed that the one time Monty would finally succeed in catching one of us off guard and causing a broken ankle, it would be in a mobile phone dead zone.

Several times the previous year I had come across downed sheep and it would have been helpful to be able to call for assistance in standing them up again. Downed sheep, you would imagine, should be more than happy to see rescue coming towards them, waving a fist at the circling crows, ready and willing to pop them upright. The truth is that they are uncooperative, very heavy and have done their best to cover every part of their fleece with the muck they have been rolling around in. They are also normally slightly bloated and fart a lot.

Summoning John would have meant I could point out the ailing beast and then stand by looking weak and female while he gave himself a hernia and ended up covered in sheep droppings, as opposed to me being in the middle of nowhere and having to do it myself.

Luckily with the Great Cow Rescue the cows had been kind enough to conduct their manoeuvres where there was a signal but, I pondered, it could have been very different. A stand-off with General Cow when my phone was cheerfully flashing *'emergency calls only'* could have had one of two outcomes: I could either have waited it out in my bolthole until such time as John decided I had been gone too long and he had better come to find me; or I could have availed myself of the 'emergency calls only' technology, explained to the emergency services operator that I was being held hostage by General Cow and run the risk of being sectioned.

Explaining my predicament to my dad the next time I saw him, he came up with a brilliant solution. As a retired aircraft engineer he had built up over his career a huge toolbox of useful equipment. He had a pair of walkie-talkies and a base unit. He would charge them up and I could collect them the next time I visited. I beamed. Not only did this solve my communication problems but I also saw the opportunity to liven up daily dog-walking no end.

A few days later, two walkie-talkie handsets took pride of place on the kitchen windowsill and I was consumed with uncharacteristic enthusiasm for heading out into the lashing rain with Megan and Monty. Togged up, I clipped my handset to my pocket and headed off.

At the gate I checked in, "Roaming Pooch to Pooch Base, come in Pooch Base. Over."

The microphone crackled, "What are you on?"

I glared at the set and huffed, "No, it is Pooch Base to Roaming Pooch, actually, and you didn't say 'over'"

"Are you driving a truck? Or flying a plane then?"

"ROAMING POOCH to POOCH BASE, what has that got to do with anything? OVER!"

"Okay, Pooch Base to Roaming Pooch, you don't need to say 'over', it is not a CB radio. And are you actually roaming with the dogs anywhere, or are you still fannying about in the lane talking to me on this thing? Over and out!"

He had a point. Megan was looking cross standing at the gate and Monty was whingeing quietly at this change in routine. We started our normal playtime and began skirting the fields.

About half an hour in, I saw a new reason to call in, "Roaming Pooch to Pooch Base, we have dropped the payload on the western flanks, maintaining cover."

"You what?"

I stared at the handset in disbelief then pressed the transmit button twice so John got a crackle of annoyed static.

"Sorry, Pooch Base here, what the hell are you burbling on about Roaming Pooch?"

"Work it out Pooch Base. Over."

There was a long pause, long enough for me to get to the top of the hill and stand for a while surveying the fields, then my walkie-talkie crackled into life again.

"Pooch Base to Roaming Pooch here, you actually called in to tell me the dogs have had a crap under a tree?" I was immensely pleased that John was cottoning onto walkie-talkie speak but I now had something else to occupy my attention.

"Roaming Pooch to Pooch Base, maintain radio silence, combatants from previous skirmish in the vicinity. They haven't seen me yet. Heading for Pooch Base."

"The cows are back?"

"Roaming Pooch here, what part of 'maintain radio silence' are you not maintaining, exactly?"

"Pooch Base here, have you joined The A-Team or something?"

"Roaming Pooch to Pooch Base, have reached the perimeter. ETA thirty seconds."

John opened the front door as I crossed the yard. Shaking his head he retrieved my handset for recharging. I realised that an hour of dog-walking had passed in a flash, I hadn't even been bothered by the rain. Never had traipsing through the muddy fields been so much fun and we had been in constant contact so no emergency could have arisen unnoticed. Walkie-talkies were the way to go in field communication from now on.

THE STREAM EATS
MY WELLIES

"What's all this lot?"

"Presents, John. It's Christmas."

I was sat on the floor of the office wrapping a mountain of gifts a week before the big day. Distributing them into bags, I explained the chaos.

"Pet presents are in this pile, our presents are in this one, family pressies are here."

"I thought we agreed to keep to a budget this year?" John queried.

"Indeed we did but I've sort of gone a bit off piste with the budget idea and adapted it slightly. There is still one involved but it is what you might call a female concept budget."

John winced slightly then asked, "These pet presents? Are they for or from the pets?"

"Both. If they all have something to play with it means we will have peace and quiet to unwrap our own. Besides, you know the animals get involved in celebrations, don't you remember Valentine's Day?"

"How could I forget," John commented. On the first Valentine's after Megan's arrival a large pink envelope had plopped onto the doormat. This was in addition to the two cards waiting to be exchanged by us and John was quizzical as he saw it was addressed to him. Opening it, an impossibly cute and fluffy border collie puppy decorated the front of the card, surrounded by a ribbon heart and a cascade of little foil cupids had scattered everywhere as John read out the message, '*Smoochy, smoochy from the poochy woochy xxxx*'.

Now, as he prodded the huge Santa sack of pet presents with his foot, he sought further clarification, "Just so I know for when I start my shopping, which pets exactly are buying gifts this year?"

"Meg, Mont, Micky, Goebbs, Bobs and the budgies," I replied. "Then there are the big fish, little fish, snails and shrimp. But they are only little things, mini presents," I explained hurriedly, as John looked as though he was about to pass out. "What do you mean 'for when you start your shopping'? There is only a week left!"

"It is what you might call male concept shopping," John smirked. "See what's left in the coffers after the female has blown the finances out of the water and then try to come up with a decent present in the total hell that is town at this time of year."

"But Christmas shopping is fun: you need to browse, amble, pick and choose, tick people off your list, go for lunch and sing along to festive tunes in shops."

"In, park, shop, home. What exactly is fun about being elbowed off the pavement by rampant women whacking you with their carrier bags, queuing for about three weeks in every shop you go in and singing along to Christmas songs that have been playing since August?"

"Humbug," I said, going back to my wrapping. "Men have no idea."

"Um, excuse me!" John defended, "I think you will find that men invented Christmas shopping. But it was a case of 'Right lads, gold, frankincense and myrrh okay with you? Great, sorted! Off we go then'. You don't read anywhere that it involved them faffing about on Bethlehem High Street for a day."

We each did our shopping in our own way as usual and a week later exchanged gifts. I dished out treats to the birds and gave each dog a chew designed to keep them occupied for hours, loosely wrapped so they had to work to find their prize. Megan settled down to play with hers while Monty destroyed his in seconds and then decided to help us unwrap ours. I barricaded our bags behind the coffee table and then sat on the beanbag to stop Monty gaining access to what he had obviously assessed as a whole pile of chews we just had not bothered to give him yet.

Thwarted he circled the table but was blocked from our present unwrapping area.

"Oh look, this one is from the budgies," said John, reading the label and standing a bottle of red wine on the windowsill.

"Ah, thanks big fish," I said, taking the lid off a bottle of bubble bath and sniffing the scent.

"Monty, what on earth do you think you are doing?" John demanded, as Monty climbed up onto the coffee table and walked across it. "Get down."

My main present to John had been a new phone to replace his antiquated specimen. It was a brand he had wanted and all the bits that came with it were dotted about as he checked features and set it up to charge.

"Are all those black lead things with your phone vital?" I asked. "Because Monty is trying to pinch one?"

John made a snatch for the end of a cable and chucked a wadded piece of paper at Monty. I made the most of the pause in proceedings to gather all the discarded wrapping and place it in a bin liner. The dogs promptly joined forces to empty the bag and relocate its contents back to the floor; furthermore, they now felt that it needed urgent shredding.

"Pack it in you two," I muttered, as I gathered all the bits up again and tied the top of the bin bag. "Right John, back to our pressies."

Megan went back to her chew while Monty sneakily dragged the refilled bin bag out of the lounge and down the hall.

The pets had surpassed themselves on both sides with little gifts. As John put his trio of festive chutneys from the snails, and Himalayan pink salt mill from Micky on the windowsill, I cooed over silver earrings from Megan and chocolates from Goebbles.

My main present from John was a tablet computer, which he undertook to set up for me as I found one last little offering at the bottom of my bag.

"What's this?" I read from the label and realised that John had shown that men do actually have the best grasp of Christmas shopping. A fine bottle of sparkling wine was clearly labelled *'thank you for checking on us, from all your hairy and woolly farm friends'*.

Working in retail means time off over Christmas is non-existent. Luckily, our branch of the shop was one of the lucky ones that did not open on Boxing Day so I actually had two precious days of relaxation. Flushed with festive feelings after an indulgent Christmas Day I took over all the preparations for our Boxing Day lunch while also offering to do the afternoon pooch run. This offer was made in the morning, which happened to be well before all my chopping, stirring, baking and roasting was liberally lubricated with a couple of hefty Bloody Marys, loaded with all the essential seasonings and heavy with blue Smirnoff and splashes of sherry.

"Are you sure you're going to be all right walking these two?" John queried, as he watched me dancing in the kitchen, using a sprout tree as a microphone and singing along to a festive medley on the radio.

"No problem," I assured him, as I left everything cooking and layered up in walking gear, feeling distinctly merry.

I headed off into the murk with Megan and Monty.

"Jingle bells, jingle bells," I warbled, as we slithered through the mud to the gate.

"Rockin' around the Christmas tree," I squawked happily, as Monty promptly became entangled in the gorse bushes in search of some yummy fox poo to hoover up.

Mellow with generously portioned vodka, I was immune to the driving rain and wind and even felt the sudden urge to work off an excess of festive treats by trying to race Megan to the corner of the field, yelling, "Driving home for Christmas," as I plunged across the cow-hoof pocked ground.

This was fun. Never before had traipsing round in the semi-gloom of a miserable winter afternoon been so enjoyable.

Then the pooches got wind of interlopers. Some people had decided that our deserted lane, late Boxing Day afternoon, just as it was becoming dark, was the perfect spot for a chat and a stroll. Megan shot off across the field to howl and woof a lot at the fence just as the interlopers made some comments about how utterly peaceful the countryside was. Monty, attached to me by his lead pranced about but maintained some modicum of control.

"Good dog," I praised, patting him on the head and yelling for Megan to come away from the fence.

We then reached the stream and Monty decided that it was high time he was allowed to contribute his own rabid Christmas greetings to the walkers. Clearing the channel in one leap, he hurtled to the end of the extending lead and lunged happily, which meant that I had little choice but to follow. As I plunged through the water I found that the muddy bed, churned by tons of prime beef stock hooves, had assumed all the characteristics of quicksand.

One foot stuck fast in the mire as the stream swirled with murky intent around my ankle. With Monty still hauling the lead taut, my forward momentum continued unabated as my other foot squelched down into the clay. I suddenly found myself welly-boot-less as my socked feet emerged from the slime but my wellies didn't. Not wanting to think too hard about the contents of the green brown gloop oozing between my toes I looked across the field to the distant beacon of light glowing from our living room window.

Acutely aware that I was about a quarter of a mile from home in socks with the stream energetically slurping down on my footwear I had no choice but to ring home. The phone was answered after a couple of rings, "What's up?"

When I could stop giggling I issued a plea for help, "Hello, can you meet me at the gate with some shoes, I have been sucked off."

"I beg your pardon?" John said, incredulity in his voice.

"The stream ate my wellies, tee hee. I need shoes."

"Where are you now?"

"I am standing in the mud by the stream."

"And where are your wellies, exactly?" John appeared to be having difficulty grasping the situation.

"In the stream. I just told you, it ate them. Monty jumped over the stream, pulled me after him and my feet came out but my wellies didn't."

"Can't you pull them out?"

"No! I have tried, but Monty is pulling me one way, Megan is half a mile away barking at some strolling interlopers and the stream has no intention of letting me have my wellies back. My feet are cold and squidgy, I dread to think what is in this mud, and so I am heading up to the gate."

"On my way."

John duly showed up at the gate shaking his head as I squelched my way across the field, by now chortling with high good humour at the silliness of the proceedings. With admirable lack of comment, he handed over replacement wellies and took control of the dogs for me. I then discovered, with even more hilarity, that I could not get the new wellies on owing to my feet being wet and clammy, plus being covered in sheep dung, cow dung and mud.

The best I could manage was to squash my toes in and flail my arms to keep my balance on the uneven ground. Realising that I had the entire gait and bearing of a zombie, I tottered up the lane on tiptoes, half in half out of wellies, with arms outstretched, yelling, "I neeeed youur braaiinns."

John, by now eyeing me with his best 'must ring the doctor' look, followed with Meg and Monty.

It wasn't long before we were all back in the warm house, my utterly rancid socks were thrown in a bucket of disinfectant and we settled down to our Boxing Day dinner. John promised to retrieve my wellies the next time he was in the field.

He then opened a bottle of fizz. "Best stick to wine from now on," he declared. "Odd things seem to happen when you've been on the vodka."

COLD STORMS AND HOT ROCKS

January had seen some of the worst storm surges in living memory. Propelled by high tides and strong winds, the waves had devastated the Victorian seafront promenade of our local town. We live up in the hills so we were spared the impact but February brought more storms and gales. My shop had been closed for a refit so I was commuting from town two hours by coach to another store.

On the twelfth February it was already blustery and torrential downpours slowed the coach as it made its way through the hills. By the time I reached my destination I found out that the weather forecasters had issued a rare red weather warning for the whole of the West Wales coast. This meant a serious risk of death or injury arising from the weather conditions and a warning to avoid all but essential travel. It was time to batten down the hatches and I was two hours from home.

Through the store windows I gloomily watched the weekly market traders fight a losing battle to keep their stalls intact. As one stall was lifted bodily and twisted by the gales, its tarpaulin shredding in the gusts, the market traders decided as one to pack up and go home. I thought that this was an eminently sensible idea so I arranged to skip my lunch hour and catch the next available bus.

Leaving at two fifteen, I should have been safely home by five. I actually arrived in a stressed out, tearful heap somewhere around seven thirty. The journey had been a nightmare with three diversions for fallen trees and one for an unstable roof. We had sat and watched while the fire brigade removed someone's chimney from the middle of the road and experienced our bus being shifted bodily from our side of the road to the oncoming side by a particularly vicious gust that took all control from our driver.

Arriving back at the bus terminal we saw walls crumbled, trees down, slates all over the place, with an auditory backdrop to the whole calamitous scene of emergency sirens, whistling wind, shop alarms and various crashing sounds of bits of town hitting other bits of town. The storm had chosen to hit while our car was in the garage being fixed so I needed to find a taxi to make the last leg home.

Unsurprisingly, most of the local taxi firms had declined to sit their cars on the rank in the hope of picking up passengers as opposed to chunks of masonry and had sent their drivers home. Most businesses had closed early in the face of the weather warning so town was deserted. It took a while but eventually I found a cab, then it was just a case of finding a route home that was not blocked by trees.

The normal route up the hill was impassable due to a particularly massive specimen so the driver went around the houses. Everywhere we tried we got so far and then had to find an alternative route as we came across trees, bushes and pieces of house, or a cluster of emergency workers waving us down to warn of trees, bushes and pieces of house, blocking our path.

Before long, it dawned on me that there was only one option left, a winding lane that crawled up the side of a hill through a thickly wooded area. In summer, this was a pretty lane that led home while allowing lovely views of mature woods and natural wildlife. At this moment in time its charms were slightly less appealing as several million tons of unstable hardwood waved menacingly in the gales, creaking a challenge to us.

As the crow flies I was only a couple of miles from home by now so I gave the taxi driver the option of letting me out and I would walk the rest of the way. Being a chivalrous type he was having none of it. I got the impression that, come hell or high water, he was going to get this quivering jelly in his passenger seat home. In our favour was the fact that the bulk of the wood was on the sheltered side of the hill, and although the concept of sheltered was largely academic in the face of this storm, nevertheless there was the slightest respite from the brunt of the gales.

Ten minutes later I was being dropped by my gate. Although he didn't ask for it I insisted the driver took double the fare and wished him luck getting home, along with my heartfelt thanks. In the brief time I was outside I felt the winds rip around the yard and against my face, the air was full of tiny stinging pieces and a couple of slates were smashed on the ground, but at least I was home in our cosy warm house.

There was no electricity and hadn't been since two in the afternoon so the house was neither cosy nor warm, it was pitch black and freezing. John had lit some candles and had dug the camping stove out of the shed so we could make hot drinks and cook the basics. Monty, unimpressed by the flickering flames, had taken to curling up on the floor in random places so you fell over him in the dark. After such a traumatic day we decided that the best thing was to settle down for the night and let the storm blow itself out.

The electricity company knew about the power failure, it would be all right in the morning.

Next day we woke to slightly calmer gales and our battery powered radio burbling about widespread damage, devastation on the roads and the fact that the greater part of Wales was without power owing to the storms, which the helpful newscaster informed us were amongst the most damaging since records began. We were not surprised to find that we were still without electricity but now we had no water supply or landline telephone either. Our car was now trapped at the garage by a fallen tree across the access road so John and I went into siege mode.

I started fretting about my tropical fish. Assuming that it was only a brief interruption to the power I did not feed them that morning to avoid spoiling the water when there was no filtration going on. The tank temperature was stable in both tanks, and although it had dropped a couple of degrees it was still within a healthy range for the breeds of fish. Without lights the fish were less active but did not seem too affected and we had completed water quality checks a couple of days before so we knew that there was no imminent problem with chemical pollution. As long as the outage was resolved quickly the fish would be fine.

John used his mobile and rang the helpline for an update; owing to the extensive damage and the still risky conditions there would be no reconnection before four that afternoon. We wrapped the tanks to conserve heat. The house was rapidly taking on the characteristics of a fridge, so our other main concern was Micky.

Birds can tolerate low temperatures as long as they are protected from drafts and are dry but their inbuilt survival techniques do rather depend on them having feathers. Micky was bald, apart from his wings, tail and head. I had piled on extra blankets when I had covered the birds' cages the night before and had left three sides covered when they had been fed that morning, but Micky was morose and goose pimpled on his perch, his normal pink skin showing a faint purplish hue. With trees still being cleared on all the roads and lanes, and with our car stuck three miles away I could not even get him over to my parents' house which had had its power restored.

I dredged up my best Girl Guide training, something had to be done to keep Micky warm. As I plodded over the kitchen tiles in my socks, feeling the chill seeping through to my feet, I suddenly thought of something. Heading outside with a bucket I ferreted about in the garden, searching for the large flat, round pebbles and pieces of slate that dotted the ground. Back inside I placed half the rocks in a pan of water on our camping stove and brought the pan to the boil. Once the stones were heated through I took them to

Micky's cage and placed them on the newspaper on the tray that sat under the base grill of the cage.

"Who's a posh parrot then?" I said, as he looked quizzically downwards. "You've got under floor heating now."

With the other half of my haul of stones now boiling on the stove I had a ready supply to swap over when the first lot cooled. John came to find me to let me know that the latest estimate for possible reconnection was now late evening.

"I've just had a peek at what you are doing for dinner. It doesn't look very appetising."

I gestured at the cage, "They are the next lot of Micky's hot rocks."

Micky had climbed down to the cage floor to investigate and was now sat on the grill about an inch above the rocks, munching a cashew and basking in the welcome warmth. He had also started chattering away again, a sure sign that he was feeling happier.

"At least someone is cosy," John commented.

The next problem was the fish. With the latest possible reconnection time we were looking at an outage verging on thirty hours. John fetched some water from the spring that fed the natural pond down the lane and we heated it up on the camping stove. I then slowly added it to the tanks in a vain attempt to halt the continuing drop in temperature showing on the gauges. The little fish did not seem too bothered by the situation but the large ones had taken to hanging near the top of the water gasping.

"The oxygen levels are getting lower," I muttered gloomily.

I tried to remedy this new disaster by pouring subsequent warm water additions into the tank from a height. It did not seem to make any difference but it was the best I could do.

We moved into the lounge as the daylight faded and lit candles. By closing the door we could actually make the room quite warm. The dogs were still uneasy with the flames so after dinner *a la can* we all moved to settle down for the night. It had to be all right in the morning.

Come the next day there was still no power or water, our mobiles were nearly out of battery, I had used up practically all our camping gas on hot rocks and water for the fish, we still had no car and the house was arctic.

"All we need now is for the zombie apocalypse to start and our day is complete," I fumed, staring at the two dead big fish that had given up the ghost overnight. This survival mode lark was beginning to get on my nerves.

Finally, some good news, the trees on the road had been cleared and the garage was able to get our car back to us. As I commenced funerary rites and transferred the dead silver dollar and shark into a bucket, in the vain hope that a ten degree temperature drop and no oxygen meant that they were just having a protest kip until it was all back to normal, John went off to try and find a generator.

He returned a couple of hours later with water supplies, gas bottles and a petrol generator. "The power had better be off still," he grumbled, having had to travel all over the county to find one available.

Before too much longer my fish had light, heat and the yard reverberated with what sounded like an airliner engine maintenance depot. It was a close call but we did not lose any more fish. If anything, the little fish did what is traditionally done in a power cut and found their own way to keep warm; a couple of weeks later there was a new crop of tiny fry zooming around.

Later that day, over forty-eight hours after it first went off, the power was restored. After a flicker or two it came back on properly, which also meant the local water pumping station now had power, and shortly afterwards the water supply returned.

In our newly warm house we took stock; the tiled floors were filthy with grime trodden in from numerous trips to the spring, there were candle stubs everywhere, the dogs now thought it was normal to cuddle up under the duvet, Micky's cage looked like a rockery and when I fed the fish after their enforced fast they acted like piranha and nearly took my hand off. Furthermore, their ex-mates had completed their lying in state and had joined the 'too big to flush' club.

We sat in the lounge later after long hot baths and made a list of essentials. Water had not really been a problem and we had managed to stay warm by wrapping up. In fact I had been particularly snug as I had made use of an unusual birthday present from my brother and his family, but an emergency kit was essential. On the next trip to town we would buy oxygenating tablets from the pet shop and start enquiries about the cost of a generator. As the camping stove was moved back to the shed it was the final move back to normality after a stressful couple of days.

I poured wine for us both as John made a proper dinner. Handing him his glass, he glanced at my jumper and skirt.

"You know, I am going to miss you in your fluffy parrot onesie," he said.

SUMMER WALK

It was the middle of June and I'd had a headache all week. Going into work was a struggle and I came home each night drained and in pain. Finally, in the early hours of Friday I woke up with the most excruciating agony in both temples. Summoning up the energy to creep to the bathroom to raid the medicine cabinet for painkillers, I downed a couple of paracetamol and fell back into bed.

In a semi-dozing state I lay as still as I could as every movement inflamed more spikes of pain in both sides of my head. At around six I felt horrifically nauseous and could feel every palpitating heartbeat banging erratically in my ears and chest. I'd had palpitations before and they normally passed, but when it came to eight o'clock and there was no change I knew that this was something different and a bit worrying. John was already up and about and when he appeared with a cup of tea for me he was immediately concerned.

"I think I might need to go to casualty," I moaned, from the depths of the pillow.

John was ready in ultra-quick time; he took the dogs out for a quick walk to do the necessary while I dragged myself into some clothes. We were then on our way to the local hospital and I found myself ensconced in the resuscitation bay for pretty much the rest of the day.

It turned out that I had a very fast and irregular heartbeat that needed immediate treatment. This could also have been the source of my headache, as the atrial fibrillation had not been providing my brain with an adequate source of blood and oxygen. As repeated intravenous shots of beta blockers were administered to try to bring the situation under control monitors beeped, blood pressure cuffs expanded and I sat in the middle of it all feeling dreadfully ill and not in control. Then it was announced that the drugs were not working. The doctors proposed an electro-cardioversion, which would involve a brief general anaesthetic followed by shocking my heart back into a normal rhythm. All being well this should work and I would possibly be able to go home after a few hours monitoring, with some medication to take if the problem recurred.

The irony of the fact that it was Friday the thirteenth was not lost on me. I should have been at work selling jewellery and accessories to happy holidaymakers and townsfolk, not sat in accident and emergency signing consent forms for cardiac procedures. Luckily things seemed to go to plan and when I came round the monitor was beeping happily, with the trace showing a much more regulated heartbeat. The nurses and doctor were still bustling around me but now with decidedly less urgency than before.

Once they were satisfied that I was recovering well, the oxygen mask was removed and I left resuscitation for a conventional bay under twenty minute observations. I was finally allowed a couple of cups of very welcome tea and I waited for the all clear to go home. Early evening saw me finally back in my own bed, reflecting on the day's events. This had been an unexpected and frightening turn of events that had shaken both me and John.

Megan and Monty had also been more subdued than usual, sensing all was not quite well with me. They had taken to coming up to me and placing their heads on my knee, looking up and whimpering, while giving reassuring little licks to my hands. Whereas Monty normally took a flying leap onto the bed regardless of the position of the occupants, now he walked up to the edge and climbed up, with as little disturbance as possible, creeping up my side and settling with his head on my shoulder and a worried little sigh.

I'd had a wakeup call and resolved to make some lifestyle changes; no more rushing or missing lunch, no more eating total crap for lunch, no more getting to home time and realising that the last time I had drunk anything was my pre-work cups of tea, no more stressing about work and winding myself up long after the working day was ended and finally, no more assuming that I could pass off my consumption of five fruits a day as a couple of glasses of wine every evening. I also resolved to take more notice of the minutiae of the beautiful world around me. There was nothing like a heart scare to focus the mind on the fleeting fragility of your existence.

With this in mind and with firm instructions from John to take it easy and not to overdo it, a day or so later I decided to take the dogs out for their morning walk. I headed out into the flatter of the fields around the house, it was gearing up to be a hot day and the air was sultry and still.

For once Monty was a dream to walk. As if aware that hauling me round could be hazardous to my health, he was happy to amble along sedately. For quite a while I had got into a bit of a rut with my contributions to dog-walking. I loaded up with treats and my phone, waved a goodbye, disappeared for an hour to walk round the fields, and then came back, job done. I realised that sometimes it was becoming a necessary chore to be completed rather than an enjoyable experience in itself. On this day I intended to see it differently.

The farmer had long since given us permission to amble through all his fields. We did not do any damage, respected his crops and livestock, and it had the added bonus for him that we could spot any problems and report back. The flat fields had been planted with barley but there was a border around the edge that had not been cultivated. It was along this border, in the shadow of the hedgerow that we walked.

Megan trotted ahead, stopping every few yards to glance back over her shoulder to check that we were still behind her. I followed with Monty on a long lead, as he snuffled and scented his way along the verge. When we caught up with Megan and Monty joined her in investigating something particularly interesting in among the hedge roots, I took the time to look around me. I marvelled at how the barley seemed to have sprung up by several inches in just a couple of days, the overnight rainfall working its magic.

Rather than urging the dogs on I let them inspect while I looked deep into the hedge and by chance saw the blackbird hen, motionless on her nest but alert and watching me with beady eyes. I stepped back so as not to worry her but I was still able to see the intricacy of the nest construction in its protected spot, hidden from the crows and completely sheltered from the elements. As I took my cue from the dogs and moved on I had no idea if she was on her first or second brood, or whether she had eggs or chicks tucked in the depths, but I wished her 'good luck' as I left her to it.

As we skirted the longer edge of the field and the hedgerow diminished into grassy banks I noticed that the foxes had been indulging in a spot of housekeeping. Fresh earth, scuffed from the burrows, lay on the ground spotted with bones. Both dogs sniffed animatedly and then scented the entrances.

"Be nice you two, how would you like it if the fox peed in your house?" I murmured, coaxing them on.

A skylark sang overhead and I registered the song as I had done many times before but on this occasion I stopped and scanned the endless blue expanse of sky until I located the tiny black speck, fluttering far above. It took a while and the brightness made me sneeze repeatedly so I perched on the bank to catch my breath. It was green. Except that it wasn't green, it was an acid, olive, emerald, moss, lime green and here and there, dotted amongst the waving grasses were the tiniest, most delicate, brilliant scarlet flowers.

The barley was less well grown here, being in the windier part of the field and there were more flecks of red on the dry earth around the base of the plants. These were moving specks – ladybirds – that I had acknowledged enough on previous walks to try to avoid stepping on but had not really noticed beyond that. Now I wanted to know how many spots they had. As Megan checked on the lambs in the field next door and Monty did his best to excavate a long gone mole from a fresh molehill, I crouched down and wheedled a ladybird onto my fingertip.

"Right bug," I muttered, in my best Dirty Harry drawl. "Now do you have seven spots or only five?"

It was a seven spotter. I returned it to the ground and tried again with a different specimen, this also had seven spots. So did their mates a few paces further on. Leaving the seven spot bug convention to its business I wandered on. The dogs were only too happy in the heat to amble slowly along at my pace, in fact they seemed to relish the chance to examine every interesting find at leisure without being urged on, but they were getting warm and panting. I made my way up to the lower vantage point of the barley field. Here the breeze wafted across the hill and Megan and Monty lay down in the grass and savoured the cooler air.

Leaning on the fence post I surveyed the view; looking west the sea sparkled in the distance – mill pond still by the looks of it and reflecting the cloudless sky; north lay our little hamlet half hidden in trees with the lane snaking down the hill. To the south the fields rolled endlessly, filled with sheep and cattle, to the far distant communication mast just visible in the shimmering haze, completely different to the glimmering beacon of lights that you could see shining brightly on a clear night. Finally, to the east were the mountains beyond the fields. The wind turbines on their flanks were still and they loomed green grey and timeless. Above them clouds gathered in white roiling banks.

"See that," I said to no-one in particular. "If you look three ways there are no clouds to be seen anywhere but there they are, lurking. That's what has happened to me. What on earth have you got there Monty?"

Obviously uninspired by my philosophical musings, Monty was scratching around the base of the post I was leaning on. With a few treats I persuaded him to let go of the owl pellet he was about to eat and then saw another opportunity. Instead of casting it aside as another rescued piece of contraband and hurrying quickly on before Monty could make a return pass, I found a bit of stick and prodded the pellet apart.

I had no idea what animal the tiny bones and fluff I teased out had come from, or when their unfortunate owner had become dinner, but I relished the chance to be in a position to examine an owl pellet, in the sunshine, with nothing but birdsong around me. I could hear no traffic or industry, see no other people and I was only five minutes from home: what city dweller with all the urban bustle, traffic fumes and chaos had the same privilege? Eventually, with the dogs now cool and restless to continue, we moved on.

Heading down the western flanks of the field I discovered more ladybirds and did another spot count on a few individuals. All had seven spots. No five spot interlopers for me to find today. I checked off the meadow flowers; purple and white clover, celandines, daisies, dandelions and buttercups and watched the back ends of bees bumbling in the flowers of tall pink foxgloves and dog roses. I took photos of a spider's web, hanging in a shaded spot and still festooned with droplets of water that caught the light and glistened brighter than the most perfect diamonds.

We visited the little slate quarry so Megan and Monty could drink from the deep puddle that never drained away and while they did so I examined the steep angles of the strata of slate. Millions of years ago they would have been lying flat until some primeval earthquake caused the upheaval that led to their new position. I realised that I would also have been standing on the seabed at that time so I looked for fossils. I found none but what I did find was that the quarry was not just grey slate. Chunks of quartz lay around along with stone shot through with reddish glints that sparkled in the sun. Dull brown rocks littered the floor but when you passed them and looked back from a different angle they too shimmered as if coated with metallic copper frosting.

The puddle was surprisingly deep, cool and clear considering the heat of the day; the dogs cooled their paws and I joined them for a paddle, my ankles chilled as the heat reflected off the quarry walls and warmed the back of my neck. I wondered if the puddle was fed by a spring seeping up from below, there was no obvious bubbling source but the water seemed too fresh to be left over rain water given the hot still air contained within the steep walls. Crunching across the stone, with wet foot and paw prints drying almost immediately behind us, we made our way up to the path that led into the field that adjoined the house.

We were now back onto grass and Megan and Monty bounced around, chasing each other and rolling on their backs. The cattle had been gone for around two weeks and it was amazing how the pat-strewn pasture had recovered. Cropped to within a few inches of the soil by hungry mouths, the grass and clover were already growing back. The beetles and worms that digested dung had been busy and the many cowpats had already been reduced to crisp husks, disappearing back into the earth and making the field a pleasure to walk once more.

We crossed the little brook by the oak tree on the last lap home. There had not been a lot of rain so the water was low and strings of green algae clung to the rocks and waved in the current, dappled by flickers of sunlight breaking through the leaves above.

There were three options for crossing the stream; by the oak, which was the prettiest; in the middle of the field where the stream was at its most muddy and shallow, here the cattle had pocked the damp earth into clay craters that trapped stagnant water and fed the midges that rose and swarmed as you passed; and by the gorse bushes where a long ago farmer had made a makeshift bridge with a dozen railway sleepers, now bleached by years of sun and wind, the gaps between them showing glimpses of the stream meandering over its dark stony bed.

We crossed the field, heading for the gate to the lane. Crows voiced their annoyance at a red kite that wheeled at treetop height overhead and one brave individual took off to mount an aerial challenge. The kite swooped away, banking so the sun glinted off its russet feathers, and continued its search for prey lower down the valley. Once endangered, they now flourished in our part of Wales and it was a privilege to be able to view this magnificent bird at close quarters. It was rare that a walk did not result in the opportunity to see red kites and to marvel at their sheer size and beauty.

Leaning on the gate to catch my breath as the dogs gratefully lay down in a patch of shade I watched the air shimmer slightly above the bars and felt the warmth of the sun-heated metal against my back. The fields spread out before me, sloping down the valley towards the sea, green and peaceful in the late morning heat. It really was a lovely part of the world to live in and I realised, as I opened the gate to tread the last few steps back to the house, that I had seen more on that one walk than I had for months. I resolved there and then that no walk would ever be a chore again. My eyes open approach was here to stay.

REVENGE OF THE SHEEP

Recall with Monty was the one area of training that he seemed to have a mental block with. After a year and a half he was still obsessed with trying to get away to bond with his woolly friends and had all the recall skills of a straight boomerang. I had pored over behaviour guides, sought help from fellow dog owners and scoured the Internet for advice; the nuggets of training had sunk into my brain, it was just that Monty, with the attention span of a peanut, refused to take them on board.

In my dreams Monty ambled free with Megan, instantly presenting at my side whenever I called, as we made our way through the eternally sun dappled fields. In reality, he persisted in hauling away at his lead as anything and everything proved more interesting than listening to me.

It was not that he did not have recall because he did. He could hear kitchen activity through solid walls and about sixty feet of house and you only had to whisper 'Monty' for him to skid to a halt in front of you to see what you wanted, in a blur of drool and wagging tail, if he even sensed movement of the treat box. So, to have the perfect stress free walk I had two options: either venture into the fields dressed like a sheep and making a noise like a fridge or this field training lark was going to be cracked once and for all.

"I think I've done it this time," I reported, on my arrival back from the latest walk. "The field is secure."

For the past few sessions I had been obsessively walking the perimeter of the field nearest the house, attempting to make it Monty-proof. This would give us about six acres of training area in which Monty could run safely and learn to come back on command.

Two sides of the field had been sorted by the farmer with new fencing and a run of barbed wire along the bottom. One edge ran alongside the lane and the fence was mainly secure with the trees and hedgerow that bordered the tarmac providing a secondary border. Mature and spiky gorse bushes were a further deterrent but even so, I prowled in search of escape holes and plugged anything larger than a mouse hole with tree branches and tufts of dried gorse. The fourth side skirted the neighbouring farmer's land; the fencing was fine and had withstood the onslaught of his Welsh Black cattle using the posts to scratch. It had been patched up in places but there were no breaches, the only problem was the access gate had a large gap showing underneath it. Half a dozen Montys could get through this so between us John and I dragged a redundant roll of left over fence wire across the field and attached it to the gate with cable ties.

I then took every opportunity to check and recheck the four sides of our training field until I was satisfied that it was secure. John checked and rechecked my checking, then I went out and did the same to his. Finally we arrived at the point where we decided we would take Monty out and let him off the lead before my obsession drove us both mad.

In preparation for the big event we had been calling Monty's name at random times when he was in the house or yard. As soon as he gave us his undivided attention we praised and rewarded. On walks we had been doing the same, having him respond and return from the end of his training tether, within the limits of his deficient attention span.

One fine July evening we all made our way to the field. I made one last circuit of the perimeter before reporting back.

"It's like Alcatraz, we're good to go. Let loose the Mont."

We started with some basics. John held Monty's lead while I backed off a few paces and called him. Megan lay down in the grass to watch. Monty trotted over to me and was rewarded with a piece of steak. I then sent him back to John for the process to be reversed.

Gradually we increased the distance between us so that, before long Monty was running the length of his lead between us in search of treats.

Then it was time to bite the bullet and let him go. We shortened the distance and repeated our training, but this time Monty was off the lead.

"Good boy," we praised, as he dutifully bounced backwards and forwards. "Good recall. Good, good dog!"

For about fifteen minutes Monty showed perfect recall skills. We did not want to over stretch him so kept the session short but fun. In high spirits we finally took him home where he revelled in the ongoing rewards of being a newly amazingly well trained dog.

The next morning John and I prepared for a repeat session. We walked Megan and Monty for an hour as usual before returning to the training field. It was a hot, still day without a cloud in the sky. The idea was to finish the walk with ten minutes of recall before heading home for a well-earned rest and a cooling snooze in the shade.

As before, we practiced on the lead and all went brilliantly.

As before, we practiced off the lead and all went brilliantly.

As before, we then decided to bring our short but fun training session to a close and it all went spectacularly tits up. Monty suddenly made an unexpected bee line for the fence, promptly squeezed his sixty-five pound bulk through a tiny two inch square hole that I had missed and cleared off to say 'hello' to the ram lambs sunning themselves in the clover about half a mile away.

"Alcatraz huh?" John sighed. "Well, it looks like we've got ourselves a jail break."

The sheep separated into two groups as Monty forged through the knee-high clover towards them. I called Megan to me and headed for the gate while John climbed into the clover field and followed the black head he could just see ploughing off into the distance.

As Megan and I walked quickly along the path that ran

alongside the sheep field towards the access gate I could see John attempting to round up Monty, who was bouncing round the clover trying to persuade the lambs to form one big flock. The sheep refused to cooperate, one group gathered in the corner of the field and one clustered by the gate where Meg and I were watching the proceedings. Monty was flying between them, diverting off every now and then to hurtle in mad circles, his panting head appearing above the clover while the sun beat down with relentless heat as we neared midday.

Megan sniffed at the sheep gathered on the other side of the gate and sat, casting a look at me that seemed to say, '*What the hell does he think he is playing at, it is too hot for this?*'

Finally Monty stopped bouncing and disappeared. John headed for his last seen position and then bent down, attaching the lead and bringing him to the gate. The sheep ambled back into one big group and carried on grazing while Monty came out of the field and collapsed in a heap in the grass at the side of the path.

He was a complete state; his chest was heaving as his tongue lolled from his mouth and his eyes rolled, foamy spittle flecked his side and rimmed his mouth as he gasped for breath, while his legs paddled aimlessly in the dust.

"Stupid dog has given himself heatstroke," I muttered. "We need to get him cooled down."

John looked back along the path. "There is still water in the stream by the house."

Feeling the sun burning down on the back of my neck, I held my scarf up to give Monty a bit of shade while he tried to catch his breath.

"Too far, the quarry is closer," I said.

Megan had inspected Monty, prodding him with a foot and sniffing his face. She then sat by the gate and eyed the sheep, who were gradually wandering back in our direction to see what was up. Torn between keeping an eye on the sheep and watching over an ailing Monty, she cast her gaze back and forth before seeming to make a decision and trotting a few paces off down the path towards home.

Between us, we coaxed Monty onto his feet and, very slowly, helped him along the path. "Take it nice and slow Mont," urged John.

Repeatedly, Monty stopped and lay back down on the grass, reluctant to move. We let him catch his breath as much as possible but what he really needed was to have his core temperature lowered. He was too squirmy and too heavy to carry, so we had no choice but gently to keep him moving. Megan was already in the quarry when we arrived and circled as I pulled Monty into the middle of the deepest pool and started scooping water over his back and head. He stood with his legs submerged up to his knees, head drooping, as I poured tub after tub of cool water over him using the treat holder we had brought out for his training.

John splashed water up from the pool onto Monty's tummy and legs and I soaked my scarf and plonked it over his head. Every few minutes I checked Monty's temperature by putting my hand into the hairless patch in his groin. After what seemed a very long time his breathing calmed and his chest stopped heaving. His groin went slowly from red hot to a more normal heat and eventually, he raised his head, looked around groggily and licked some of the foam from his lips.

Even then we carried on dousing his fur with water until he was completely saturated. Only when Monty showed signs of being more alert did we slowly coax him on wobbly legs back to the house.

"Now see Monty," I admonished, as he gratefully lay down in a patch of shade in the breeze that wafted through the yard. "That's what you get when you chase around in boiling weather, the sheep nearly killed you. I hope you remember this next time you spot your woolly mates and want to play."

"I wouldn't bank on it," commented John, watching from the front step. "Thick as two short planks, that dog."

Monty snoozed for most of the day, either in the shade in the yard, or on the bed in the cool draughts that wafted through the open windows. We had the vet on standby but by evening he was completely back to normal, gobbling his tea and hassling Megan.

The next morning I took both dogs out for their walk. Monty was firmly attached to his lead once more. As we approached the fence where he had made his great escape he lunged to snuffle hopefully at the hole as the sheep grazed contentedly on the other side.

"Out of luck pooch," I told him. "John has plugged the fence."

Seeing that his route was blocked Monty settled for planting his paws on the wire and watching the sheep, some of whom came forward a few paces and stomped their feet at us. He panted happily, sniffing in their direction, and his tail began to wag so violently that his whole back end wobbled from side to side.

I shook my head at him. "John was right, completely forgotten about yesterday already have you? Sheep are hazardous to your health."

Pulling him off the fence I added, "And while we are at it, your shenanigans are hazardous to ours, I don't think our blood pressure could have got much higher."

We went back to our walk. Megan brought over a stick and dropped it in front of me hoping that I would throw it for her, Monty lunged to the end of the lead and bounced around, tugging a loop of it in his mouth with a force that swivelled me on my feet. I lobbed the stick and watched as Megan used it to tease Monty, the two of them chasing each other in circles, sheep now completely ignored. Finally, both dogs rolled happily on their backs, cooling down on the rich grass as one of the lambs poked its head through the fence and started munching the pasture on our side.

I sat on the bank of the stream and watched. Life in Alcatraz wasn't all bad.

GUNS AND CROWSES
(AND A WOOD PIGEON)

The farmer had arranged for a crow cull. There were thousands of them and they were causing havoc and injury amongst his livestock. As a bird lover I was not too happy about it but knew that it was a necessary evil to keep the population under control every now and then.

So one late summer morning, a couple of marksmen set up a hide in the field. Passing the time of day with them as I brought the dogs down the hill at the end of their walk I arranged to avoid the area for the rest of the day. They would be shooting until about four in the afternoon, which meant that the fields would then be accessible for the dogs' second walk.

Lures fluttered around the hide and the guns popped away as the marksmen started work. Megan and Monty were safe in the yard although Meg took it upon herself to bark her disgust at the gunfire. Monty, watching Meg bouncing angrily around the yard after the latest volley, settled into the kennel for a snooze out of harm's way.

Every now and then, one of the shooters would head out into the field to collect up the corpses and dispatch any injured birds. I used binoculars periodically to check on proceedings and watched as they walked in criss-cross fashion across the field, searching for their downed quarry.

It was in the middle of one of my checks that John came to find me. I had the binoculars trained on a patch of hay, mid-field.

"They have missed one," I said.

"They have probably missed lots, I thought it was the ones that they hadn't missed that you are worrying about."

"No, they have missed collecting one." I handed the binoculars over, with agitated instructions for him to concentrate on a particular area.

John peered through the lenses for a moment before announcing, "It is a weed."

"It is not a weed, it is a shot crow!"

I surveyed the field regularly in the countdown to four o'clock, hoping that the marksmen would find the injured bird and put it out of its misery but the crow, in an act of self-preservation, burrowed itself into the mown hay and hid. I was ready with leads and dogs the second the shooters had dismantled their hide and cleared away their lures. I was at the gate ready to enter the fields as their Land Rover disappeared down the track to the farm.

Counting the rows of hay, I headed towards the site where I thought the crow to be but could not find anything. The weather was grey and blustery with frequent heavy rain showers and my scarf whipped around my head. It was looking hopeless, the field was huge and the crow had obviously gone to ground. Still prowling the area, I decided to employ Megan as a crow-dog.

"Come on Megan, find it," I commanded.

Megan looked at me perplexed. I did not have a stick or a ball so I could not be asking her to find either of those, there were no sheep in the field so she came and sat at my feet, looking at me and wondering what I was going on about.

I waved my arm at the rows of hay and sent her away. Monty charged round tugging at his lead as Megan reluctantly wandered off and half-heartedly sniffed at a pile of straw. She then took her lead from Monty and upended onto her back for a good roll and a wriggle. Then, standing up and shaking herself, she seemed to sense something. Trotting off she began to sniff animatedly just as there was a commotion and a black, feathered shape flapped forlornly out into the open. Monty froze while Megan ran towards the crow.

"Keep it Megan," I called after her.

Crow-dog circled this strange thing she had been asked to keep and very gently, as it flapped along the ground with a surprising amount of energy, placed a paw on its back and held it still.

"Good girl," I praised, as she sat back to let me inspect the casualty. The crow tried to drag itself away, trailing a wing so I placed a towel over the bird and scooped it up. Covering its head to keep it calm I looked for injuries and soon found that it had a bad flesh wound in the area where its wing met its chest. The wings themselves and the rest of the bird seemed to be unhurt. I tested the reflexes of both feet and yelped as it clamped two entirely healthy and very strong sets of toes around my fingers, sinking its needle claws through my glove. Adjusting the towel to have a quick look at its head I was fixed with a baleful, beady black-eyed stare as the ungrateful crow whipped its beak round to tweak a chunk of my bare wrist.

"Ouch, bird. Do you mind? I am trying to help you here," I complained, as the crow refused to let go and began twisting. "Now this is why you have got a bad reputation. Let go, I am not a sheep. Hello John."

John was coming across the field towards me. "Why is that manky old crow wrapped in one of our best towels?"

"It is my crow rescue kit, told you it wasn't a weed," I replied, still trying to ignore the beak firmly clamped to my flesh.

"And what do you propose to do with it now you have rescued it?"

As usual, John was far too obsessed with the practicalities, but I had it all worked out. Luckily it did not seem to be too badly hurt. The crow would go into a hospital cage after I had cleaned up the wound. Birds healed quickly and I would then let it go again. A rigorous hygiene regime would have to be in place so that neither the crow nor anything it touched came into any sort of contact with our other birds. It would live in the bathroom where it was easier to disinfect and where the dogs and the cat could be excluded.

So our bathroom was duly commandeered as a Crow Hospital. I gently cleaned the blood and dirt from the wound and offered water and a meal of dried mealworm, dog food and chopped raw beef. The crow peered out at me suspiciously but I could see that it was interested in the food. Covering one half of the cage with a blanket so the bird had somewhere to rest I then withdrew and shut the bathroom door.

After a few seconds there was a thud and then the unmistakeable sound of beak against pottery as the crow hopped off its perch in search of dinner. A while later, I reopened the door to find the food bowl empty, the crow back on the perch and there seemed to be no fresh bleeding from the wound site. I covered the cage with a heavier blanket and settled the bird for the night.

Next morning I headed down the hall to find John emerging from the bathroom, grumbling.

"It's like living in a bloody Hitchcock movie in this house," he complained.

I looked through the door. He had uncovered the cage and the crow was beadily surveying its surroundings with that glittery, sinister stare that all corvids have. It looked alert and healthy apart from one slightly drooping wing. Gently catching it up in a towel I found that the wound was healing but there had been some seepage during the night. Without disturbing the forming clots I once more carefully disinfected the site and popped the bird back in the cage.

It tucked into breakfast with gusto and I removed the pungent evidence of the healthy digestion of the previous night's dinner in response to John's pointed observation, "The bog stinks of crow poo."

This was the routine for the next few days. The wound healed up well and I persuaded the crow to exercise the wing by holding its feet and bringing it downwards so it was compelled to flap. It was getting close to being moved to a bigger outside cage in preparation for release when the gunmen set up their hide again for another cull.

Several hours later we were returning to the house with the dogs when a squawking black shape flapped across the ground in front of us. Megan relished the opportunity to assume crow-dog duties once more and stopped it in its tracks with a paw.

John hauled Monty onto a short lead and planted a look of resignation on his face as I homed in on the latest casualty. Once again the bird had a wing injury but this time it was to the outer joint where the wing flexed.

As we all made our way home John seemed keen to discuss living arrangements.

"And where is this latest specimen going to go then?"

Cradling the bird against my sweatshirt I told him, "Crow One can move outside into the aviary cage and Crow Two can move into the hospital cage in the bathroom." I had a thought, "Do you think they will be shooting every week?"

"I hope not. How many half-dead festering birds do you think our house will hold?"

So Crow One was duly moved out into its new lodgings. Here it could reacclimatise to the outside temperature and it had enough room to flap its wings and hop from perch to perch. A tarpaulin was anchored to the top and back of the cage to protect it from rain at night and give it the safety of a roost.

The hospital cage was given a blast with the shower nozzle and hygiene spray and was then set up to accommodate Crow Two. As before we cleaned its wounds but this time, carefully taped its wing into position with surgical tape to allow the joint to heal. Crow Two proved to be a feisty little character. Whilst our first guest had been happy to eat, poop, glare at us and fill our bathroom with the unmistakeable aroma of *'eau de crow'*, its follower did all this but was also imbued with all the escape intent of a prisoner of war.

Hearing a crash John had gone to investigate one morning to find it out of its cage and in the toilet bowl. Being not in the slightest bit grateful for the latest human help in preventing it meeting its maker, it pecked John as he hauled it out of the bowl, wriggled free and made a break for the bathroom door, where it promptly met a very interested cat.

On another occasion I was in the middle of checking the healing process when the bird decided to jump onto the windowsill and upended itself in the ferns, feet waving in the air as it scuffed compost all over my pile of cotton wool and surgical tape. It was with some relief that Crow One was soon released to re-join its friends in the wild blue yonder and Crow Two made the transition to the outside cage.

I cleaned the bathroom and the hospital cage was returned to the shed. It was lovely to use the facilities without being watched and although we were pleased to be able to rescue and successfully return our beady-eyed lodgers to the wild it was an experience we were happy was over.

That night John picked me up from work. "Grab hold of this," he said, handing me a large bundle as I climbed into the passenger seat.

"What is it?" I wanted to know.

"It was flapping about on the lane, I couldn't leave it. It is a pigeon."

Arriving home, I brought the bundle inside and we carefully unwrapped the coat John had used to scoop up our latest guest. It was a very beautiful and very fat little wood pigeon.

"Yum!" John said.

I gave him the evils and sent him off to bring the hospital cage back out of the shed. The bird did not look injured apart from a tiny bit of blood from a broken wing feather but it did seem dazed. We concluded that it had probably been clipped by a vehicle and just needed to rest.

Pigeon One was duly settled into the cage with a little water and it was covered with a heavy blanket to give it peace and darkness. Our bathroom was a bird repository once more. By morning the pigeon was much perkier. As it had been found on the lane not far from the perimeter of our garden we let it go into a bushy tree opposite the kitchen window where it seemed quite happy to sit on a branch in the sun and watch the world go by.

Eventually it flew off and that brought to a close our brief but successful stint as a Wild Bird Hospital.

WINTER WALK – THE SONG OF THE GATE

Owning dogs, especially two energetic specimens like Monty and Megan means there are walks to be undertaken, regardless of the weather. Every season has its own appeal but a walk in the hills around our house in winter has a wild and often very dramatic beauty.

It begins with layering up in the hallway – sweatshirt and then fleece under a full length wax coat, skirt over joggers with thermal socks and knee high wellies – then gloves and a heavy scarf wrapped around my head. Opening the door to driving rain and a howling gale in the relative calm of a yard enclosed by buildings on all four sides only gives an inkling of the conditions at the top of the hill.

Heading for the fields the lane is muddy but lies in the shade of the house. It is when you reach the gate that the first force of the wind hits you as it blows up the valley straight off the sea. Seagulls wheel overhead, buffeted as they screech defiance to the leaden skies and it is here that the first biting sting of rain catches you on any uncovered skin.

Megan remains largely unbothered by all but the worst downpours. Monty sometimes needs coaxing over the threshold if the rain is particularly heavy, possibly as a throwback to when he was abandoned and a tiny concern raises itself, briefly flickering insecurity, in his brain. Out and about there are bushes to provide cover for wet dogs, but there is little to give shelter to the person with them.

It is normally at this point that the mantra of the necessity of the winter walk is trotted out, "Whose stupid idea was it to get a bloody dog?"

One such day I had given up waiting for the weather to improve, if anything, it was getting worse by the minute and the radio forecaster was cheerfully warning of day-long storms.

"Come on then, you two. Let's go," I muttered, glancing gloomily at the yard puddles that actually had little waves breaking across them.

We made the gate. The grass, sodden and blown flat, was slippery underfoot and I was glad of my new wellingtons with their deep tread as we made our way around the field's edge towards the gorse bushes and the protection they provided for essential activities. Their gnarled branches creaked together and the dogs were careful to skirt the fallen twigs, bristling with paw-pricking thorns, old and brown but still painful if caught between pads.

Megan came running up to me to find what I was going to throw for her on this outing. I normally brought out a ball thrower or an old glove but on this occasion, caught up in my wrapping and layering up with coats, scarves and thermals, I had forgotten to bring anything.

Megan was unimpressed. She circled me, barking.

"Sorry Megan, we'll have to have a normal walk today," I told her, just as a particularly strong gust straight off the sea caught her side on and knocked her onto the grass, winding her up even more.

Monty had sneaked under a bush and was using the relative shelter to conclude his business. He then crept out and trotted towards me before stopping dead and sitting, one foot held off the ground. With ears flat and worried, he dangled the offending paw and whimpered.

"Caught a thorn, have you Monty?" I crouched, back to the wind with one knee in the mud, "Let me see then."

Wiping clean his upturned foot with what I found was my only tissue I probed for the embedded splinter of gorse. Monty breathed hotly in my ear as he inspected what I was doing and I realised how much he must have grown to trust me. With his teeth millimetres from my face I found the end of the thorn and pincered it between two nails, pulling it free with only a tiny bead of blood to indicate its exit.

Monty gingerly placed his foot back on the ground and his relief in suddenly being pain free was comically palpable. I patted him and went to pick up my gloves, one of which was now twenty feet away being dead-rat-head-shaken into submission by Megan.

"Give me my glove," I ordered.

Megan brought it to within a few feet and dumped it. As I bent to retrieve it, she pounced and disappeared off to the other side of the field.

I sighed and followed with Monty. I had made a classic dog training error, which meant I couldn't be annoyed at Megan. I could not expect her to differentiate between one glove and another. A glove was a glove in her mind, and something that I used to get her to play with on walks. The fact that the one I usually brought out was an ancient, holey, woollen effort and she had just cleared off with my expensive patented, technologically designed, hiking glove, was my problem not hers.

It was something that dog owning had taught us and which we normally tried to apply: the need for consistent rules and instructions. Once we had made the decision to allow the dogs on the furniture, it was unfair to then tell them to get off if they hopped up with muddy paws. Offering the dogs table scraps meant we could not complain when dogs gathered hopefully and drooled while we ate. Allowing Monty on the bed in the early months of owning him, because sometimes it was the only way we could get him, and therefore us, to sleep meant it was entirely our doing when Monty then saw the bed as a refuge.

We apply far too much reasoning to dogs; expecting them to know the difference between rough and tumbling a teenager (smiled on and filmed for social media) and doing the same with the new baby (sadly filmed by a solemn news crew); encouraging the dog to bark at strangers to protect the house and then yelling at it for barking at the postman; laughing when the puppy pinches food from the toddler, then crying when a fully grown dog does the same more forcefully later and bites a child.

So the fact that my hand was bare and frozen and scrunched up into my fleece sleeve was entirely my fault.

At the top of the hill I took stock, barely able to stand upright as the force of the wind funnelled straight up the valley. In the distance the sea churned as breakers formed off the coast and then crashed ashore, grey water foaming as the noise of the waves breached even the howl of the storm.

Turning my back to the gale I watched the clouds scudding towards the mountains, which were wreathed in veils of rain swirling with silvery menace across the landscape. At once hiding and then revealing sodden, grey green hills, it was possible to track the progress of the showers, as they slowly engulfed the nearby fields and announced their arrival with stinging drops.

The dogs came to shelter under my coat, Megan bringing my glove with her. We stood out the worst of the shower and then made our way down the hill. The hedgerow provided shelter, gaps in the hawthorn allowing the wind to punch through with a boxer's force, no less diminished by the lower slopes we now crossed on our way to the gate.

Megan bounced and nipped at my glove, which was now firmly back on my chilled hand. I sent her away, "You're not having it, go find me a stick."

Megan looked around her. No sticks in the vicinity.

"Go find a stick," I told her.

She charged off, scouting the ground as I persuaded Monty to come away from the side of the hedge and run with me.

"I'm not going to abandon you. You need to run, get moving," I encouraged.

Monty circled me in speedy laps, charging through the rain up to me and then away again. Panting, he took a break after a while and sat, cocking his head.

"Can you hear it too Monty?" I said. "It's the song of the gate."

When the wind blew in winter, in a certain direction, and with a certain strength the gates sang. A mournful but beautiful moaning vibrated off the bars and serenaded us. Drops of rain clung in crystal desperation to the underside of steel bars, chased up and down by the gusts in a Newton's Cradle race; joining, dropping, forming again. Watery diamonds in a musical dance; transient and fragile, with a ghostly orchestral backdrop of whispering, softly spectral song.

Normally, this sort of thing would freak me out; my imagination was more than capable of seeing a sinister choir but I found it uplifting. An affirmation of nature that would outlast me, the dogs, all I knew, and still be there for generations to enjoy.

"We're just here for a moment," I told Monty as he listened still to the gate and I pondered life.

Then Megan backed into view, back legs pumping and putting some effort into something. She reversed round the bushes up to my feet and gave me a satisfied stare. I looked down.

"What the hell is that? I told you to find a stick," I laughed, as Megan plonked a foot on her find and gave me a look that indicated that she felt her mission was complete and what was I complaining about?

Next to Megan was what could only be described as a large branch. A central trunk, with several branching offshoots, that had scuffed a trail through the wet ground and clustered grassy tufts on the end of numerous twigs. It was about five feet long.

As Monty peed on the larger part of Megan's offering and tugged loops of lead in dashing circles around us, I broke off a reasonable length of stick and threw it for Megan. As she darted off to fetch it I crossed the sleeper bridge with Monty.

The wind plucked at my scarf, the rain dampened my hair, and the gate sang us home.

TRIBUTE TO A DYING EWE

I drew back the curtains one early spring Sunday to be met with an absolutely beautiful day. The skies were cloudless and the sun shone down with unseasonal warmth. There was no wind to chill the air or dull the birdsong that greeted the end of winter. It was the type of day that cheered the soul and I resolved to make the most of it.

The doors could be open to air the house, I would clean through and catch up with some paperwork and the washing could go outside for once. We would have a barbecue for tea, relishing this unexpected treat in March. John would pop into town for the papers, which we could then read in the sunshine on the bench table in the back garden with a glass of wine. It was going to be a productive day.

First though, we would do the morning dog walk together. I had given John a reasonably decent camera for Christmas and he was keen to make the most of its features, taking pictures of the wildlife and scenery while he was out and about. This was easier said than done with Monty on the other end of a lead. Several times he had morosely reported that he had just set up the perfect shot of a red kite or attractive rural scene to find that Monty hauled at the lead just as he clicked the shutter. Checking the digital recall, he would find that his 'nature in the raw' snap was actually a view of his big toe.

"No problem," I said. "We'll go out together. I will take Monty, Megan will do her own thing anyway, and you can bring the camera and zoom and click away without hindrance."

So, on this lovely Sunday we set off as the sun climbed high. There was none of the haze or dust of a warm summer's day, everything was defined in the sharp relief of new colours emerging for spring, washed by recent rains and as yet not faded by days of sunshine. Our little group skirted the field closest to the house and then made our way through the gate, across the marshy patch with its reeds and midges and along the hedgerow of the nearby meadow. The dogs made the most of the sniffing and scenting opportunities left by the overnight badgers and foxes whilst John snapped away, unencumbered by Monty.

Megan trotted ahead to the far fence where she could watch the sheep on the pasture of the neighbouring farm and wait for us to catch up. From a distance we saw her demeanour change as she fixed her gaze on something we could not yet see.

"Meg has found something to interest her," murmured John, as the distant form dropped into a collie crouch.

As we approached the fence we saw the ewe, stretched out on the grass with her lamb tucked in beside her; not an unusual scene for the time of year except that the ewe's face was streaked red. Hopping over the wire while John gathered the dogs I calmed her with a hand on her fleece and inspected the damage. From the ruin of her eye socket, fresh red trails tracked down her cheek, shining wetly in the sun and mingling with viscous jelly spatters. She had gone down and the crows had done their work, two of them mocking us from a nearby tree with their caws.

I lifted her head to look at her other eye; it was intact but milky and vacant. The ewe focussed briefly and paddled her legs; I tried to get her on her feet as her lamb backed off and bleated but she sank back down onto the grass, her mangled eye turned upwards to an azure sky she could not see. Her legs stilled again and we noticed one foot was misshapen; the cloven toes forced apart by the black, grossly granulated mass of an untreated infection. A back foot was swollen too. Her fleece was discoloured, the wool dry and rough under my touch, as she lay silent and uncomplaining on the grass.

"That is one sick sheep," John stated flatly.

I climbed back over the fence. The crows sat waiting.

"As soon as we leave her, that lot will be back to finish the job," John said, "They'll take the other eye and her back end out."

We looked around, there was no one apart from us, the dogs and the sheep. Far, far overhead a heavy jet droned its way out to sea on its long haul to the United States, trails from its engines scarring the blue of the sky, its occupants unaware of the pastoral tragedy unfolding below.

As we assessed our options I heard engine noise back in the yard by our house, followed by bleating. Our farmer neighbour was moving sheep into the fields. I decided to run back and enlist his help while John maintained his vigil and warned the crows away. Sprinting soon turned to trotting but I made speedy progress back across the meadow and caught the farmer just as he was about to leave. Panting, I explained that Megan had spotted a downed sheep but that the crows had injured it and we had no number for the farmer who owned the land. He invited me to hop into his Land Rover and we sped back to John.

"The crows have done a good job," John warned.

"Aye, crows are bad this year," the farmer said, as he made his assessment. "Young ewe, probably about four, her teeth are good." Then he felt her fleece, "Wool's rough though." Examining her teats, he produced the merest smear of milk. "She's lambed recently but there's nothing here, not good, she's nearly dry."

Standing up he looked around. "Did you see the lamb?"

"It's over there, it looks quite healthy and it is a decent size. It was with her until we came near."

The farmer looked down at the motionless ewe again, "Lamb will survive as long as it's around a month old, don't know about her. She's probably been ill for a while. I'll let the farmer know, he'll come and collect her, give her a shot."

We thanked him for his help. He climbed back into the cab and then gave us a quizzical look.

"We'll stay until he gets here."

He nodded, "Aye, crows are bad this year, very bad."

And so we waited. I made a trip back to the house and made a flask of tea and one of coffee. Also picked up a bottle of water and the portable dog bowl. Then I returned to John. I attached my scarf to the fence to give the ewe some shade from the midday sun and perched on the grassy bank.

It should have been lovely; a warm day in the countryside, nature blooming with new life, no sounds other than birdsong and the bleating of lambs checking their mothers were nearby. And it was; it was beautiful, life affirming and joyous. We watched birds collecting nest material and felt the sun warm our necks. Megan and Monty made the most of this unrestricted opportunity to investigate the scents that surrounded the foxholes in the bank and John and I chatted about anything and everything as we waited for the owner of the sheep to come to its rescue.

But it was also awful. As we drank tea and coffee the ewe was lying in silence a few feet away, the crimson tracks on her face marking the passage of time by turning slowly darker and drying into a russet crust. She hardly moved save for the occasional feeble paddling of her swollen feet, the only good thing coming from her blinded incapacity was that she did not have to stand on the obscenity of the infections in her toes. When I poured water into the bowl I had brought for the two panting faces in front of me, the sheep stirred and mumbled her tongue over her lips. I used the lid of the bottle to dribble a little water into her mouth and she stirred more. John supported her head to allow her to drink from the bowl and she lapped eagerly before sinking down again.

The farmer wouldn't be long, we thought. A sheep is not a particularly valuable animal but it was ill and injured. It was a busy time for farmers, and sometimes it was hard to get around in the available hours in a day, to all the jobs pressing for attention. We had nothing important planned for the afternoon, so once we had left the casualty in its owner's care it wouldn't take long to catch up with the housework and our barbecue.

As the clock ticked past three our neighbour came back with more stock. He seemed surprised to see us still on our watch.

"He must be on his way, I rang him as soon as I left you last time. I'll call him again when I get back."

We nodded. The slightest chill was beginning to edge into the afternoon. The sun still shone brightly but now a breeze wafted my scarf shading the ewe and the shadows began to creep outwards from the hedges and fence posts. John shifted and stretched uncomfortably and when I stood up to join him I realised that I too was stiff from our long wait. The crows still watched us from the trees, sometimes moving away for a while but never far enough that they could not see the ewe, who seemed now to be sliding deeper into her terminal reverie.

"I don't think he's coming," John murmured, training his camera on another heavy jet way above us, its four engines powering it out over the sea into the setting sun that glinted off the fuselage. "Bet those pilots have a fantastic view of the sunset."

"Better view than we've got," I looked at the comatose sheep.

We waited another hour. The air continued to cool as the sun dropped lower in the west. By now the ewe was going for longer and longer periods of increasingly shallow breathing, held in the clutch of the long grey fingers that shadowed out from the fence posts, creeping across the dampening grass to embrace her. She gave the occasional gasp as if giving a last defiant kick against the inevitable but now her chest stilled as she sank deeper, unaware now and hopefully out of pain. The crows gave up as the day ended and evening took over, flying away to roost.

The farmer was not able to come and the ewe died. When it came down to her last fight against illness she had given everything to her lamb and had kept nothing back for herself. It was a very busy time for farmers, and she was only a sheep. To her lamb though, she was everything. As we finally accepted that there was nothing more to be done and moved across the darkening fields with the dogs towards home, the lamb scuttled along the edge of the field and tucked into her mother's still and silent flanks.

The ewe was still there next morning, tinged with an early morning frost. The lamb moved away as John approached with the dogs, bleating but receiving no reply. Hopefully, it was at least a month old. When John made a return circuit on the afternoon walk the carcass had gone, only a few tufts of wool and an indentation on the grass marking her existence. The farmer had been at last.

MONTY IS A LEGEND AFTER ALL

A couple of weeks of heavy showers, sun and then showers again had meant that the fields were taking on the attributes of a virgin rain forest. I had completed a few circuits with the dogs, wading through thigh high clover and rye and trying not to think about the creepy crawlies that no doubt thrived on the verdant vegetation, but finally wimped out and stuck to the field closest to the house that had recently been grazed by cattle.

So when the farmer made the most of a week of dry weather to bring in the barley and mow the clover fields for haylage I was relieved.

"See you later," I called, heading out one morning for an amble.

We made our way across to the gate to the barley field. The combines had harvested the crop and the ground was strewn with rows of straw. Heading up the hill along the hedgerow both dogs relished this chance to renew their acquaintance with the scents of the undergrowth and I wandered along, letting them take their time exploring. It was a cloudy day and the breeze was quite cool as I crested the hill and looked across to the sea. Monty sniffed at the base of a fence post and then cocked his leg as I pulled the hood of my sweatshirt up around my ears and looked around the sweep of the bay, all shades of olive and granite on this dull summer day.

Then, as Megan ran back over with the ball and dropped it at my feet I looked down. In amongst the damp barley stalks, close to the grassy border, was something black, about an inch long, fluffy and crawling. Beating a hasty retreat I coaxed both dogs further along the edge of the field only to spot another fluffy black inch. Putting a row of straw between me and the caterpillars, I sought sanctuary in the middle of a bare patch of ground, spotted only with the odd broken stalk and more creeping fiends.

Feeling the old sense of chill I stomped my feet. I only had ankle wellies on and when I felt a touch on my skin above my socks I sprang about a foot into the air. Of course there was nothing there but now the goose bumps were breaking out on the back of my neck and I automatically glanced over every part of my fleece and joggers.

"Seriously you lot, it's almost September. Aren't you supposed to be hibernating or pupating or whatever it is you do?"

The caterpillars quivered their fluff at me and charged.

"Right that's it. Monty, Megan, come on. I'm done with barley."

The dogs trotted ahead as I mentally talked myself down, "They are just babies. Little baby butterflies. We need butterflies. Butterflies are lovely."

By the time we were halfway through the massively shortened clover next door I was just about back to normal, although I did still stamp my feet occasionally. The farmer had breached the bank to allow access to heavy machinery so there was another field to explore. Megan raced off to find the ball I had thrown for her while Monty disappeared into the depths of long grass in one shaded corner and refused to come out. I gave the lead a little tug, but there was no response.

"Come out of there Monty."

Nothing.

"Whatever it is you are eating, stop it and come here."

Nothing.

"Monty! Here now."

Still nothing.

I surveyed the grass with trepidation; if it was long enough to hide sixty-five pounds of stone-deaf dog it was long enough to be a haven for millions of caterpillars. However, Monty could have got his lead caught and be unable to comply. I would have to go in and fetch him, but woe betide him if he was just ignoring me.

Shivering slightly, I took the plunge and waded into the grass. Monty was sat by the fence intently staring through the wire and turned his head to look at me as I tiptoed towards him. He sat quietly but his tail was wagging furiously, his ears were pricked and his eyes danced as he looked away again.

"You had better be looking at something worthwhile," I muttered, brushing feverishly at my coat.

When I saw what he could see I patted him on the head. "You are such a good, good dog," I praised, as his tail wagged even faster but he maintained his focus.

On the other side of the fence, hidden from view in a thicket of spiky hawthorn branches was a huge ewe caught fast by her horns. I climbed out of the grass and tried to find a way over the fence. Having alerted me to his find Monty trotted after me so I tethered his lead to a post and called for Megan to come over. When both dogs were sitting nearby I tested a couple of fence posts. They wobbled alarmingly as I tentatively put a foot on the aging mesh which sagged and bowed. In addition, the fence was topped by vicious looking rusted barbed wire.

"I hope my bloody tetanus is up to date," I worried, as I found a section of fence in a slightly less distressed state with wire attached to a fence post that stood reasonably firm. The barbs plucked and snagged at my joggers as I climbed over, before approaching the ewe.

I looked at the thicket in dismay, it was low and dense. There were branches and foliage everywhere and in order to help the sheep I would have to crawl into it. The back of my neck pricked as I sensed its inhabitants dropping on my head. I thought of ringing home for help; no mobile signal. I gauged how long it would take to run home and then back but ruled this out as an option when I heard the cawing of a nearby crow.

Finally I gave myself a little pep talk, "Just pull your finger out and get on with it, you silly moo."

"All right girl," I soothed, as I walked over. The sheep was stuck fast in an almost sitting position but tried to struggle free. "Take it easy, there's a good girl."

I crept under the branches and put my hands on her fleece.

"Good girl, let's see what we have here then."

She sat quietly as I gave her the once over, talking softly to her all the while.

"There's a brave lass," I said, checking both eyes were intact. Luckily it looked as though the crows had not yet discovered her predicament, but they would also attack the back end so I ran my hands under her rump and down her tummy.

"You are being such a good girl," I told her, as I found all was undamaged and then encountered two enormous furry testicles.

"Eww! I've just felt up a sheep!" I groaned to myself. "Oh my! Okay, take it easy good boy."

The ram was a fine, handsome beast in every sense. I had no idea how he had managed to trap the branches under his horns because it was no easy job freeing him. A large thorn was millimetres from one eye so I began breaking off smaller twigs until I could twist and bend green wood under the curve of his horn. He didn't move as I worked until the moment when I was struggling to flex the last branch away. As if sensing freedom he gave an almighty buck and wrenched his head clear. I shoved as he wriggled and tottered out of the thicket on shaky legs.

"Good lad," I called, as he stumbled away.

Megan and Monty were watching as the ram made his way into the middle of the field, unsteady at times but unhurt. I scrambled back over the fence and the thicket was now completely hidden once more.

I waited a while, watching as the ram met up with the rest of the flock and regained its balance and composure. Halfway across the field, he turned back and looked at us for a moment. I scratched

Monty around the ears and put my hand on Megan's head. When I glanced back up at the sheep they all looked the same.

"Well done Monty. Shall we go and tell John what a hero you are," I stroked his face and we turned for home.

"You did what to a sheep?" John wanted to know.

"Rescued it."

"No, the bit before the rescuing part," John smiled.

I was proudly relaying our story as Monty sat at my feet looking suitably heroic. Animatedly I told of our survival of the killer caterpillars and of Monty discovering the hidden ram as we skirted the borders of the bad-lands, miles from assistance or succour.

"And then, parched and ailing, but not wanting to leave our trapped friend, Meg and Mont stood guard, unfailing in their duty while I dragged my weary body through the barren landscape, across the sharp basalt flints that tore at my combats as I reached the casualty."

"Hang on a minute," John said. "You were a mile from the house. Basalt is volcanic, I think a volcano would have made it into the local paper somehow."

"To continue…" I gave him a look. "…With his last energy Monty urged our downed comrade to hang on, just hang on while I tried to free him. But if he couldn't hang on then we would use the last bullet on him, from our trusty Luger, to stop him falling into enemy hands and the tortures that awaited."

"Luger, eh? Don't think the farmer would have been very pleased, somehow. Not usually the protection of choice for the farm rambler. I'm partial to a crook myself."

"So anyway," I stared. "I'm across the flints and Monty has still got my back, and I creep in and check him over and…"

"Feel his bits?"

"Free him so he can fight another day, actually."

John looked at us.

"Don't you remember when we named Monty, there was that legend programme on the telly?" I asked.

John nodded.

"Well, that Monty may have been a legend in the desert but ours is a legend in the fields."

"Or the volcano," John finished.

After dinner that evening we all relaxed together; John in his chair, me on the settee, Megan on the armchair and Monty next to me, doing his best to kick me off so that he could have more room.

"Do you realise," I said. "In a month we will have had Monty for three years?"

"Really?"

"Yes. Do you remember how he was?"

John looked over, "Oh yes, there was nothing of him."

"He crapped all over the place," I said.

"And peed!" responded John.

"He drove the cat up the wall."

"He tried to eat everything in sight."

"Including us," I said.

"He had nightmares…"

"…When he finally started sleeping."

We both looked at a dozing Monty, nose twitching and feet paddling as he chased rabbits in his dreams. Between us, we concluded that he had not turned out too badly. He was big, bold and confident. He was selectively deaf and very naughty on occasion. A few things still spooked him but he knew all the basic commands. He still had the recall of an amoeba but we would carry on working with him for as long as it took.

I looked at our little pack, snoozing happily and asked, "Do you actually remember a time when we didn't have dogs?"

"What? You mean a time when we had clean carpets and no paw prints on all the tiles? And when everything wasn't covered in dog hairs? And when going away didn't involve more planning than a NATO summit?"

"And a time when you could go to the loo in peace, or wake up without a ton of dog on the duvet?" I offered.

"And a time when it didn't cost more to insure the animals than our house and car combined. And when every spare minute isn't spent wandering round the fields in a howling gale or rain?"

We paused for a second to think.

"Or a time when we went to sit at the top of the hill and really looked at the views and admired where we live on a daily basis?" I said.

"Or a time when we always, without fail, have a paw, or a lick to cheer us up or welcome us home?" John added.

"Or before we knew we could make such a difference to a couple of manky mutts who had a bad start in life, because their eyes tell it like it is? Yes, that time." I said.

"No, can you?" John replied.

"Nope," I said.

"And I have to admit, even the second dog idea worked out well in the end," John conceded.

I pulled a magazine out from under the coffee table. "It's funny you should say that, because I've been reading this article," I started.

John's eyebrows flickered upwards.

"Yes, it says that one dog is great, two dogs are brilliant, but in actual fact," I paused, as John began to cast a wistful look at the drinks cabinet. "The optimum number of dogs for a happy pet pack is three!"

I got the look, big time.